SUPERVISION

SUPERVISION
The Management
of Organizational
Resources

STERLING H. SCHOEN
Professor of Management
Washington University
St. Louis, Missouri

DOUGLAS E. DURAND
Associate Professor of Management and Organizational Behavior
University of Missouri
St. Louis, Missouri

PRENTICE-HALL, INC., Englewood Cliffs, N.J. 07632

Library of Congress Cataloging in Publication Data

SCHOEN, STERLING HARRY
  Supervision, the management of organizational resources.

  Includes index.
  1. Supervision of employees. I. Durand, Douglas E.
1944–   II. Title
HF5549.S247   658.3'02   78-10461
ISBN 0-13-876235-X

© 1979 by Prentice-Hall, Inc., Englewood Cliffs, N.J. 07632

Printed in the United States of America
10 9 8 7 6 5 4 3 2 1

Editorial/production supervision and interior design by
   Alice Erdman

Cover design by Jorge Hernandez

Manufacturing buyer: Harry Baisley

Prentice-Hall International, Inc., *London*
Prentice-Hall of Australia Pty. Limited, *Sydney*
Prentice-Hall of Canada, Ltd., *Toronto*
Prentice-Hall of India Private Limited, *New Delhi*
Prentice-Hall of Japan, Inc., *Tokyo*
Prentice-Hall of Southeast Asia Pte. Ltd., *Singapore*
Whitehall Books Limited, *Wellington, New Zealand*

CONTENTS

Part IV
ORGANIZATIONAL SKILLS

Part V
DECISIONAL AND ADMINISTRATIVE SKILLS

Part VI
THE SUPERVISOR'S PERSONAL AND CAREER DEVELOPMENT

Part VII
SOME PARTING THOUGHTS

CASES

PREFACE

Managers and business educators alike agree that the quality of managerial performance is critical to the success of an organization. Managerial effort is directed toward accomplishing productive work by organizing and motivating the efforts of other people. In our society managers are also expected to create the type of work climate that will enable subordinates to achieve their personal goals and a sense of satisfaction from their work.

Middle- and lower- level managers are important members of the management team, and first-line supervisors occupy a particularly critical position in the organization. It is at this level that managerial and non managerial employees meet face to face and work in a close relationship with one another. They are "the company" to the large number of unskilled, semi-skilled, and skilled workers, and to the large number of specialists and professionals employed in every part of the organization. They are the principal point of contact for labor unions. Compliance with many government regulations depends upon the knowledge, attitudes, and skills of these supervisors. Finally, it is also at this level that such matters as leadership, motivation, communication, and labor relations become crucial and seem to present the greatest problem for the organization. *Supervision: The Management of Organizational Resources* is about these supervisory positions and the men and women who work in them.

Our objectives in writing this book are threefold: First, we wish to describe the manager's job and to analyze and discuss the skills most important for performing that job; second, we focus on the actual behavior and analytical reasoning required at the first-line supervisory level up to the middle managerial level—while theory and "principles" are important, they are not quite enough; and third, we attempt to present sophisticated ideas in a simple and straightforward manner. We have enjoyed writing this book and we want students and supervisors not only to understand it but also to enjoy it.

Supervision: The Management of Organization Resources is directed toward students in two - and four-year colleges who are enrolled in their first course in management and who wish to develop or improve their supervisory skills. The practical orientation of the text and the large number of realistic case studies will make this book especially interesting and helpful to mature students who are continuing their education on a part-time basis. Since it is oriented toward the practice of management, it will also be of interest and help to practicing supervisors enrolled in training programs in their organizations. Supervisors of production, sales, finance and accounting, and technical and engineering groups will find this book equally helpful.

To develop a better understanding of managerial work, the book begins by summarizing pertinent findings about what managers actually do. From this analysis comes the conclusion that supervisory work is characterized by such elements as decision making under great time and information constraints, reliance upon verbal communication, and the open-ended nature of job responsibilities. The subsequent seventeen chapters focus on the important functions, responsibilities, and behaviors required of those who occupy these supervisory positions. Chapter 19 is designed to help supervisors with one of their major problems—managing their time. Chapter 20 is directed toward helping supervisors establish personal goals and plan their careers.

A book is the product of many people. We are indebted to the many supervisors and educators who have provided the storehouse of research and experience from which we have drawn. Many of our colleagues have assisted us in our work. The case studies at the end of each chapter were collected in the course of our consulting and conference leadership activities. However, the names of all individuals and organizations have been disguised. We thank Mr. William A. Beltz, Executive Editor, Bureau of National Affairs, Inc., who permitted us to adapt the two case studies from Labor Arbritration Reports which appear in Chapter 18. We especially want to thank Mrs. Ruth Scheetz of the Washington University staff and Mrs. Janice Archibald of the University of Missouri–St. Louis staff, who diligently and patiently deciphered and typed many drafts of copy to produce the completed manuscript.

SUPERVISION

I

Introduction

1

THE NATURE OF MANAGERIAL WORK

LEARNING OBJECTIVES

This chapter discusses the nature of managerial work. After you have read this chapter, you will

1. Know why organizations are important in our daily lives
2. Know why managers are important in the success of organizations
3. Have a better understanding of the meaning of such terms as man-ager, supervisor, and leader
4. Know which organizational functions and activities relate to man-agers
5. Know why certain characteristics are identified with managerial work
6. Understand why managers typically like their work

ORGANIZATIONS ARE PERVASIVE IN OUR LIVES

We live in an organizational world. Each of us is a member of many organizations. Some of these organizations are immediate and affect us deeply. For example, most of us are members of a family, which is a small and personal organization; many of us are members of a formal religious organization; and many of us are also members of a work organization. All of these organizations embrace a set of values, beliefs, and sentiments which determine and define their policies, procedures, and practices, some of which are openly expressed and others of which are only felt. Each of these organizations has developed a set of behaviors that are expected from members.

Some organizations touch us only incidentally, and we are scarcely aware of their existence. We hear of them only when they embark upon a fund drive or when their activities produce some dramatic outcome, such as the discovery of a polio vaccine or the development of a spaceship that can land on Mars.

Some organizations are large and others are small. They range in size from a two-person partnership to a community of nations. They may be simple in their structure, such as a corner grocery store; or they may be complex, such as an international conglomerate. They may be very informal and devoid of structure and rules, such as a bridge club; or they may be highly bureaucratized, such as General Motors or the federal government.

Organizations differ in their objectives, too. Some seek to make a profit for their owners; some want to render a service; others attempt to satisfy the spiritual, aesthetic, or humanitarian needs of their members; and still others exist to establish and maintain systems of individual rights and responsibilities among members of a society.

We are the willing members of some organizations; we are born into others; and we may be enlisted into still others, sometimes against our desire. Thus we belong to one or more "voluntary" organizations which exist in large numbers to protect the health and safety of members of communities and to promote the recreational, aesthetic, cultural, political, educational, religious, and familial quality of life in our society. We are also members of government organizations—local, state, federal, and international. Finally, most adults work in an organization that not only provides them with the means for earning a livelihood but also enables them to satisfy their need for creativity, achievement, responsibility, growth and development, recognition, membership, and the utilization of their talents and skills. In summary, we live our lives as members of many organizations of all kinds, each serving one or more of our individual or collective needs.

　　While we typically take organizations for granted, they should inspire us with awe and admiration. For example, it seems only short of a miracle that the 150,000 employees of IBM are able to plan, organize, and control their behavior to the end that the company can innovate, design, produce, and market computers that meet the needs of many people with widely divergent needs and expectations. The IBM employees not only produce computers, but they do so efficiently. But this company does more than create, manufacture, and sell computers; it also engages in a wide range of ancillary activities designed to meet, even anticipate, the many demands of society for social change. For example, IBM's philanthropic activities include the support of community action, social welfare, and educational organizations. The company's equal employment opportunity policies and practices antedate federal law and far surpass the minimum requirements of federal, state, and local statutes. It is even more impressive to consider that the millions of people in these United States are able to assemble themselves into more or less formal and structured groups to meet their many and varied needs. The ability of human beings to associate themselves into goal-oriented groups in order to satisfy their many needs should be viewed as one of the universal and fundamental abilities of humankind.

MANAGEMENT: THE CRITICAL FACTOR IN ORGANIZATIONAL SUCCESS

Organizational behaviorists, like economists and security analysts, assess the viability of organizations by the quality of their managers. It is the managers who make things happen in the organization and who determine whether or not it will be successful in meeting its objectives today, tomorrow, and a decade from now. It is the manager who is the catalyst in bringing the organization's resources together in such a way as to create an innovative, productive, adaptive entity serving the needs of its members, its clients, and the community.

Management, Managers, Leaders, and Supervisors

　　The terms <u>management</u> and <u>manager</u> are often used interchangeably. This practice will be followed when traditional usage demands it, such as in the chapters that discuss unions and collective bargaining. The terms are not synonymous, however.

Management consists of the process of developing objectives and striving to attain them. It includes all those activities directed toward enabling the organization to assemble and utilize effectively the human, material, financial, and ideational resources necessary for attaining these objectives.

Management is a dynamic concept. It includes not only the formal and rational planning, organizing, staffing, and controlling activities that go on in organizations but also those creative, political, nonformal, and even nonrational behaviors inherent in organizational life.

A manager is the individual in charge of an entire organization, one of its divisions, or one of its subunits. The manager may be the president of the corporation or the first-line supervisor in charge of production, sales, the office, or the laboratory. In other words, a manager is a person who is held finally responsible for achieving the objectives of a particular work unit. The organization may be large or small, public or private, profit-oriented or not-for-profit.

In this book we are concerned with managers in formal organizations. They occupy positions to which they have been appointed or elected. These positions are located within a hierarchy in the organization.

The manager is vested with formal authority over an organizational unit, and this person is held accountable for achieving its goals, designing and maintaining its continuous operations, adapting it to changes in the environment, and serving as a communications link between the organization and its environment. For the president, the environment is composed of all the other organizations with which he or she has contact in the community and in the industry. For all managers below the president, the environment includes all other subunits within the organization plus all the external organizations with which the president has contact.

Managers and Leaders

The task of the manager is (1) to determine what is to be done and (2) to see that it gets done. It is the manager who provides the dynamic force or direction that combines static resources into a functioning productive system. The manager is constantly concerned with profit or productivity for the organization and proficiency and performance from its members. Managers are keenly aware that they will obtain none of these outputs if they do not develop within their subordinates competence and motivation.

Every manager is also a leader, but leadership is only one element of the overall managerial job. Leadership pertains to the behavior of the manager that stimulates others to submit to his or her influence. Leadership is not so much a function of position or authority as it is of the quality of the relationship between leader and follower.

Management is directed toward the achievement of organizational goals. Leadership may be exercised either to achieve *or* to thwart attainment of these goals. Furthermore, management—in both theory and practice—is oriented toward the logical, the factual, the financial, the material, the impersonal. Leadership, on the other hand, is associated with feelings and with the quality of the relationship that exists between leaders and followers.

Managers and Supervisors

All managers are supervisors, although the term supervisor is frequently reserved for the lowest managerial level in the organization, the "first-line supervisor." On the other hand, supervisors are also managers. All managers, including first-line supervisors, perform the important management functions of leading, planning, organizing, staffing, and controlling. The amount of time devoted to each of these functions tends to vary from one managerial level to another, but managers perform all functions. The relationship between organizational level and time devoted to each function is illustrated in Figure 1-1.

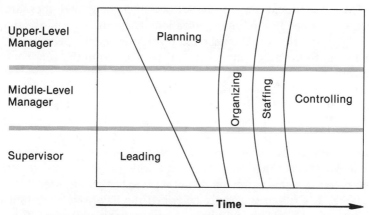

Figure 1-1   Time Devoted to Managerial Functions Related to Managerial Level

MANAGERIAL FUNCTIONS AND ACTIVITIES

We have already stated that the manager's job is essentially that of taking inputs in the form of people, money, materials, and ideas and converting them into outputs in the form of products and services as efficiently as possible. The manager also has other responsibilities, such as introducing innovation and adapting the organization to changes in the environment.

The manager's job is usually studied in terms of formal responsibilities:

1. Leadership, which includes motivating employees, determining assignments, setting standards, training and developing subordinates, appraising employee performance, and distributing rewards.

2. Planning in order to anticipate the future so as to control it, if possible, to capitalize on the opportunities that the future always offers the astute.

3. Organizing people, machines, materials, money, and technology so that the organization's objectives will be met with maximum efficiency.

4. Staffing the organization not only to get today's job done but, more important, to ensure that the human resources will develop so that the organization will remain highly productive in the future and so that employees will obtain satisfaction from their work.

5. Controlling the efforts of subordinates by maintaining a system of standards and budgets—time, quality, output, cost—against which actual performance can be compared in order to discover discrepancies, take corrective action, and evaluate results.

These functional responsibilities are important, and they are performed in the operation of an organization. They suffer from oversimplification, however; they are too neat and tidy. As every manager knows, they seldom seem to describe fully what actually goes on in the conduct of the organization.

When we look more closely and analytically at managerial work, we see that managers are intricately enmeshed in a system of relationships with subordinates, peers, superiors, and staff and service specialists who occupy much of their time and energy. Managers often have little control over the manner in which they spend their time and the persons with whom they spend it. We also see that they engage in a wide range of activities that are necessary to the organization but do not seem to be "managerial."

James J. Cribbin succinctly described the day-to-day job that managers perform. According to Cribbin, managers are people who

1. *Work to implement* their personal career plans, using the firm as a vehicle for so doing while seeking to meet its requirements.

2. Endeavor to be *sensitive* to the expressed or, more often, implied expectations of their immediate superiors. They seek to tune in on new pressures, new developments, and new requirements that may subtly or sharply alter how they go about their work.

3. *Negotiate* continuously with their peers in other departments on whom they depend and who depend on them and their work group to get the total job done effectively.

4. *Cultivate* good relations with staff and service groups whose attitudes and actions can make their jobs easier or harder, for they realize that at times support groups have the ear of the throne.

5. *Respond* to the requests, demands, and requirements of significant individuals and groups in their occupational life spans so as to retain their goodwill or at least not alienate them. They must be flexible in adjusting to an astounding variety of personalities, cliques, and in-groups, parochial loyalties, expertise, and eccentricities.

6. *Oversee* the flow of work into, within, and out of their departments to insure that it proceeds with a minimum of interruption or static that may draw unwanted attention from superiors.

7. *Are alert* to the work output, needs, desires, and morale of their subordinates, interacting with them, yet maintaining their own managerial position.

8. *Represent* their people and their views in dealings with their superiors and other departments.

9. *Try to remain their own person* while accommodating themselves to the legitimate demands of the organization. They must establish a valid order of priorities balancing out what is rightly due the firm, their families and themselves.

10. *Attempt to cope* adequately with their own tensions so as to receive a fair share of psychic as well as economic income from their work.[1]

If managerial performance is so important to organizational success and if managerial work is so complex and demanding, we shall at this point ask two major questions: What are the general characteristics of managerial work? and How do managers feel about their jobs?

CHARACTERISTICS OF MANAGERIAL WORK

Theorists and practitioners have discussed and studied the content and functions of managerial work at great length in an attempt to better select, develop, and assess managerial talent and to predict individual performance in an organizational setting. Mintzberg has identified six characteristics of managerial work:

1. The pace and pressure of managerial work

---

[1]Reprinted by permission of the publisher, from *Effective Managerial Leadership,* by James J. Cribbin. ©1972 by American Management Association, Inc., pp.4–5.

    2. Work patterns characterized by brevity, variety, and fragmentation

    3. Preference for action and the here and now

    4. Attraction to verbal media

    5. Maintenance of the communications network

    6. A complex blend of rights and duties[2]

Pace and Pressure of Managerial Work

Studies of managerial activities reveal that executives seldom escape from their jobs. Mintzberg's studies of organizational presidents disclosed that their days were fully occupied. Telephone calls, mail, and scheduled and unscheduled meetings accounted for most of their workday. Similar studies of lower- and middle-level executives indicate that the pace is almost as grueling, although the workdays are not quite so long. Lower-level executives nevertheless feel that the pace is fast, the pressure ever-present, and the amount of production required of them very high.

Why the heavy work load, constant pressure, and rapid pace? The answer is that the manager's job is never done—it is open-ended. The manager is responsible for the success of the organization, and there are few benchmarks by which to judge success. There is always an additional improvement that might be made or an extra unit of output that might be produced. In addition, the future is always uncertain—extra work might help ensure success, forestall disaster, beat out a competitor, or ride out a recession. As a consequence, the manager is perpetually preoccupied with the job.[3]

Work Patterns Characterized by Brevity, Variety, and Fragmentation

Managers are generalists. They are unable to concentrate their efforts on a narrow range of skills and knowledge at any one time. An earlier study of production foremen revealed that they engaged in 583 incidents each day—forty-eight seconds per activity. In another study, Ponder found that middle managers averaged about two minutes per activity.[4] Mintzberg reported that half of the presidents' activities were completed in less than

---

[2]Henry Mintzberg, *The Nature of Managerial Work* (New York: Harper & Row, 1973), pp. 28–53.

[3]R. H. Guest, "Of Time and the Foreman," *Personnel,* 32 (1956), 478–86.

[4]W. D. Ponder, "The Effective Manufacturing Foreman," *Industrial Relations Research Association Proceedings of the Tenth Annual Meeting* (1957), 41–54.

nine minutes; only scheduled meetings, which constituted only one-tenth of the daily activities, averaged more than one hour. The major problem associated with becoming a generalist is that detailed knowledge of a specific topic is virtually impossible due to the time constraints. Thus one of the occupational hazards of the manager is tendency toward superficiality.

While managers could probably lengthen the duration of their activities, there is some question as to whether they would wish to do so. Again, studies indicate that they thrive upon brevity, variety, and fragmentation, just as they thrive upon the pressure, rapid pace, and never-ending nature of their work. They find it stimulating and interesting.

Mintzberg also offers the thought that managers possess a keen recognition of the value of time. A few minutes devoted to each of several activities may have a higher payoff than all those minutes devoted to only one of them.

Preference for Action and Operating in the Here and Now

Managers devote their energies to those activities that are "current, specific, and well defined, and those that are nonroutine." Their jobs demand that they manage the specific and current issues that continually confront them. Mintzberg discovered few occasions in which managers engaged in abstract discussions or in general planning.

Research has shown that chief executives express a strong need for the most current information, especially about concrete life situations. Routine reporting, and reporting that deals with historical situations, are of less interest. It has been found that these managers want information quickly and seem willing to tolerate a high degree of uncertainty in order to obtain it. Thus gossip, hearsay, and speculation form an important part of their information.

Attraction to Verbal Media

Managers employ face-to-face contact with others inside and outside the organization as their chief means of communication. Telephone calls, unscheduled meetings, scheduled meetings, and plant or office tours are the principal devices employed. The manager's world is a verbal one—face-to-face contact provides two-way communication, having a very personal and immediate quality. Through these face-to-face contacts the manager can learn much, not only by listening to what is said to him but also by observing the behavior, including body language, voice inflection, and facial expression, of the other person. Written communication, on the other hand, is slow in providing feedback; it is laborious both to prepare and to read. It is no accident that managers insist that memoranda be brief, and that when length is necessary they be supplemented with a brief summary!

Maintenance of a Communications Network

Managers must maintain communications links with superiors, subordinates, and outsiders. Maintenance of these contacts consumes much of the manager's time. They are complex and demanding, but they are important in enabling the manager to complete the prescribed work. Mintzberg and others consistently report that whatever the level in the hierarchy, managers spend 33–50 percent of their verbal contact time with subordinates, 10–20 percent with superiors, and 33–50 percent with outsiders. Sometimes they spend more time with outsiders than with subordinates.

Complex Blend of Rights and Duties

From top-level executives to first-line supervisors, managers are customarily considered to have wide discretion over the use of their time and the use of their decision-making power. Recent studies, however, seem to indicate that this is not so. One group of foremen were found to initiate 60 percent of their contacts, another group of lower and middle managers initiated about 50 percent, and a group of senior managers only 32 percent. Thus managers can be governed by their jobs unless they assume initiative in determining those activities in which they will be involved or not involved. They maintain autonomy by determining the ends they will achieve in the process of engaging in desired activities. However, it is evident that managerial positions permit much more latitude in the performance of the task than does most machine-paced, nonmanagerial work.

The above description of managerial work suggests that the work pace and the open-ended nature of the job can greatly influence a manager's behavior. For example, the effective use of the scarce resource of time becomes critical. The speed with which decisions must be made leads to a somewhat superficial understanding of the specific details surrounding a problem or issue. The use of feedback and written communications may be downplayed in favor of the more immediate, but possibly less accurate, verbal communication mode.

Overall, it appears that to be successful a good manager must be competent at verbal communications, be able to make decisions under conditions of great uncertainty, be able to organize both personal time and work schedule, and have a high tolerance for ambiguity. Persons who perform these tasks poorly can expect to have great difficulty as managers.

MANAGERS LIKE THEIR JOBS

If you were to ask a group of managers, "Do you find your job interesting, stimulating, and challenging?" they would almost unanimously say yes, and it would generally be an enthusiastic yes.

     If you were to ask them, "What is it about your job that makes it so positive for you?" their answers would include the following:

Solving nonroutine problems
Taking initiative and being creative
Making decisions
Learning and growing on my job
Having power or influence
Having freedom to work in my own fashion
Meeting the challenge of motivating my subordinates
Having a feeling of accomplishment from a job well done
Making contacts with other people

     The above list reflects some of the positive aspects of the job. Comments regarding problems or the less positive aspects of managerial work would include the following:

Coping with the pressure of the job
Realizing that the work is never done
Having to juggle so many things at once
Being caught in the middle (the company president would mention government regulations, stockholders, employees, and customers as a source of problems; the production foreman would mention an immediate supervisor; the union, the personnel department)

This list is typically shorter than the preceding one; however, note that the general tone even of these responses is positive and optimistic.

     In general, managers like their jobs. Although they often experience heavy work loads and frustration at resolving all the problems and conflicting demands placed upon them, managers seem quite willing to accept these difficulties as things that "come with the territory." They seem very willing to tackle difficult problems. In fact, it often appears that managers are willing to tackle difficult assignments in order to obtain the satisfaction of having solved the problem or overcome the obstacle—one goes with the other.

SUMMARY

Everyone is a member of many organizations which touch upon almost every human activity. Almost everything people achieve during their lives they accomplish as a member of an organization, either as a manager or as one of the managed.

Managerial work is complex and demanding. It cannot be adequately described in terms of planning, organizing, staffing, directing, and controlling. The work is characterized by constant interactions with subordinates and outsiders, rapid pace and pressure, brevity and fragmentation of activities, concern for action and operating in the here and now, and the imposition of structure and control by the demands of the organization.

Managers like their jobs and find them interesting, stimulating, and challenging. They accept the negative features as a small price to pay for the rewards they receive from their jobs—feeling of achievement; opportunity to earn recognition; opportunity to grow, develop, and be creative; feeling of being influential and helpful; and the challenge, autonomy, and variety that the job offers.

The chapters that follow will describe and discuss the functions, responsibilities, and activities of middle- and lower-level managers.

DISCUSSION QUESTIONS

1. List all the organizations to which you belong, placing them under the following headings: family, work, social, educational, religious, government, other.

2. Define *management, manager, leader, supervisor.*

3. Describe the broad range of duties a manager may perform beyond those listed under leading, planning, organizing, staffing, and controlling.

4. How does the job of a sales manager differ from that of a salesperson? A director of a research laboratory from that of a research chemist? A production foreman on an assembly line in an automobile plant from that of an assembler?

5. According to Mintzberg, what are the major characteristics of a managerial job?

6. Why do managers typically like their jobs? What disagreeable features might be present in a managerial position?

7. Would you like to be a manager? Why, or why not?

CASE 1-1. The Foreman Candidate

Tom Powers works on the assembly line of the small-motor division of the American Electric Company, which produces fractional horsepower motors for manufacturers of such household appliances as fans, heaters, hair dryers, dishwashers, and clothes washers and dryers. He learned a few days ago that the company planned to select a new foreman for the line to replace the current foreman, who is retiring in about a month.

Tom had thought on several occasions of leaving American Electric. The pace on the assembly line is fast, the work is repetitive and monotonous, and it offers him little challenge. Even worse, he feels that future prospects seem dim. He took the job five years ago after graduating from high school because the pay was good, and it was about the only job available at that time, other than unskilled laborers' work. He has been rather lucky in that he has worked on almost every part of the line, and for about nine months he also worked on the maintenance crew. His present supervisor likes Tom. At his supervisor's suggestion, the plant manager allowed Tom to work as a temporary foreman while his foreman was on vacation. Tom liked the assignment, although he was surprised at the heavy work load and the constant pressure from top management to get out production. He found that the union steward was also constantly "on his back." In fact, he did not realize, as an employee and a union member, how much work the steward creates for the supervisor. Then, too, the quality control department was always harping about the number of motors that did not pass inspection.

On the other hand, Tom liked the contact that he had with other supervisors during the two weeks he substituted as a foreman. There seemed to be more freedom to get the job done, more variety, and more challenge. He could see where he might enjoy the planning and scheduling involved in a management job. Besides, he had always been something of an "idea man." Maybe that is why the present foreman likes him.

There is one problem, though. He notices that his friends on the assembly line were less friendly during his two-week stint as temporary foreman. In fact, they still seem somewhat distant, even though this temporary assignment occurred six months ago.

Tom has always enjoyed working with people. He did not especially like academic studies in high school. He was captain of his football team but was too lightweight to compete in college. He was appointed to serve on the union negotiating team two years ago but decided that he was not interested in pursuing a union leadership position. He has been studying electronics one night a week at the local high school, hoping that this might enable him to either get ahead at American Electric or prepare him to open an electrical repair shop of his own.

Tom has been wondering whether he has the ability and qualifications necessary to become a supervisor, especially a supervisor in this plant. He has been thinking about discussing this with his supervisor.

QUESTIONS

1. What major duties and responsibilities are involved in the position of foreman at American Electric?

2. Does Tom Powers seem to possess the interest, abilities, and skills necessary to fill the position of foreman?

CASE 1-2.   The Hard-Working Supervisor

Warren Brown, manager of the accounting department of the Mutual Insurance Company, noticed that Sheila Boyce, who was in charge of the accounts payable section, devoted a considerable amount of her time to production work in her section. He was concerned about this because she supervised nineteen typists, file clerks, keypunch operators, accounts payable clerks, and junior accountants, who seemed to require her constant attention. He was especially concerned because he had received several complaints from other supervisors that some of the work coming out of her section was of poor quality. They stated that there were many errors resulting in overpayment or underpayment of bills. These errors also both delayed and made inaccurate the work performed in their sections. They also stated that it took so long to process work through her section that the company frequently lost discounts offered by suppliers for prompt payment.

Before arranging a meeting with Boyce, Brown reviewed the following provisions in the *Supervisors' Handbook:*

Supervisors and other members of management must *not* perform nonsupervisory manual work normally performed by personnel under their supervision, except under the following circumstances:

1. Instructing employees.

2. Operating new or revised equipment or processes. This enables the supervisors or other management personnel to learn the new process or equipment. It also enables supervisors or other members of management who are transferred to new equipment, processes, or work group to learn their new assignments.

3. Emergencies endangering the safety of personnel, equipment, or property or seriously interfering with production.

4. Experimental work.

While discussing these problems with Brown, Boyce stated that she spent about one-third of her time processing accounts payable. She said that she pitched in when work was behind schedule because of periodic heavy work loads and when work fell behind schedule because of heavy absenteeism. She also told him that she helped out for short periods of time when one or more persons arrived late. Boyce also pointed out that she knew much more about some of the operations than anyone else in the department. Her ten years' experience in the department had enabled her to learn most of the "tricks of the trade." It was much more efficient for her to take over temporarily than it was for her to stand over another person to ensure that the work would be performed properly.

QUESTIONS

1. Why did the Mutual Insurance Company have a policy limiting the performance of production work by supervisors? Does this policy seem reasonable?

2. Might Boyce's processing of accounts payable contribute to her problems? How might she better use her time?

3. Did Boyce use the appropriate methods for dealing with heavy work loads, tardiness, and absenteeism?

4. If you were Brown, what would you say to Boyce?

II

Interpersonal Skills

2

LEADERSHIP

LEARNING OBJECTIVES

This chapter discusses various approaches to the leadership process. After you have read this chapter, you will

1. Know what role influence plays in the leadership process
2. Understand the trait approach to leadership and its limitations
3. Understand task-oriented and employee-centered leadership
4. Understand the situational approach to leadership
5. Know how to analyze work situations to select effective leadership styles

Although leadership is one of the most widely studied concepts in management, there is substantial disagreement as to what leadership is and how a person should act as an effective leader. Part of the problem stems from the fact that leadership is a very general and vague term. At times, when speaking of leadership, we refer to *levels* or positions of leadership. From this perspective, a middle manager is more of a leader than a first-line supervisor, and a company president is more of a leader than a middle manager. At other times we refer to certain *qualities* or *characteristics* of a leader. These qualities may be either innate or developed within the person (e.g., intelligence, self-assurance, etc.). Finally, leadership at times is described as a *kind of behavior.* In this sense, a leader may be characterized as considerate or warm versus hard-driving or autocratic. But defining leadership in so many different ways can result in increased confusion as to what a leader actually is.

INFLUENCE

We define leadership in organizations as a process in which one person successfully exerts influence over others to reach desired objectives. A person who has the *ability* to influence the behavior of others and who *uses* this influence to alter their behavior will be called a leader. It should be recognized that influence utilized by a leader may stem from several sources (e.g., hierarchical position, organizational policy, informal relationships, expertise, and physical strength).

Leadership is not so much a question of having power over subordinates as it is a matter of having influence *with* them. A leader must meet the general needs and expectations of the followers (e.g., psychological or monetary rewards) and in return can receive status, esteem, and increased influence from the led. Thus leadership is a process of mutual influence and reward; it reflects a situation in which leaders lead at the consent of the governed. From this point of view, the title to supervise others is a gift of the higher echelons, but the title to lead others is a gift of the followers. The preceding sentence makes it clear that leadership is a process of influence and power. Obviously, that influence or power might be used for either personal or organizational ends. Frequently, a "good" leader is differentiated from a "bad" one by identifying whether he or she is predominantly concerned with personal or organizational goals.

As stated in Chapter 1, the concept of leadership should be distinguished from that of management or supervision. Supervision is a broader concept, which comprises a process of mental and physical activity. In supervision, subordinates are brought together to perform specific formal duties and to accomplish organizational objectives. Thus leadership is but one element of the overall job of supervision.

APPROACHES TO LEADERSHIP

This chapter will focus on *understanding* leadership in an organizational context and *developing* effective leadership skills that lead to the attainment of organizational goals. To accomplish this, a supervisor should understand what has been learned from studies of leadership so that effective leadership behaviors may be selected. In this regard, we will discuss several approaches to leadership about which there is substantial knowledge. These approaches include the trait approach; the task, or production-oriented approach; the supportive, or employee-centered, approach; and the situational approach.

Trait Approach to Leadership

Over the years many studies have attempted to identify the characteristics or traits of leaders, and especially those essential traits of effective leaders. Although some progress has been made, no general conclusion has been reached as to the necessary traits for all work situations. For example, leaders were reported to be generally more intelligent than the group average, but they were not substantially more intelligent. Obviously, a leader's intelligence would need to vary with the intelligence of the particular group. Most important, the trait approach tends to emphasize existing personal attributes and identifying (selecting) persons possessing such traits rather than the process of leading; it does not focus on developing leadership skills or attributes. Because of its limited utility, the trait approach to leadership has had a restricted impact.

Task-Oriented and Employee-Centered
Leadership Approaches

With few exceptions, the most widespread approaches to understanding leadership focus on two dimensions of leader behavior. One dimension concerns the leader's efforts to accomplish organizational tasks, and it is described by various names: task-oriented leadership, concern for production, and initiating structure. We will use task-oriented leadership to designate this dimension. The second dimension focuses on the relationship between the leader and the subordinates, and it is also described by various names: employee-centered leadership, concern for people, and consideration. We will use employee-centered leadership to designate this dimension.

By focusing on these two dimensions, leadership effectiveness is usually determined through measures of productivity and of worker satisfaction. Supervisors have been led to believe that if they have a high concern for getting the job done and for maintaining good relationships with employees, they can expect to have both a productive and a satisfied work group. Frequently, this prescription for effective leadership has been applied to almost every leadership situation. But what have studies of these approaches revealed? The following summary provides some clues.

Task-Oriented Leadership. Some of the most significant research work focusing on task-oriented leadership is that reported by the Ohio State Leadership Group. These researchers identified a leadership dimension, "initiating structure," which has great importance for task-oriented leadership; this leadership orientation focuses on the degree to which a leader schedules or plans the method of work. The leader may also develop methods for measuring or monitoring work output or job performance. Leaders who emphasize these concerns are usually rated very highly by their supervisors; also, they usually perform well on objective measures of cost reduction and high productivity.

Although leaders who are high on "initiating structure" tend to be rated as superior by their own supervisors, research has shown that when such leaders have little concern for people or low "consideration," their subordinates tend to be dissatisfied with the working environment and with their supervisor. As a result, it appears that an emphasis on "initiating structure" alone may lead to short-run increases in productivity at the expense of having higher rates of grievances, absenteeism, and turnover. Such leaders also are perceived as being "authoritarian" or "autocratic."

Leaders who emphasize consideration along with initiating structure tend to have work units that are highly productive; these units do not have the negative attributes associated with the leadership styles of persons with a low concern for people. As a result, high initiating structure by itself has some unfortunate and negative consequences, whereas high initiating structure when coupled with high consideration for employees tends to produce results that are desirable in terms of task accomplishment and desirable in terms of work group morale. It should be emphasized, though, that these findings are of a general nature; it is not clear exactly how high one's initiating structure or consideration should be.

Employee-Centered Leadership. Over the past two decades, much attention has been given to the supportive, or employee-centered, style of leadership. Many adherents of supportive leadership styles argue that a "democratic," participative, or employee-centered atmosphere is useful in almost every organizational setting. Although some studies have demonstrated that supportive leadership styles can have desirable effects on organizational performance and subordinate satisfaction, this conclusion is not unanimous among researchers. Specifically, while some studies advocate a more general or participative leadership approach, other studies have found that close supervision is also effective.

A comparison of a few representative studies highlights the lack of agreement concerning the effects of employee-centered leadership. One study found that general supervision was accompanied by employee-centered supervision; employee centeredness tended to improve subordinate satisfaction with the job. (Frequently, it has been *assumed* that high subordinate satisfaction is associated with high output.) By contrast, another study found that close supervision may be perceived by some subordinates as being an expression of the supervisor's concern for them or interest in their welfare. It has been reported that subordinates with certain personalities (i.e., authoritarian types) preferred more direct leadership styles to the employee-centered styles. Evidently some subordinates view the participative leader as someone who is weak and who should be avoided. Thus the findings reported by researchers advocating employee-centered leadership styles seem to have certain limitations. The effective use of employee-centered leadership styles is dependent upon the needs and perceptions of the persons involved. At this time, the most useful conclusions seem to be that employee-centered leadership styles are most effective when

1. Decisions are not routine
2. The information required for effective decision making cannot be standardized
3. Decisions need not be made rapidly, thus allowing time to involve subordinates in a participative decision-making process
4. Subordinates feel a strong need for independence
5. Subordinate participation in decision making is legitimate
6. Subordinates see themselves as being able to contribute to the decision-making process
7. Subordinates are confident of their ability to work without the reassurance of close supervision

In general, employee-centered leadership styles are appropriate under certain conditions (e.g., among professionals), but these conditions are not found in all work situations (e.g., routine clerical jobs).

Situational Approach to Leadership

The situational approach to leadership focuses on effective leadership behavior as a function of the leader's personality, the needs and expectations of subordinates, and the environment in which the leader and subordinates perform their work. By simultaneously taking these three variables into account, the situational leadership approach is able to help point out an appropriate style in a given situation. One expert, Frederick Fiedler, has analyzed leadership styles in terms of (1) the leader's personal relationship with group members, (2) the formal power or authority that the leader's position provides, and (3) the degree of structure or repetitiveness in the assigned task. Through proper analysis, a selection between employee-centered leadership and a task-oriented style can be made according to the demands of the situation.

According to Fiedler, in very favorable conditions where the leader has (a) power, (b) informal backing, and (c) a relatively well outlined or structured task, the group is ready to be directed—a task-oriented style is effective. In addition, the task orientation is appropriate under conditions very unfavorable to the leader because the group will lose effectiveness unless the leader actively intervenes and keeps the members on the job. By contrast, employee-centered styles get more desirable results under moderately unfavorable conditions. That is, when an accepted leader faces an ambiguous task or his or her relationships with group members are unsatisfactory, a "people orientation" and helpful attitude may reduce anxiety or intergroup conflict and thereby permit the leader to operate more effectively. Thus an employee-centered leadership style is most appropriate where a leader has good relationships with group members and has high position power. This is so because it helps the group work on an ambiguous task (see Table 2-1).

In a different situation, a leader who has moderately poor relationships with group members and little position power but who has a highly

Table 2-1.   Situational Leadership Analysis

Group Situation			*Leadership Style Correlating with Productivity under Condition in Column 1*
(1)	*(2)*	*(3)*	
Leader-Member Relationship	*Task Structure*	*Position Power*	
Good	Structured	Strong	Task-oriented
Good	Structured	Weak	Task-oriented
Good	Unstructured	Strong	Task-oriented
Good	Unstructured	Weak	Employee-centered
Moderately poor	Structured	Strong	Employee-centered
Moderately poor	Structured	Weak	No data
Moderately poor	Unstructured	Strong	No relationship indicated
Moderately poor	Unstructured	Weak	Task-oriented

structured task would probably find an employee-centered leadership style to be appropriate because the leader would most likely be trying to guide and suggest solutions rather than attempting to manage and control the group. By contrast, when a leader can expect support from group members because they personally like him or her *and* when the leader can enforce his or her will because of a position of power *and* the situation is one in which the leader and the group members understand their duties, then the appropriate general leadership style is one that provides direction and relies on authority. Under these conditions, the group members understand what they should do and the leader is the one who directs their behavior. In a different way, the leader who is faced with a very poorly structured task, little formal authority, and unsatisfactory relationships with subordinates would find, also, that a more directive leadership style would be most effective. This occurs because the leader will have to be assertive to gain recognition from the group and because the task is ill defined; the group needs direction or a suggestion from someone who appears to know how the problem should be tackled. In summary, for different reasons, then, both a very favorable and a very unfavorable leadership condition or situation call for more directive leadership styles; moderately or intermediately favorable situations call for more participative styles.

In a different way, the situational leadership theory provides an explanation for the *sequence* of leadership styles needed as a project progresses. For example, a research project becomes more structured over time. During the planning phases, a research project is more tentative and unstructured, but it becomes more highly structured or programmed once the design is decided and the experiment begins. In the initial stages, it is appropriate for the leader to play a more permissive and "democratic" role as planning proceeds. But as the project progresses and the procedure for completing the task becomes more programmed or well known, it is appropriate for the leader to become more autocratic or directive. In this later phase, control is more necessary. Thus the leader should change the leadership style in order to meet the requirements of the situation.

It should be evident that the situational approach to leadership provides much promise as a practical tool for managers and supervisors. It requires, though, that the supervisor be able to analyze situations effectively and change his or her behavior to fit situational requirements.

With the findings that a single leadership orientation or style is not appropriate for all situations, two questions then arise: How should the manager go about analyzing situations and selecting an effective leadership style? and How is the supervisor to behave in any given circumstance? The following discussion provides some valuable insight into answering these questions.

CHOOSING A LEADERSHIP STYLE

Most supervisors are aware that effective decisions are made by utilizing various degrees of participation by subordinates. At times individual supervisors solve problems and take action with little participation from others, while at other times a group or a committee is used. Supervisors must consider the situation they face in order to select an effective leadership style.

To select an effective leadership style, it is important to recognize the complicated contributions and limitations of groups in problem solving. Supervisors want to make high quality decisions. While the rational model of decision making concentrates on the manager as the appropriate focal point in the decision-making process, many modern approaches have suggested that a group, or participative, mode holds much promise. As mentioned earlier in the chapter, the participative approach involves subordinates in solving problems; this results in developing employees who are more likely to implement effectively the conclusions reached to solve a particular problem. But, as we have seen, there are several limitations to these participative approaches. What is a supervisor to do? What leadership style should be adopted? How does a leader know whether the appropriate amount of involvement is being developed in subordinates? To resolve these questions, the following system is recommended.

Types of Leadership Decision Styles

At the outset it is important for a leader to understand that there are several intermediate styles between that which could be called directive or task-oriented and that which could be labeled as fully participative or employee-centered. Table 2–2 lists various types of leadership decision styles. It can be seen that of the five leadership decision styles included in the table, only the last one is a completely participative, or "democratic," one. Supervisors should realize, however, that they do not have to select any *one* of the styles or approaches for *all* problems. That is, at times style A is appropriate, while at other times problems require style C or style E. These styles form a continuum of leadership decision styles, as shown in Figure 2–1. An understanding of the factors that influence the choice of leadership styles makes it possible to select an appropriate one with confidence.

Diagnostic Questions for Analyzing a Problem Situation

Table 2–3 lists seven diagnostic questions that a supervisor should ask himself or herself in selecting an appropriate leadership style. By answering the questions in the table with a simple yes or no, the manager can analyze the situation and determine the appropriate leadership style.

Table 2-2. Types of Leadership Decision Styles

A. You solve the problem or make the decision yourself, using information available to you at that time.
B. You obtain the necessary information from your subordinate(s), then decide on the solution to the problem yourself. You may or may not tell your subordinates what the problem is in getting the information from them. The role played by your subordinates in making the decision is clearly one of providing the necessary information to you, rather than generating or evaluating alternative solutions.
C. You share the problem with relevant subordinates individually, getting their ideas and suggestions without bringing them together as a group. Then *you* make the decision, which may or may not reflect your subordinates' influence.
D. You share the problem with your subordinates as a group, collectively obtaining their ideas and suggestions. Then *you* make the decision, which may or may not reflect your subordinates' influence.
E. You share a problem with your subordinates as a group. Together you generate and evaluate alternatives and attempt to reach agreement (consensus) on a solution. Your role is much like that of chairman. You do not try to influence the group to adopt "your" solution and you are willing to accept and implement any solution that has the support of the entire group.

Reprinted from *Leadership And Decision Making* by Vroom and Yetton by permission of the University of Pittsburg Press. © 1973 by University of Pittsburgh Press.

Table 2-3. Diagnostic Questions for Analyzing a Problem Situation

1. Is decision quality important? Is one solution likely to be more logical, functional, or desirable than another?
2. Do I have enough information to make a high-quality decision myself?
3. Is the problem structured (is there a systematic method, policy, or formula for solving the problem)? Do I know where to gather the appropriate information? Must I define the problem?
4. Is acceptance of the decision by subordinates critical before it can be implemented effectively?
5. If I were to make the decision by myself, is it reasonably certain that it would be accepted by my subordinates?
6. Do subordinates share the organization's goals or objectives to be accomplished by solving this problem?
7. Will the preferred solution likely cause conflict among subordinates?

Leadership Decision Process Analysis

The analysis questions from Table 2–3 are listed along the top of Figures 2–2A and 2–2B. To select the appropriate leadership style, the supervisor should ask himself or herself these questions and move along the appropriate decision path until a final leadership style is indicated.

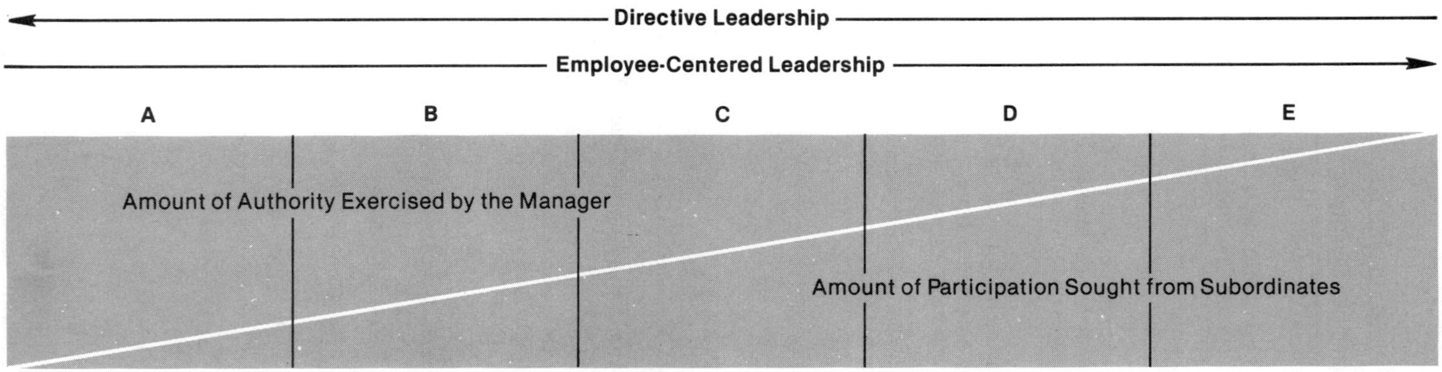

A	B	C	D	E
Manager Makes Decision	Manager Makes Decision	Manager Makes Decision	Manager Makes Decision	Group Makes Decision
Seeks no information from subordinates	Seeks information from individual subordinates	Seeks information from individual subordinates	Seeks information from subordinates as a group	Seeks information from subordinates as a group
	May or may not share problem with subordinates	Shares problem with individual subordinates	Shares problem with subordinates as a group	Shares problem with subordinates as a group
				Group and manager Generate and evaluate alternatives
				Group and manager Reach agreement (consensus)

Figure 2-1 Leadership Decision Style Continuum

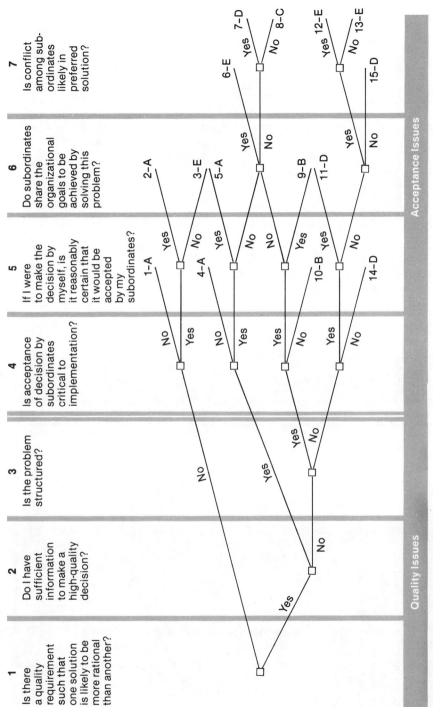

Figure 2–2A Decision Process Flowchart

31

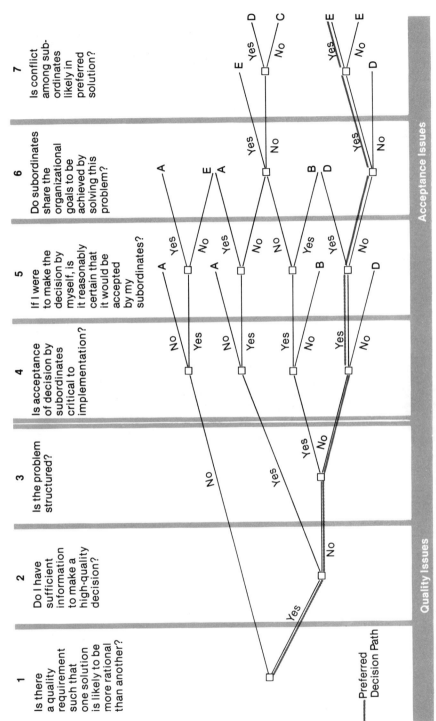

1

Is there a quality requirement such that one solution is likely to be more rational than another?

2

Do I have sufficient information to make a high-quality decision?

3

Is the problem structured?

4

Is acceptance of decision by subordinates critical to implementation?

5

If I were to make the decision by myself, is it reasonably certain that it would be accepted by my subordinates?

6

Do subordinates share the organizational goals to be achieved by solving this problem?

7

Is conflict among subordinates likely in preferred solution?

Quality Issues

Acceptance Issues

—— Preferred Decision Path

Figure 2–2B Decision Process Flowchart Example

32

Although some situations call for more than one leadership style, Figure 2–2A designates the leadership style that is the most time-efficient. Thus, if a supervisor could appropriately make a decision alone or involve subordinates in the decision process, it would be more time-efficient to make the decision alone and forgo the time necessary to involve others. Figure 2–2A reflects this logic.

If enough time is available, other leadership styles *could* be used. For example, even though a leader has enough information to make a high-quality decision and group acceptance is unnecessary, a more participative leadership style usually *could* be used. The leadership styles shown in Figures 2–2A and 2–2B were selected by taking into consideration the important factor of time. However, in Table 2–4 all of the feasible leadership styles are presented regardless of the time needed to implement them. Thus, even though the most time-efficient approach is shown in Figures 2–2A and 2–2B, other feasible styles can be implemented if enough time is available.

To provide an example of how Figure 2–2A could be used, the reader is asked to consider the following short case and answer the seven questions in Table 2–3. By noting, in Figure 2–2B, the path indicated by the answers to these questions, the analysis of the reader can be compared with that of hundreds of other managers who have been asked the same questions.

Table 2–4. Problem Types and the Feasible Set of Leadership Styles

Problem Type	Acceptable Styles	Most Time-Efficient Style
1	A,B,C,D,E	A
2	A,B,C,D,E	A
3	E	E
4	A,B,C,D,E*	A
5	A,B,C,D,E*	A
6	E	E
7	D	D
8	D,E	D
9	B,C,D,E*	B
10	B,C,D,E*	B
11	D,E*	D
12	E	E
13	E	E
14	D,E*	D
15	D	D

*E is an acceptable style only when the answer to question 6 is yes.

EXAMPLE

You are the manufacturing manager in a large electronic plant which has always been searching for ways to improve efficiency. Recently, new machines have been installed in addition to a new simplified work system. But to the surprise of everybody, including yourself, the expected increase in productivity did not occur. In fact, production has begun to drop, quality has fallen off, and a number of employee separations have occurred.

You do not believe that there is anything wrong with the machines. Reports from other companies that are using the same equipment confirm your opinion. In addition, you have had representatives from the company that built the machines check them out, and the report has been that the machines are operating at peak efficiency.

You suspect that some part of the work system may be responsible for the change, but this view is not widely shared by your immediate subordinates. These subordinates consist of four first-line supervisors, each in charge of a section, plus your supply manager. The drop in production has been variously attributed to poor training of the operators, lack of an adequate system of financial incentives, and poor morale. Clearly, this is an issue that involves considerable anxiety within individuals and potential disagreement among your subordinates.

This morning you received a phone call from your division manager. He had just received your production figures for the past six months and called to express his concern. He indicated that the problem was yours to solve in any way you thought best, but that he would like to know within a week what steps you plan to take.

You share your division manager's concern as to the falling productivity and know that your workers are also concerned. The problem is to decide what steps to take to rectify this situation.

Analysis

Questions to address:

1. Is there a quality requirement such that one solution is likely to be more logical, functional, or desirable? Yes, you wish to find a solution to the problem of falling production. Just any solution may not solve the problem.

2. Do you have sufficient information to make a high-quality decision by yourself? No, you are not certain of the specific cause of the production problems; since the problem cause is not clear, the solution also is not known to you.

3. Is the problem structured? (Is there a systematic method, policy, or formula for solving the problem?) No, though you may have some idea as to how to begin to uncover the problem cause, this is a problem that was unexpected. Thus, no company policy, system, or formula has been developed to solve it.

4. Is acceptance of the decision by subordinates critical before a solution can be implemented effectively? Yes, since there is disagreement among subordinates about the causes of the problem and since they must implement the decision, their acceptance is necessary.

5. If you were to make the decision yourself, is it reasonably certain that it would be accepted by your subordinates? No, on this issue there are deep feelings and disagreements among subordinates.

6. Do subordinates share the organization's goals or objectives to be achieved by solving this problem? <u>Yes</u>, you know that your subordinates are also concerned.

7. Will the preferred solution probably cause conflict among subordinates? <u>Yes</u>, at this point subordinates have disagreements among themselves. They would be unlikely to agree among themselves as to the appropriate steps to take to remedy the problem—hence conflict is probable.

Effective leadership style (see the indicated decision path in Figure 2-2B): *E.*

The above case points out the situational aspects of group versus individual decision making; the selection of group or individual decision making depends upon the problem being confronted. For example, whenever mere short-run compliance with the dictates of the leader or supervisor is sufficient for successful decisional implementation, acceptance is not so critical. But as experienced supervisors know, acceptance of a decision by subordinates is frequently essential to the effective implementation of the decision. The need by the decision maker for acceptance *and* commitment to the decision by subordinates eliminates the A and B styles. Moreover, when the supervisor needs acceptance plus commitment, and conflict can be expected over whatever solution is chosen, the A, B, and C styles are inappropriate. The fully participative mode (style E) is the most appropriate leadership style when the supervisor desires acceptance plus commitment from subordinates *and* many acceptable solutions exist. Thus, by answering the questions in Table 2-3, a supervisor can chart the appropriate leadership style by using Figure 2-2A.

Significantly, many writers on the subject of leadership advocate very participative leadership for most situations. Although Figure 2-2A reveals that some degree of participation is a frequently (even usually) appropriate style, these are not the best approaches at *all* times. The usefulness of this leadership style selection system in determining the appropriate style is that it effectively helps the supervisor sort out the crucial elements in a situation. And since there are only seven questions involved, they can be mastered in a relatively short time. By utilizing this approach, a supervisor may promptly experience an improvement in effectiveness as an appropriate leadership style is adopted.

SUMMARY

This chapter has discussed several approaches to leadership. An analysis of research studies has revealed limitations in adopting only the task-oriented *or* employee-centered leadership styles. To assist the supervisor in selecting an appropriate leadership style, a practical system was provided which can be used to analyze almost any situation based upon information, group acceptance, and time usage considerations.

DISCUSSION QUESTIONS

1. In what way is influence related to leadership?

2. What have studies revealed about the use of the trait approach to leadership?

3. Define *task-oriented leadership*.

4. Compare task-oriented leadership with employee-centered leadership.

5. Under what conditions is employee-centered leadership most effective?

6. From personal experience, describe a situation in which task-oriented (employee-centered) leadership was effective.

7. What are the three major components of the situational leadership approach presented in the chapter?

8. Describe the relationship between authority exercised by a supervisor and participation sought from subordinates.

9. What is the importance of quality and acceptance issues in the leadership decision process?

10. In what way does time affect the choice of leader behaviors?

11. Apply the leadership decision model presented in this chapter to the role of teacher of the course using this text.

12. What factors might cause you to use a leadership style that is not the most time efficient, as specified by the flowchart in this chapter?

13. What is a "structured" problem as defined in the chapter?

CASE 2-1.   Driemeier Construction Company

You are the general foreman in charge of a large gang laying an oil pipeline, and you have to estimate your expected rate of progress in order to schedule material deliveries to the next field site.

You know the nature of the terrain you will be traveling and have the historical data needed to compute the mean and variance in the rate over that type of terrain. Given these two variables, it is a simple matter to calculate the earliest and latest times at which materials and support facilities will be needed at the next site. It is important that your estimate be reasonably accurate. Underestimates result in idle foremen and workers, and overestimates result in tying up materials for a period of time before they are to be used.

Progress has been good, and your five foremen and other members of the gang will receive substantial bonuses if the project is completed ahead of schedule.

CASE 2-2.   Markland and Beatty, Inc.

You are supervising the work of twelve engineers in a large engineering firm. Their formal training and work experience are very similar, permitting you to use them interchangeably on projects. Yesterday your manager informed you that an overseas affiliate had requested that four engineers be sent abroad on extended loan for a period of six to eight months. For a number of reasons, he argued and you agreed that this request should be met from your group.

All your engineers are capable of handling this assignment, and from the standpoint of present and future projects, there is no particular reason why any one should be retained over any other. The problem is somewhat complicated by the fact that the overseas assignment is in what is generally regarded as an undesirable location.

QUESTIONS

1. Is there a quality requirement such that one solution is likely to be more rational than another?

2. Do I have sufficient information to make a high-quality decision?

3. Is the problem structured?

4. Is acceptance of the decision by subordinates critical to implementation?

5. If I make the decision by myself, is it reasonably certain that it would be accepted by my subordinates?

6. Do subordinates share the organizational goals to be accomplished by solving this problem?

7. Is conflict among subordinates likely in the preferred solution?

8. Utilizing the answers to the above questions and the decision process flowchart of Figure 2-2A, what leadership style would you use for this case?

3

UNDERSTANDING YOURSELF AND OTHERS

LEARNING OBJECTIVES

This chapter discusses how people become what they are. It also discusses the needs that people hope to satisfy at work. After you have read this chapter, you will

1. Have a better understanding of how heredity and environment shape our lives
2. Understand how and why each person is like every other person in some ways, like some other people in other ways, and like no other person in still other ways
3. Be familiar with A. H. Maslow's "hierarchy of needs" and Douglas MacGregor's "Theory X and Theory Y"
4. Understand how employee needs can be satisfied on the job

Every person is in certain respects like all other persons, like some other person, and like no other person. The ability to understand similarities and differences in human personality, and the needs, attitudes and perceptions of people, is one of the manager's principal skills.

While it is important that supervisors understand themselves and others, it is also difficult to accomplish this. Very few people understand themselves even when they attempt to do so. Those parts of our personality that we definitely should understand are the very parts that lie buried deepest in our unconscious self. Understanding is further complicated by the fact that people do not readily reveal themselves to others.

The attempt to understand oneself and others involves developing a sensitivity to one's own behavior, as well as to the behavior and feelings of others with whom one associates. Managers who have some understanding of why they behave and feel as they do find it easier to understand the feelings and behavior of the persons whom they supervise. They also find it easier to motivate them, to satisfy their needs, and to deal with them fairly, constructively and empathetically.

HOW WE BECOME WHAT WE ARE

Personality

We are all products of both our heritage and the experiences we have had in the process of growing up. As a result of our heritage and lifelong experiences with our physical and social world, we develop sets of values, beliefs, and sentiments, which are deep-seated and which determine how we perceive, feel, and think about events in the world about us. These ways of feeling, thinking, and behaving are patterned and quite consistent over time and are unique to each of us.

These patterned and consistent ways of feeling, thinking, and behaving, plus our physical and mental capacities and structures, become our individual identifying mark—our personality. Personality includes behavior that we cannot consciously control, such as blushing, as well as that which we can control, such as a decision to work late in order to complete an assignment. It also includes our tendency to behave in a particular way in a given situation, as well as our actual behavior in that situation. For example, a harsh and undeserved reprimand from a supervisor may cause a subordinate to want to respond by punching the supervisor in the nose. However, the subordinate may have learned that such aggression leads to discharge; and, instead of hitting the supervisor, the subordinate may behave humbly and promise to be more careful in the future. Personality also includes our aspirations and goals, as well as the means for achieving them. In other words, by personality we mean the total person—all that the person has been, is, and hopes to be.

Heredity

Certain physical and mental qualities or traits are passed on from parent to child. Physial characteristics, such as height, body build, color of hair and eyes, muscular coordination, and sensitivity to sound, sight, or taste, are inherited. Sometimes heritage also determines mental abilities. Thus a person who inherits the physical capacity for rapid, coordinated hand movements, and the mental abilities of reading musical scores and of keen sensitivity to sounds, may possess the talent necessary to become a concert pianist. Such a person does not inherit the skill for playing a piano, but rather inherits the talent or aptitude for doing so. The combined traits, capacities, and talents with which a person is born are referred to as heredity.

The fact that each person inherits certain traits and qualities, and that the inherited combination is different from that of every other person, makes each person unique. The supervisor's first step in understanding people is recognizing that each person is different and that everyone possesses a unique combination of strengths and abilities, and weaknesses and limitations.

Environment

While heredity is a major determinant of our physical and mental characteristics and of our personality, we are also molded by our environment from the moment of conception.

Family as Environment. The family is the most significant part of a human being's environment. Attitudes toward authority are shaped through the types of experiences children have with the authority figures in their lives, particularly with their father and mother. Parents who treat their children in an autocratic and arbitrary manner, and who force them to remain overly dependent, breed in them deep, though often unexpressed, hostility toward authority and those in positions of authority. For example, many behavioral problems in organizations, especially insubordination, stem from the deep hostility formed during adolescense toward persons in positions of authority. Supervisors are also authority figures and under certain circumstances they may "trigger" this latent hostility, which can be expressed in the form of refusal to follow orders, "backbiting," carrying rumors, or even—in extreme cases—physical attack.

The Influence of Culture. While the family is the principal institution responsible for instilling values and attitudes, it is part of a broader set of institutions that influence and mold personality. These institutions influence the individual both indirectly through the family and directly in the individual's interaction with them. The values, beliefs, and sentiments shared by individuals in an organization or society constitute its culture. Culture, at any point, is a product of their response to the problems they encounter in their journey through life. It is learned and is transmitted from one generation to another. It includes the philosophies, customs, beliefs, and attitudes that reflect the value system that a group of human beings have developed in order to survive within their environment and to give meaning to their lives. It includes all those forms of social organization and technologies that people have devised to achieve their individual and group goals. Finally, it includes the natural environment, climate, natural resources, and other natural factors that affect patterns of behavior. Culture tends to make people similar to each other, and it also shapes the various organizations within its boundaries.

Subculture. While the members of a culture or society may share many values, beliefs, and sentiments, few "universals" exist. Such cultural traits as language, dress, housing, and life-style vary from one individual to another, depending upon age grouping, occupation, geographic area, religion, and the social class to which one belongs. These groupings constitute subcultures within the larger culture. Members accept the values, beliefs, and sentiments of these subcultures or smaller societies. They become committed to them; hence these subcultures influence the behavior of their members.

The Organizational Subculture. Every organization operates within a larger cultural environment, and the values, beliefs, and sentiments held by those constituting the society set the limits within which the organization must function. From the point of view of society, the organization may be considered a subculture. At the same time, the organization may be considered a culture. The business organization acquires its own unique value system and patterns of conduct, which, although not identical to those of the larger culture, are consistent with it.

No two organizations are exactly alike. Thus, two businesses producing the same product, serving the same market, and operating in the same community may be quite different from one another as a result of the unique personalities and philosophies of the founders, method of organization, production processes, competitive pressures at critical times in the history of the business, and similar other variables. Furthermore, each major functional group within an organization tends to have a unique value system. The values and orientation of the research and development group in an organization tend to be quite different from those of marketing or production, and those of accounting and finance tend to be quite different from all of the other three. For example, research groups tend to be individualistic and idealistic. They place high value on perfection, "theoretical yield," "100 percent purity." Finance and accounting groups tend to be conservative in orientation and are usually identified as those that always seem to ask, "But who will pay for it?" The differences in value and orientation among these organizational subcultures frequently cause misunderstanding and conflict.

Implications of Culture for Supervisors. An awareness of the culture concept is useful to supervisors in three major ways. First, it enables them to understand the behavior of the people in their organizations. Perceptions, attitudes, and behaviors are in large measure learned from cultures. For example, Southern workers, many of whom come from farms and small towns, have usually resisted unionization. They tend to look upon an employer's right to control wages, hours, and working conditions as being natural and proper. They have not found authoritarian leadership styles as onerous as have workers from large metropolitan areas, and they have not experienced the discontent that is often a prerequisite to unionization.

Second, the patterned life experience of people in large measure determines how they will behave in a certain situation. For example: a professional or a supervisory employee will be more likely to oppose the unionization of an organization than will a blue-collar worker; American supervisors will be more likely to utilize participative techniques in carrying out their management functions than will German supervisors; a group of coal miners will be more likely to share the available work in a time of unemployment than will a group of automobile workers.

Third, the culture concept aids supervisors in understanding change, as well as in facilitating change in their organizations. It is difficult to effect changes that run counter to culturally based expectations and behavior. For example, factory workers feel that they accumulate increasing rights to a job the longer they work on it. Thus they expect that length of service, or seniority, should govern the order of layoff during cutbacks in production. A supervisor who violates this expectation can anticipate strong resistance from workers.

Let us now examine a situation in which an understanding of culture is important for supervisors.

Motivation and Culture. Supervisors value highly such traits as punctuality, responsibility, and the desire to achieve and succeed. They emphasize and advocate these qualities in supervising their subordinates. These personal qualities have been learned through a lifetime of experience. Family, friends, teachers, and supervisors rewarded them for exhibiting desired behaviors until these traits became a part of their personality.

On the other hand, underprivileged workers from low socioeconomic backgrounds generally have not learned punctuality, responsibility, and the desire to achieve. They, too, are acting in accord with the values of their subculture. The habits of "lack of ambition," irresponsibility, absenteeism, and quitting the job are normal responses that these workers have learned from their lifetime of experience. If the workers from underprivileged backgrounds are to behave like those from middle-class cultures, they must experience rewards on the job which will reinforce these desired behaviors. In other words, they must unlearn the values and behaviors of one culture and learn the values and behaviors of another.

The implications of culture extend beyond those of motivation. Culture also influences leadership style, organizational structure, and policies and procedures with respect to selection and placement, layoff and termination, promotion and transfer, collective bargaining, wage and salary administration, discipline, fringe benefits and social security, and the employment of women and minorities. The attitudes and expectations of employees are in large measure determined by how they have been molded and shaped by the culture.

UNDERSTANDING HUMAN NATURE

In attempting to understand why individuals behave as they do in organizations, it becomes necessary to make some basic assumptions about the nature of people. This section reviews several major concepts that have influenced the analysis and discussion of people's behavior at work. Three eminent psychologists, A. H. Maslow, Douglas McGregor, and Frederick Herzberg, have noted that people seem to be motivated by the need to achieve, to increase their competence, and to grow and develop as individuals. These theorists believe that the basic nature of human beings is such that they will strive toward those goals when given an opportunity to do so. Given the basic nature of man, the problem becomes one of designing organizations and creating the type of environment under which this inherent inclination of human beings can be nurtured and stimulated for the mutual benefit of the individual and the organization.

Maslow's Hierarchy of Needs[1]

Maslow viewed individuals as complex and changing beings. If an individual is motivated to act and if that individual's behavior is rational and purposeful, then that action must have been stimulated by an attempt to achieve some desired goal or end result. Maslow thus directed his attention toward those needs, wants, or drives that stimulate an individual to act.

Maslow conceptualizes a set of universal needs arranged in ascending order from the most basic, the <u>physiological</u> needs, through <u>safety</u> needs, <u>social</u> needs, <u>egoistic</u> needs, to the highest, <u>self-actualization</u> needs. An individual is thought to move successively up this need hierarchy in such a manner that each higher level of need is activated only after the needs below it are reasonably well satisfied. This view of a hierarchy of needs follows from Maslow's assumption that a satisfied need is not motivating.

Physiological Needs. The needs to survive, grow, and procreate are basic. They are powerful determinants of behavior when they are not satisfied. No other human need receives attention until these survival needs are met.

Safety Needs. The safety or security needs center on a person's desire to achieve a measure of control over the environment. People need to feel that they have a degree of mastery over the forces at whose mercy they may find themselves. Thus human beings strive to gain a degree of mastery over their own destinies.

For example, a basic physiological need is satisfied when one has had a nourishing meal. A person will then be concerned about making certain that this basic physiological need will be met the next day, the next month, the next year; but in modern society, food is purchased with money which, in turn, is received through employment. Workers who perceive their supervisor to be arbitrary and their job tenure to be unpredictable will feel threatened and insecure. They might then turn to a labor union to help make future employment less insecure.

Social Needs. The social or belongingness needs occupy the third level in Maslow's hierarchy. This set of needs includes the need for acceptance by others, the need for companionship, and the need to love and be loved. The social needs are those satisfied through association with others. Because the need to be accepted by the members of one's group is so strong, the group is able to exert strong influence over its members by threatening to ostracize or exclude the member who may not conform to group standards of acceptable behavior. For example, a group that has established what it considers

[1]See Abraham H. Maslow, *Motivation and Personality* (New York: Harper and Brothers, 1954) for a full discussion of The Hierarchy of Needs.

to be a fair level of output will "punish" a member whom it perceives to be either a "rate buster" or a "chiseler."

Ego Needs. An individual wishes not only to be accepted by others but also to be recognized as someone special or different. The ego or esteem needs include the need for recognition, status, achievement, competence, and self-respect. While the social needs are related to the need for belonging to a group, the ego needs are concerned with an individual's need to establish his or her unique identity within the group.

While ego needs may be strongly felt, they typically remain unsatisfied for many people in organizations. Many jobs, as now designed, do not offer individuals the opportunity to attain a sense of self-worth, achievement, or competence. In addition, many supervisors fail to satisfy this need through recognition for work well done and providing the type of feedback that indicates to people that they are needed and that they are achieving.

Self-actualization Needs. The need for self-realization and self-fulfillment is the highest order of need on the hierarchy. It refers to the need to become all that one is capable of becoming. In self-actualization, individuals measure their actual performance against their internal concept of the greatest performance of which they are capable. At this level, individuals do not measure themselves by the amount of acceptance they receive from their group nor by how well they achieve and distinguish themselves, but rather by how well they do compared with their concept of what they are capable of doing.

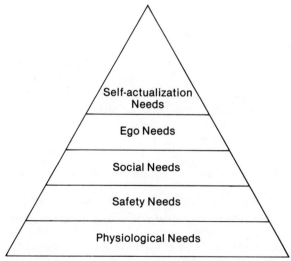

Figure 3-1 Maslow's Hierarchy of Needs

Is There a Hierarchy of Needs? While little direct evidence exists to support Maslow's strict application of a hierarchy of needs, there is definite evidence that the higher-order needs (social, ego, self-actualization) will not be strongly felt until the lower-order needs (physiological and safety) are reasonably well met. Once these lower-order needs are met, the social, ego, and self-actualization needs probably come into play more or less simultaneously, with the actual force of each being uniquely determined for each individual. Thus a person might be motivated to satisfy simultaneously two, or all three, higher-order needs, the exact strength of each need being unique to each individual.

Since most U.S. citizens' lower-order needs have more or less been satisfied, supervisors will obtain better results by attempting to motivate them through activation of their social, ego, and self-actualization needs.

McGregor's Theory X versus Theory Y

Douglas McGregor postulated two contrasting sets of assumptions about the nature of people. These assumptions are important to us because the set to which a supervisor subscribes in great measure determines how that supervisor will design an organization and supervise people. Theory X and Theory Y represent polar positions along a continuum of possible sets of assumptions about the basic nature of people in work situations.[2]

The Theory X assumptions are:

1. The average human being has an inherent dislike of work and will avoid it if he can.

2. Because of this human characteristic of dislike of work, most people must be coerced, controlled, directed, and threatened with punishment to get them to put forth adequate effort toward the achievement of organizational objectives.

3. The average human being prefers to be directed, wishes to avoid responsibility, has relatively little ambition, and wants security above all.

The Theory Y assumptions are:

1. The expenditure of physical and mental effort in work is as natural as play or rest.

2. External control and the threat of punishment are not the only means of bringing about effort toward organizational objectives. Man will exercise

---

[2]Douglas McGregor, *The Human Side of Enterprise* (New York: McGraw-Hill Book Company, 1960), pp. 33–34 and 47–48.

self-direction and self-control in the service of objectives to which he is committed.

3. Commitment to objectives is a function of the rewards associated with their achievement.

4. The average human being learns, under proper conditions, not only to accept but to seek responsibility.

5. The capacity to exercise a high degree of imagination, ingenuity, and creativity in the solution of organizational problems is widely, not narrowly, distributed in the population.

6. Under the conditions of modern industrial life, the intellectual potentialities of the average human being are only partially utilized.

According to McGregor, the supervisor who perceives people as being lazy, avoiding work, requiring coercion, and seeking direction will control behavior closely and motivate through the use of money, discipline, and authority. In other words, a Theory X supervisor will tend to perceive people as being rather limited in the needs they expect to satisfy on the job and will attempt to motivate them by appealing to Maslow's lower-order physiological and safety needs.

It is also reasonable to assume that the supervisor who perceives people as being capable of exercising self-direction and self-control toward the achievement of worthwhile objectives will tend to provide a participative style of leadership, will be supportive of employee attempts to accept responsibility, and will design jobs so that people can develop a sense of achievement, growth, and competency. The Theory Y supervisor will tend to appeal to Maslow's higher-order social, egoistic, and self-actualization needs which people hope to satisfy on their jobs.

Theory X or Theory Y? Which assumption about people is correct, Theory X or Theory Y? In some instances Theory X might be correct, for we all know that some people do not like work, require close supervision, have little ambition, and seek only security. In other instances Theory Y might be correct, for there are many people who are energetic, enjoy work, and are self-actualizing in their basic orientation. Furthermore, we have also observed people whose basic need orientation has changed as a result of changes in their life and career situation.

The Theory Y assumption is appealing to many people in our culture because it is consistent with the American democratic ideal, with the desire for participation and consultation and with the belief in individual freedom. It holds strong appeal also because it emphasizes the concept of growth, competency, and self-actualization. Theory X assumptions, if carried out in practice, would deny individuals the types of experiences that would enable them to learn how to solve problems, make decisions, develop self-confidence, and improve their mental and physical capacities. Most supervisors make Theory Y assumptions about their own behavior but make Theory X assumptions about their subordinates' behavior.

SATISFYING NEEDS ON THE JOB

Can Needs Be Satisfied on the Job?

Maslow's concept of a hierarchy of needs is based upon the assumptions that a need can be satisfied and that when this occurs people cease seeking outcomes to satisfy that need. This seems to apply principally to the physiological and safety needs.

Evidence indicates that the satisfaction of the need for ego esteem and self-actualization is difficult to achieve. By their very nature they seem to continually proliferate and elaborate upon themselves by seeking, even demanding, countless degrees and forms of expression.

Figure 3–2 indicates the importance attached to five needs by nineteen hundred managers, and Figure 3–3 indicates the degree to which these needs were being satisfied in their jobs.[3] Note that it was those needs they considered most important that were being the least well met! This study is extremely significant because other studies indicate that the higher-order needs of self-actualization (Porter's "self-realization"), ego esteem (Porter's "autonomy" and "esteem"), and social needs are even less well satisfied for lower-level nonmanagerial employees than they are for managers, such as those studied by Porter.

This research indicates that managers, as well as nonmanagers, experience dissatisfaction with their jobs. It also seems to indicate that managers can maintain a fully satisfied work group only if they are able to provide subordinates with increasing opportunities to satsify their needs for challenge, achievement, and self-actualization.

Employees Express and Seek to Satisfy Needs in Different Ways

Supervisors try to induce their subordinates to work hard for the organization by rewarding desirable behavior. In other words, the supervisor provides rewards in exchange for hard work. This exchange will be effective only if the supervisor knows which of the available rewards will operate to satisfy the employees' needs. This is quite difficult to accomplish, since each person has his or her unique set of needs.

---

[3]Lyman W. Porter, Edward E. Lawler, Jr., and J. Richard Hackman, *Behavior in Organizations* (New York: McGraw-Hill Book Company, 1975), pp. 44–45.

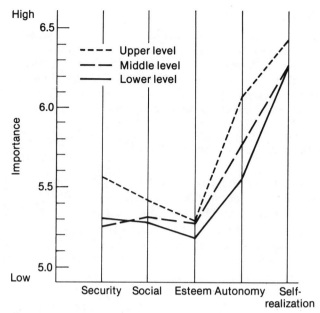

Figure 3-2 Importance Attached to Five Needs by Managers at Three Organizational Levels

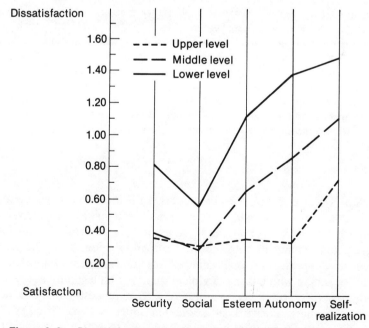

Figure 3-3 Dissatisfaction Attached to Five Needs by Managers at Three Organizational Levels

EXAMPLE

One person may seek to satisfy a need for maintaining control over his life through a seniority clause in a union contract, another through the acquisition of new skills which will ensure a demand for his services, and still another through promotion to a managerial position. The supervisor must not only learn that these three employees have a strong need for self-determination but also realize that each is seeking to meet that need in a different manner.

Some Rewards Satisfy Several Needs

Money is a reward that can satisfy many different needs. It can satisfy not only survival needs but also security and ego needs. It can be used to purchase food, clothing, and shelter, which satisfies survival needs. It can also purchase some types of personal security through such items as a pension plan or a large bank account, which will cushion the consequences of a loss of job. And a person's salary is *one* indicator of his or her achievement, growth, and worth to the organization.

EXAMPLE

Life insurance salespersons work on commission. They sometimes refuse promotion to a managerial position because as a manager they will receive a lower, though more secure, income. They have typically accumulated a large amount of assets which satisfy their rather minimal survival and security needs. They experience satisfaction of their ego, and even self-actualization, needs through their large incomes, which enable them to purchase homes, automobiles, vacations, art objects, and other amenities reflecting the level of their success. Life insurance salespersons who achieve the difficult goal of selling at least $1 million of insurance in a year are admitted to the "Million-Dollar Roundtable," an exclusive group consisting of the most distinguished salespersons in the industry. This becomes a benchmark against which a salesperson can measure himself or herself.

People Change

Supervisors find that they cannot relax the attention they give to understanding their subordinates. It is not possible to make a judgment about the "needs" of a subordinate and count on it to be valid for the future because people change in both the short run and the long run. The priority of needs they express sometimes changes from one moment to another. For example, a person who has had a violent quarrel with a spouse at breakfast may unexpectedly react very emotionally to a request from a superior regarding an emergency work situation. The supervisor may attempt to explain the employee's unusual behavior by saying that he or she "acted out of character."

50

People also change over longer periods of time. For example, a succession of successes in one's courses at college or in one's career may be expected to raise one's level of aspiration. The reverse also tends to be true.

People Are Not Fully Aware of Their Needs

Supervisors who endeavor to understand those around them in the organization often find that this can become complicated because no one is fully aware of his or her needs. Some needs remain below the level of consciousness, while we are only dimly aware of some others. This lack of awareness springs from the threat these needs present to us. By repressing or denying the existence of these needs, they can be kept below our level of consciousness. Thus they present no threat to our concept about ourselves.

In summary, it is probably overly idealistic to expect supervisors to meet fully the expectations and needs of workers. On the other hand, by being aware of the complexity of human needs and by attempting to understand their subordinates, they can offer them important rewards in exchange for excellent job performance.

SUMMARY

This chapter has emphasized those dimensions of human behavior that are important to supervisors as they carry out their leadership responsibilities. First, it discussed those principles of human behavior common to all people—causality, goal orientation, motivation, and insatiability of the important acquired needs.

Second, it focused on heritage and environment as the major determinants of personality, emphasizing the role of culture in shaping human behavior. It introduced the concept of subculture and pointed out that the organizational subculture is important in our lives. It is essential that supervisors understand the distinguishing features of these subcultures and how they affect the behavior of those who live in them.

Third, it described Maslow's hierarchical need system—the physiological, safety, social, egoistic, and self-actualization needs. McGregor's Theory X–Theory Y models of supervisory behavior were discussed as an application of Maslow's concepts of motivation.

Fourth, it explained why people expect to satisfy their major needs at work. Supervisors typically find the task of satisfying the needs of subordinates very challenging; people express many needs of varying importance to them; they seek to satisfy these needs in specific ways; some rewards satisfy many needs; some needs change from day to day and others change over long periods of time; and people are often unaware of certain needs. If supervisors understand the needs that their subordinates hope to satisfy on the job and if they provide rewards that satisfy those needs in exchange for excellent performance, they possess an important tool for obtaining a high level of motivation among their subordinates.

DISCUSSION QUESTIONS

1. What is meant by the term *personality?*

2. What do we inherit from our parents? Why is heredity important in understanding behavior?

3. What are some of the major environmental factors that mold our behavior? What is meant by the term *culture?* Give examples of culture.

4. What is meant by the *organizational structure?*

5. Why is the concept of culture important to supervisors? Give examples of the application of the concept of culture to business.

6. What is Maslow's hierarchy of needs? Define each need in his hierarchy. Give examples.

7. What is Theory X? Theory Y?

8. What are some problems faced by supervisors who wish to help their employees satisfy their needs on the job?

CASE 3-1.   Eltra Gear and Axle Company

The Eltra Gear and Axle Company is located in a suburb of a large midwestern city. It produces axles and gears for manufacturers of automobile, truck, and farm equipment. The business is highly competitive. Quality is important, and the final product must meet demanding quality standards.

The company purchases high-grade steel bars and rods, which are cut to proper size and then forged under very high pressure into approximate dimensions. Each piece is then machined and shaped to exacting specifications using a variety of precision machines, such as turret lathes, milling machines, shapers, and screw machines. The parts are then heat treated to relieve internal stresses developed within the metal during these operations. Each part is then final-machined, honed, and polished. Finally, each piece must pass from three to seven inspections before preparation for shipment. A typical gear or axle may have as many as seventy-five different operations performed on it in the course of manufacture.

The company employs approximately five hundred men and women, most of whom perform semiskilled work on high-production and sophisticated machines. While the equipment is modern, the production processes cannot be completely automated. Working conditions are excellent. Most of the heavy lifting and movement of materials is accomplished by conveyors, cranes, and forklift trucks. Machines are set up, adjusted, and repaired by a small group of skilled machinists and setup specialists, although many machine operators could perform many of the setups and most of the adjustments and minor repairs.

The company employs two industrial engineers, who design plant layout, determine the routing of the gears and axles through the various operations, and perform motion and time studies in order to set time standards. Typically, each operator performs one or two tasks, the total time of which requires from thirty seconds to two minutes. The operator's work consists largely of making certain that the parts being worked on are placed properly in the machines and that the machines are not malfunctioning, checking on the work of the machines, and calling for the supervisor if serious problems arise.

Mechanical engineers constantly work at redesigning machines and equipment in order to simplify operations and to speed up production. Metallurgical engineers experiment with heat-treating procedures in order to reduce waste and speed up the process.

Eltra moved its plant from its original location in the industrial section of the city about ten years ago when it became obvious that the old plant and equipment had become obsolete. During the fifty-five years it was located in the city, workers came from residential neighborhoods in the immediate area; many were first-generation Americans. Since moving to the new location, many of the recently hired employees have been high-school graduates with little prior work experience and few marketable skills. Many of them live a great distance from the plant—forty miles in some cases.

The president of the company remarked a few months ago that it had become very difficult to hire the "type of person we need in this plant." On the same occasion John Blake, the production manager, stated that the workers were "a restless lot." According to Blake they were "always stirring something up." Absenteeism has been averaging about 8 percent, and on some days it reaches 12 percent. Lateness is also a problem, even though the plant is located adjacent to two superhighways and has a parking lot that surrounds the plant. A commuter train brings passengers within three blocks of the plant gates.

Blake has felt for some time that the newer employees are relatively dissatisfied with their work. They have called three wildcat strikes within the past two years. The first strike was over the discharge of a union official who had reported to work drunk on three occasions; the second was over the "excessive" heat in the plant during a summer hot spell; and the third was in protest against a backlog of unsettled union grievances. In addition, workers seem to engage in considerable horseplay and give only minimum attention to their work. Supervisors spend much of their time patrolling their departments to make sure that workers stay at their machines.

The union has recently become more militant, although it did not condone the wildcat walkouts. Union officials have been urging the company to do something to "make work more tolerable." When pressed for specifics, they generally talk about higher pay, shorter hours with no loss of earnings, and more paid holidays. They have also talked about the lack of challenge and opportunity to get ahead in the company. Wage rates are above the industry average and are also slightly higher than those paid for similar work by other companies in the area.

Blake feels that most of his first-line supervisors lack enthusiasm and seem only to work to keep production at a "reasonable level." He stated that if these supervisors would really "bear down," output could be increased by at least 20 percent.

Blake recently completed a four-week Advanced Management Seminar at a leading midwestern university. He heard several experts speak on the topic of motivation; and many of the other managers talked about job enrichment, participation, behavior modification, and job design in their companies. They expressed a firm conviction that managers can influence motivation. During informal discussions, they also expressed the opinion that his company was "behind the times." He has been wondering where he should start if he were to do something about this at Eltra.

QUESTIONS

1. How do you explain the behavior of the machine operators at Eltra? Which of their needs are being met at work? Which are not being met?

2. How do you explain the behavior of the supervisors?

3. Compare the expectations of first-generation Americans with those of young high-school graduates born between 1950 and 1960. Do those of you think that expectations might affect motivation? What kind of supervision might each anticipate?

4. What changes should take place at Eltra to improve the motivation of both supervisors and machine operators?

5. How important is the attitude of the president of Eltra?

4

THE SUPERVISOR'S MOTIVATIONAL ARSENAL

LEARNING OBJECTIVES

This chapter discusses how the duties and responsibilities included in a job affect worker motivation. It also discusses how supervisors can stimulate their subordinates to work hard. After you have read this chapter, you will

1. Be familiar with Frederick Herzberg's theory of motivation
2. Understand how the design of jobs affects worker motivation
3. Understand how participation and job enrichment affect motivation
4. Know how and why positive reinforcement increases motivation
5. Know why the use of punishment as a motivator has certain disadvantages
6. Understand how money affects motivation

The preceding chapter focused on understanding human behavior in its great complexity. This chapter explores the role that supervisors and their organizations play in determining the amount of effort that individuals will put into their work.

ORGANIZATIONAL MOTIVATION

Motives are needs or forces, internal to the individual, that form the basis of behavior. In our culture most people possess a strong inner drive for growth, competence, and self-actualization. Organizational motivation refers to the creation of a work environment that stimulates and permits individuals to give full expression to these drives. Supervisors contribute most to high productivity by providing the appropriate organizational structure and job design, and by providing workers with valued rewards in exchange for their hard work.

JOB DESIGN AND MOTIVATION

Herzberg's Two-Factor Theory of Motivation

Does the content of a job affect motivation? It would seem so if the theory holds that people seek to satisfy at work most of their social, egoistic, and self-actualization needs. Frederick Herzberg concludes from a series of major studies that there seem to be two different sets of job characteristics—one set determines employee satisfaction and the other set determines employee dissatisfaction with work.[1]

The theory asserts that the primary determinant of employee satisfaction resides in a set of job-related factors intrinsic to the work itself. Intrinsic job factors are those characteristics of the work that relate to the values and goals that individuals consider to be important in giving meaning to their lives. Six job characteristics are critical in developing employee satisfaction:

---

[1]Frederick Herzberg, "One More Time: How Do You Motivate Employees?" *Harvard Business Review,* 46 (1968), 53–62.

1. Achievement
2. Recognition
3. Advancement
4. The work itself—variety, autonomy, challenge
5. Growth
6. Responsibility

This set of job factors comprises what are called <u>motivators</u> because they are effective in motivating the individual to superior performance and effort. They are motivating because Herzberg found evidence that employees have a strong need to satisfy their esteem and self-actualization needs at work.

For most of us, the need to develop and grow in our jobs and careers is one of our strongest needs in life. People will work hard to achieve goals and satisfy needs that are important to them—i.e., achievement, recognition, responsibility, growth and advancement, and challenging work. If a supervisor indicates to his or her subordinates that by working hard they can satisfy their major needs, they can be expected to put forth their best effort for the organization. The supervisor indicates to them that they can satisfy their major needs through superior effort by rewarding them for their excellent performance with recognition, responsibility, and advancement. Thus they see that by working hard (which satisfies the organization's need for productivity) they will satisfy their own needs.[2]

Herzberg's second set of job-related factors are extrinsic to the work itself. That is, they are associated with the environment and circumstances under which the work is performed. These extrinsic job factors, the absence of which can lead to job dissatisfaction in the work environment, are identified as:

1. Company policy and administration
2. Technical supervision
3. Interpersonal relations with superiors, peers, and subordinates
4. Job security
5. Personal life
6. Working conditions
7. Status
8. Salary

This second set of job factors comprises what are called <u>maintenance</u> factors. Herzberg found that the presence of the maintenance factors has

---

[2]Note that this relationship between employee performance and reward is similar to item 3 of McGregor's Theory Y (see Chapter 3, page 47).

little strong sustained positive influence upon employee effort and performance. Their presence merely eliminates feelings of inequity, injustice, and
unfairness; however, their absence in the job tends to produce feelings of
dissatisfaction. For example, paying employees salaries higher than those
paid by other companies in the community for the same work will not motivate them to superior performance. Nor will a superior pension plan, extra-
ordinarily good working conditions, or the presence of any of the other
maintenance factors in greater than the "customary" or expected amounts
stimulate them to give their best. Most people feel that they deserve such.
On the other hand, salaries below those paid by other companies for the
same work, less desirable working conditions, poor job security, and so
forth, could be expected to produce feelings of dissatisfaction, lowered enthusiasm, and poor job performance.

According to Herzberg, companies frequently err in believing that by
increasing the level of a maintenance factor they will increase motivation.
For example, would the improvement of an already adequate pension plan
stimulate employees to superior performance? Would a five-year employment
contract for the manager of a baseball team, rather than a typical one-
year contract, make him a better manager? Would replacement of a satisfactory air-conditioning system with a superior one stimulate employees to
work harder? The answer to all of these questions is, "Typically, no."

In short, if a company provides fewer of the maintenance factors in a
job than what is typical in the job market, employees will be dissatisfied and
productivity will suffer; if a company provides more of the maintenance
factors than employees expect or feel are justified, they will not put forth
superior performance. On the other hand, the motivational factors must be
present if the company hopes to obtain superior work performance, and the
absence of motivational factors will result in only satisfactory performance
at best. Whether or not job performance will be satisfactory in the absence
of the motivational factors will depend upon the degree to which the maintenance factors are present up to the expected amount.

By now it may have become apparent that Herzberg's two-factor
theory generally parallels Maslow's hierarchy of needs. Both assume that
people seek satisfaction of their higher-order needs. Furthermore, the
maintenance factors in the two-factor theory parallel quite closely the lower
levels of the hierarchy of needs, while the motivational factors parallel
Maslow's higher-order needs, as Figure 4–1 indicates.[3]

Characteristics of a Motivating Job

Which attributes of a job would therefore stimulate employees to give
their best to their organization? Studies by behavioral scientists, including

---

[3]Reprinted with permission from Theodore T. Herbert, *Dimensions of Organizational Behavior* (New York: Macmillan, 1976), p. 237.

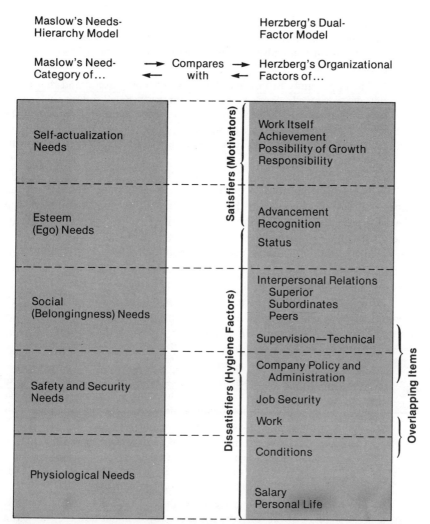

Maslow's Needs-
Hierarchy Model

Herzberg's Dual-
Factor Model

Maslow's Need-   → Compares →   Herzberg's Organizational
Category of...   ←   with   ←   Factors of...

Maslow		Herzberg
Self-actualization Needs	Satisfiers (Motivators)	Work Itself Achievement Possibility of Growth Responsibility
Esteem (Ego) Needs		Advancement Recognition Status
Social (Belongingness) Needs	Dissatisfiers (Hygiene Factors)	Interpersonal Relations Superior Subordinates Peers Supervision—Technical
Safety and Security Needs		Company Policy and Administration Job Security Work
Physiological Needs		Conditions Salary Personal Life

Overlapping Items

Figure 4-1. Comparison of Maslow's Hierarchy-of-Needs Model with Herzberg's Dual-Factor Model

Herzberg, conclude that a job provides satisfaction of higher-order needs and is motivational when it contains six major characteristics:

1. The opportunity to feel personally responsible for performing meaningful work. A job is meaningful if it provides workers with the opportunity to feel that they "own" it—that they are personally responsible for results, that their competence, creativity, skill, and interest make a difference in what is accomplished, that they can experience the joys of success and the sorrows of failure.

2. The opportunity to experience a feeling of achievement. Most individuals want to experience the successful completion of a task or assignment that re-

quires them to utilize their skills and abilities. Solving problems (especially nonroutine problems), making decisions, and taking moderate risks are challenging. Growth and advancement on the job are experienced as a dimension of achievement.

3. The opportunity to feel that the job is inherently useful and that the results are worthwhile. Workers who perform the "whole" job tend to feel useful and that their effort is worthwhile. They can see the transformation that they bring about in a product, a service, or other people. They are able to experience the feeling that their effort makes a difference both to themselves and to others.

While it is impossible to specify for each individual the types of outcomes that will be perceived as being meaningful and worthwhile, the type of work performed by skilled craftsmen, farmers, artists, professionals, and supervisors tends to provide these feelings. On the other hand, the type of work performed by most unskilled and semiskilled workers, especially those in mass-production jobs, frequently does not enable them to experience a sense of worthwhileness, usefulness, or dignity at work.

How people experience work is highly personal and is the result of the interaction between the individual and the job. Supervisors must not assume that unskilled and semiskilled jobs necessarily frustrate worker desires for feeling useful and worthwhile.

4. The opportunity to experience feelings of autonomy while performing their work. Individuals who can feel that they have a measure of control over planning, scheduling, and coordinating the work, selecting equipment, and determining procedures tend to be highly motivated.

5. The opportunity to perform a variety of important tasks utilizing different skills. Repetition tends to be monotonous. Individuals seek varied experiences for their own sake. These experiences are especially important if they utilize abilities and skills and if they tap interests, otherwise unused.

6. The opportunity to obtain feedback about what has been accomplished. The job should provide for feedback to employees about how they are getting along. Research indicates that individuals who have a strong need to achieve and grow also seek concrete information about how they are doing. Knowledge of results is important to them. This information may come from a supervisor, trainer, or fellow worker or from the task itself. Recognition, especially from a superior, provides an especially strong form of information about performance.

MANAGEMENT AND MOTIVATION

Supervisors hold within their hands most of the techniques for stimulating subordinates to make a commitment to superior performance. More than a knowledge of techniques is required, however. Supervisors can best tap the enthusiasm and cooperation of subordinates if they genuinely believe (1) that everyone can make a contribution toward achieving the organization's goals whether the person be a custodian or a president, and (2) that everyone potentially has the desire to make a commitment to the organization. This means that the supervisor should take the view that "everyone counts." It also means that the supervisor starts out with the expectation that in a motivating organizational environment, everyone will give his or her best effort. Finally, it means that the supervisor will consider the long-run potential for growth inherent in every human being.

Supervisors can provide organizational environments in which individuals will find that they can serve their own needs for growth and self-actualization best by working to meet the organization's need for productivity. Participation and job enrichment constitute two very important techniques for stimulating employees to make such a maximum contribution to the organization.

Participation

A participative leadership philosophy and style is one in which subordinates are given the opportunity to share in making decisions affecting them and their jobs. Participation contributes to increased productivity and job satisfaction for three reasons:

1. Full participation helps employees feel that "they own" their work and that they have a degree of control over their own affairs.

2. Participation enables employees to better understand the terms and conditions under which they are employed. The amount and accuracy of the information about objectives, policies, procedures, and work practices that affect them is increased.

3. People in the American culture expect to participate in making decisions. It is a part of the democratic process which affects all our institutions, including both business and not-for-profit organizations.

Participation is a process whereby employees become involved in decision making concerning those matters in the organization about which they have information and in which they are interested. For the most part, it is limited to their jobs; but as in the case of a suggestion system, it might include anything in the organization. Participation satisfies the basic needs that some people have for "being in the know," being creative, feeling a degree of freedom and autonomy, and feeling needed. They also experience feelings of competency, achievement, and growth through the process of being consulted.

Participation enables employees to receive accurate information about those matters of concern to them. Resistance to change frequently occurs through fear of the unknown. Advance information enables them to consider ways to make personal adjustments; it also enables them to influence decisions in ways favorable to their needs. It provides them with the opportunity to express their point of view, which in itself is important.

Limits of Participation. Superiors have power over subordinates; they have the ability to influence the behavior of subordinates, to produce changes that otherwise would not have occurred. It is difficult for unequals to participate openly. There are many dangers for the less powerful persons, especially if the more powerful can make decisions affecting them. Few supervisors are willing to dilute their power position to the point where they and their subordinates participate as equals.

Participation is also less useful in matters about which the subordinate possesses relatively little knowledge and expertise. In such instances the superior has much more influence than the subordinate, and subordinates usually emerge from such situations feeling powerless and manipulated. Participation is most effective when the issue of power is not significant and when participation involves areas of decision making in which all members enjoy knowledge and expertise.

The limitations cited here should not be construed to mean that participation is an all-or-nothing situation. There are many degrees of participation between these extremes, and leaders can utilize them as the situation warrants, as discussed in Chapter 2.

Job Enrichment

Job enrichment is the process of combining related tasks in such a way that employees have the opportunity to satisfy their needs for achievement, responsibility, and creativity. The organization also benefits through increased productivity resulting from increased motivation and skills of employees.

Job enrichment entails providing workers with the information required to perform their jobs and the autonomy necessary to make decisions. It includes pushing the decision-making process downward in the organization to those who perform the work. Thus the individuals performing the "enriched" jobs are able to identify with a complete assignment, product, or service over which they have control and for which they are held responsible.

Principles of Job Enrichment. Eight unifying job-design principles are critical to stimulating high job performance:

1. Assign a person a complete natural unit of work, based on such considerations as sequence of tasks, geography, numerical order, and so forth.

Sequence of tasks: A technician completely assembles a smoke detector, inspects the completed unit, and repairs any of his units that may have been returned for repair by customers.

Geography: City policemen are assigned complete responsibility for patrolling a specific area.

Numerical order: Three golf greenskeepers are assigned to maintain greens according to the number of holes: 1–6, 7–12, and 13–18.

Persons served: Financial analysts are assigned to specific industries, such as aerospace, utilities, banks, transportation.

2. Rearrange tasks and assign the total volume of work in such a way that the employee has a feeling of task identity or ownership.

3. Pull job responsibilities down to a lower job level. Sometimes decision making has been unnecessarily centralized.

4. Push routine tasks downward to lower-level jobs, and automate them completely, if feasible.

5. Increase the individual's responsibility for doing his or her own work.

6. Increase autonomy while retaining responsibility for results. Once employees have demonstrated their desire and ability to run a job, let them run it. At the same time, let them know that they have not been relieved of accountability.

7. Provide employees with regular information about their job performance as measured by mutually agreed-upon goals previously established.

8. Stimulate and encourage employees to seek additional responsibility and learn new skills. Introduce new and more demanding tasks not previously handled. At the same time, be prepared to provide both technical assistance and psychological support to minimize the danger of failure.

Limits of Job Enrichment. Job enrichment seems to be stimulating primarily to workers who have a strong need for achievement, autonomy, and responsibility. Those who are not so motivated, but rather respond to Herzberg's maintenance factors, experience a decrease in job satisfaction under job enrichment. In other words, enriched jobs may be motivating for some employees, whereas more routine jobs may be more appropriate for others.

BEHAVIOR MODIFICATION

People have many needs. Some of these needs are as basic as survival. Others are as sublime as self-actualization. Human beings are intelligent, and they can learn from experience. They can distinguish those behaviors that in the past have led to satisfaction of their needs (or to reduction of their feelings of need, want, or deprivation) from those behaviors that did not lead to satisfaction of their needs (or which may have caused them to feel even more deprived.)

Behavior that leads to the satisfaction of needs or the avoidance of pain is motivating behavior. Any given behavior that from past experience has been found to satisfy a need will tend to be repeated if that need is again experienced at some later time. Thus we say that <u>behavior that seems to lead to rewards tends to be repeated, and behavior that does not seem to lead to rewards or seems punishing tends not to be repeated.</u> When an individual discovers that some given behavior satisfies a need, that behavior thereafter will tend to be repeated more frequently than previously. Thus we say that behavior is strengthened by its consequences. Since these consequences are outside the individual, the individual's behavior is conditioned, or shaped, by the environment.

EXAMPLE

A teacher, while conducting a class, observes that one student listens very attentively, takes notes, participates in class discussion, and wears a friendly expression. The teacher also observes that another student on the opposite side of the room gazes out the window, does not participate in class discussion, and appears sullen.

Toward whom would you expect this teacher to turn and direct his or her attention, the interested or the disinterested student? Maybe the teacher should be communicating more actively with the disinterested student, if learning is the objective. But we can predict confidently that attention will be directed toward the interested student. The reasoning is as follows:

Since the teacher is committed to discussing the topic and desires approval from the students, attention will be directed toward the attentive and approving student more frequently than toward the inattentive and seemingly unapproving student. The teacher finds the behavior of the attentive student to be rewarding and that of the inattentive student to be punishing. This type of teacher behavior occurs very frequently in classrooms, and students often interpret the teacher's behavior as favoritism. In this case, neither the students nor the teacher was aware of the behavioral changes that occurred.

If we analyze the behavior of both the teacher and the attentive student in this example, we see that the teacher found the attentive student's behavior rewarding. The teacher responded by looking at this student more frequently than formerly. Thus, without being aware of it, this student influenced the teacher's behavior. On the other hand, if the student finds the increased attention from the teacher rewarding, the student will tend to be even more attentive and will participate and smile even more than previously. In short, they mutually reinforce each other's behavior.

If we now analyze the behavior of both the teacher and the inattentive student, we see that the teacher found this student's behavior punishing and responded by looking less frequently in that direction. This student, without being aware of it, also influenced the teacher's behavior, but in the opposite way. If the second student finds the decreased attention from the teacher punishing, the student will tend to be even less attentive and will participate even less than previously. Again, they mutually influence each other's behavior, but in a manner quite different from the former instance.

There are three techniques which supervisors can use to influence or *modify* the behavior of subordinates: (1) positive reinforcement; (2) extinction; and (3) punishment.

Positive Reinforcement

To reinforce behavior positively is to increase the likelihood that it will occur again in the future. There are two ways to increase the probability of a desired behavior occurring in the future:

1. Follow the desired behavior with an event or a consequence that the person considers favorable or positive.

EXAMPLE

Supervisor—I didn't think that this report would be ready until tomorrow morning.

Employee—I knew that you were in a hurry for it, so I skipped lunch.

Supervisor—I appreciate that very much. This will make the whole office look good, and especially you. Thanks.

This employee worked extra hard to complete a job. The supervisor expressed his appreciation. If the employee likes recognition for loyalty and work well done, he or she will regard the consequences as being favorable. This employee will be more likely to put in extra effort again when the need arises.

2. Follow the desired behavior with the cessation or turning off of an event or a consequence that the person considers unpleasant or undesirable.

EXAMPLE

Secretary—There has been a cold draft coming through that window for two days. I have hesitated to bother you with this problem.

Office Manager—I'll have a repairman get on it right away. Thank you for calling it to my attention.

Reporting the defective window brought prompt action which will eliminate the employee's problem. The employee can be expected to report such conditions more readily in the future.

Extinction of Behavior

The likelihood of repetition of a behavior in the future will be reduced if that behavior is followed by no meaningful consequence—i.e., the behavior is ignored; it is followed by neither reward or punishment.

EXAMPLE

Employee—I've spoken to my supervisor at least six times about the bad bearing on that motor. He says that he'll take care of it, but nothing ever happens. It's of no use to try to be helpful around here.

This employee's behavior is followed by no meaningful consequence, either favorable or unfavorable. The employee will be less likely to report mechanical defects to the supervisor in the future.

Punishment of Behavior

The likelihood that a behavior will be repeated in the future will also be reduced if that behavior is followed by an event or a consequence considered as punishing by the individual.

EXAMPLE

Salesman—I've worked very hard developing my accounts during the past year. It looks as though I'll exceed my quota by 25 percent. At last I'll make a good commission!

Sales Manager—I'm pleased to learn that you are working so hard. Incidentally, we are reducing the size of your territory effective July 1.

This example illustrates the inadvertent punishment of desired performance. Whatever the sales manager's motives may have been, the salesman will interpret the reduction in the size of the territory as punishing. Supervisors should therefore be sensitive to possible unanticipated consequences of their behavior.

Punishment as a Motivator. Punishment is very widely used for the control of behavior in our society. There are three principal reasons for this. First, it is very effective in stopping or preventing undesired behavior. Second, the punisher is reinforced (rewarded) for punishing. The punisher experiences satisfaction in the form of the successful use of power. Third, the punishment seems just. A wrongdoer receives his or her just due based on the popular principle, An eye for an eye and a tooth for a tooth.

There are several limitations or problems associated with the use of punishment to control or motivate people:

1. Punishment serves to reduce the probability of only the punished response. We know that the individual will not engage in the punishable behavior; we do not know what alternate behaviors may be employed, however, by the individual. For example, a supervisor who punished a subordinate with a one-day suspension for reporting in late for work on two consecutive days discovered that the subordinate thereafter telephoned in "sick" instead.

2. The probability of the undesired behavior is reduced only when the threat of punishment is perceived to exist. This is well expressed by the old saying, While the cat's away, the mice will play.

3. Fear of punishment may become generalized to inhibit not only the undesired behavior but also the desired behavior. For example, employees who are punished for exceeding the authority of their positions in the process of making an innovation at work may hesitate to be innovative in those matters in which their superiors want them to be creative.

4. Punishment may lead the individual to avoid, or even dislike, the punishing agent. Sometimes for this reason children avoid parents, students avoid teachers, and subordinates avoid supervisors.

Positive Reinforcement and Motivation. If employees feel a strong need to satisfy their social, self-esteem, and self-actualization needs, positive reinforcement offers supervisors a powerful motivational tool. They hold in their hands reinforcers that enable them to elicit hard work and high productivity from their subordinates. When an employee works hard, the supervisor can reinforce that behavior by following that desired behavior with an appropriate reinforcer. The motivators, such as achievement and recognition, work because they are positive reinforcers. What will be appropriate in each case is a matter for experimentation on the part of the supervisor. The reinforcer, however, will be very specific, such as "That was a job well done," or "We are granting your request to enroll in the new training program."

Money as a Motivator

Money satisfies many needs. It is typically associated with the satisfaction of needs that arise off the job. It satisfies most of the basic survival and many of the safety needs. Money satisfies many of the social needs, too. Expensive and well-styled clothes, an expensive home, a new and expensive automobile, and the cost and place of a vacation can all become important expressions of status.

For many people, money also symbolizes achievement, growth and advancement, recognition for excellent performance, and responsibility.

Herzberg identifies money as both a motivator and a maintenance factor, depending upon the meaning it has to the employee. If it is perceived by the worker as merely repayment for work performed and as a means for satisfying off-the-job survival, safety, and social needs, it is a dissatisfier. On the other hand, if it is also perceived by the worker as a manifestation of self-esteem and self-actualization, money serves as a motivator.

Do All Workers Want to Self-actualize?

The discussion up to this point assumes that all workers seek self-actualization. Furthermore, it concludes that if work is to be motivating, it must enable these individuals to feel personally responsible for results, to feel that their contribution is worthwhile, and to obtain feedback about their performance. We know from experience, however, that some employees seem content to arrive for work each day, meet the minimum performance standards, and leave at the end of the day—and to repeat this routine week after week and year after year. We suspect that if we were to work with them long enough and hard enough we might somehow motivate them to give their best to the organization, to raise their level of aspiration, to grow and develop into ideal employees. We also suspect that if we were to experiment with our motivational arsenal, we might find the key that would unlock their existing and potential talents.

Time runs out on us; and we lack an adequate understanding of these employees and their circumstances necessary to enable us to "remake" most of them. The question is, How do we manage these employees? Herzberg offers a solution by turning our attention to the maintenance factors. These employees' set of job characteristics differs from that of their highly motivated associates. They are more concerned with the environmental circumstances surrounding their work than they are with the content of it —equitable pay; good working conditions; freedom from pressure; reasonable job security; good relationships with superiors, peers, and subordinates; personal life independent from work; and fair and understanding supervisors. They measure the equity of what they receive from their jobs by comparing what they receive with what others performing similar work in their community and industry receive. They expect to receive about what others similarly situated receive. They would like more but would be very dissatisfied with less. They will not work harder or be more productive if they receive more, but if they receive less, their dissatisfaction will lead them to lowered productivity. In the present state of their emotional and intellectual development, their principal interests probably lie outside the workplace. Supervisors can expect good, but not superior, performance from these workers. They will obtain good performance if they provide a well-structured environment that satisfies the expectation of these employees for equity. If they do not provide these maintenance factors in the typical, "fair," or expected amount, productivity will decline.

SUMMARY

The supervisor's motivational arsenal is made up, first, of an understanding of the needs that people expect to satisfy on their jobs; second, of a knowledge of the effect that job design has on motivation of employees; and third, of an understanding of the power of positive reinforcement in influencing the behavior of people.

Job design affects motivation. Behavioral scientists have identified six job characteristics that seem to satisfy higher-order needs and are motivational: (1) the opportunity to feel personally responsible for performing meaningful work; (2) the opportunity to experience a feeling of achievement; (3) the opportunity to feel that a job is inherently useful and that the results are worthwhile; (4) the opportunity to experience feelings of autonomy; (5) the opportunity to perform a variety of important tasks utilizing different skills; and (6) the opportunity to obtain feedback about what has been accomplished.

A participative leadership philosophy and style often leads to increased satisfaction and job performance. It satisfies people's need to have control over their own affairs and to understand the world about them.

Job enrichment is the process of designing jobs so as to build into their content the motivating characteristics identified by Herzberg and others.

Positive reinforcement of desired behavior is a major method for influencing behavior. Since most workers seek satisfaction of their higher-order self-esteem and self-actualization needs, the supervisor can stimulate high productivity by reinforcing hard work. The supervisor reinforces hard work by rewarding it with responsibility, recognition, and advancement; by offering the opportunity for achievement, growth, and creativity; and by providing jobs that are challenging and offer variety and autonomy.

Finally, not all workers are motivated by the opportunity to satisfy their self-esteem and self-actualization needs. For them the supervisor provides an equitable wage and the appropriate amount of the maintenance factors. If supervisors provide these factors within a structured environment, they can expect adequate but not superior performance from this small group of workers.

DISCUSSION QUESTIONS

1. What is meant by *organizational motivation*?
2. Describe Herzberg's two-factor theory of motivation.
3. How do Herzberg's factors compare with Maslow's hierarchy of needs?
4. What are the six characteristics of a motivating job? Why is each motivational?

5. Why does participation stimulate a high level of motivation?

6. What is meant by *job enrichment*? What are the principles of job enrichment?

7. Why is job enrichment motivating?

8. What is meant by *behavior modification*? Give examples of its application.

9. What is *positive reinforcement*? Why is it more effective than punishment in changing behavior?

10. Is money a motivator? When is it not a motivator?

11. Do all workers want to self-actualize? How does a supervisor motivate workers who do not feel a strong need to satisfy their higher-order needs?

CASE 4–1.   United Astronautics, Inc.

Carl Hager thumbed through a thick stack of engineering drawings and project sheets in an attempt to sort out what had yet to be done today. The deadline had arrived for submission of the final drawings that were to accompany a proposal to manufacture rocket engine parts for a large aircraft company. As chief of the engineering drawing section of the engineering department at United Astronautics, Carl had felt great pressure ever since the company had been invited to submit a bid three months ago. The pressure to get out the work had been compounded by the tension that had developed between his regular crew of twenty draftspersons and the temporary design engineers who had been hired to prepare the project's more technical and important layouts. During the past few months most of the regular staff had expressed, at one time or another, considerable resentment against the outsiders, who they believed had been assigned the more interesting and challenging work. They particularly disliked taking orders from "temporary help."

Carl's deliberations were interrupted when Henry Hodgins, one of the temporary engineers, telephoned to report that Dave Vogel, Carl's most skilled draftsperson, had not completed the rather routine drawing required to complete the set. Even worse, Hodgins said that Vogel was not in the department. Hodgins also said that he found Vogel uncooperative and uninterested.

Carl was troubled by the engineer's report about Dave's attitude; he knew that it had turned sour only after the temporary engineers had been hired. Dave had led the opposition to hiring the engineers. Carl suspected that Dave had hoped to head the special project. However, he had ignored Dave's subtle overtures to direct the work because he felt that the temporary engineers, with their design training and experience, were best qualified to meet the tight deadlines.

Dave returned to his desk a few minutes later and Carl asked him to come into his office. "What's the problem, Dave? Hodgins was in here a few minutes ago complaining that you haven't completed the drawing on the left support bracket. You know that we need it by five o'clock and it's already three-fifteen."

"Well, let me tell you how it is, Carl. Those are very intricate drawings that I'm working on, and they take a long time to complete. You *do* want them to be done right, don't you?"

Carl detected a note of anger in Dave's voice. He tried to justify the assignment. "I know that you're used to doing more challenging work, but we need to save the engineers' time for the more complex jobs."

Dave replied hotly, "Hell, I haven't done anything so routine in years. I've practically forgotten how to do anything that simple. There isn't a single layout or drawing on this project that I couldn't have done as well as Hodgins. I haven't spent my life learning how to do drafting only to have my work taken over by a bunch of 'hot shots.' Why do you suppose I've been taking courses at City Tech two nights a week during the past four years? Maybe UA can't use my talents any more, but I know a couple places down the street where they really need me." With that, Dave stalked out of the office.

Carl is now having second thoughts about his decision to hire the temporary engineers. Dave is his best draftsperson, and his future with the company looks promising. Besides, Carl would certainly hate to face the work load in the department without Dave after the temporary engineers leave.

QUESTIONS

1. Why are the company's draftspersons dissatisfied?

2. Why is Dave being uncooperative?

3. Should Carl have consulted with the United Astronautics draftspersons before hiring the temporary engineers? Should he have consulted with Dave?

4. If the temporary engineers were needed, what might Carl have done to promote a better working relationship between them and the company's draftspersons?

5. What should Carl do now?

CASE 4–2.　Beacon Furniture, Inc.

Store manager Helen Willis noted that sixteen of fifty-five salesclerks had reported from five to thirty-five minutes late for work again today. In addition, three of twelve custodial and warehouse personnel, and two of the five office employees, had been late. She was also dismayed about the many absences. Four salesclerks, one warehouse employee, and one office employee did not show up for work. And today's absenteeism and tardiness have been quite typical during the year that she has been with the store. Employees never seem to lack excuses, either—car trouble, car pool problems, sick child or spouse, bus behind schedule, wait for repairmen, doctor's appointment, and on and on.

Helen reviewed those factors that might be causing the problem but could find no reason for an attendance record that was more than twice as bad as that of other retailers in the city. Wage rates and fringe benefits at Beacon Furniture are at least as high as those of other stores. Working conditions are excellent. Department supervisors have all received leadership skills training and seem to be doing a good job of managing their departments. Discipline and morale seem to be good, except for tardiness and absenteeism. The departmental supervisors have talked with the worst offenders and in the most serious cases have issued oral warnings. Attendance improves temporarily after these discussions and warnings, but in each case it reverts to the old patterns after a month or so.

Although employees are not paid for time lost, tardiness throws an extra burden upon those who arrive on schedule. It also results in understaffing whenever there are a large number of customers in the store. Some of the punctual employees have complained about the extra work required of them because of the many late and absent workers. Helen has also noticed that sick leave benefits cost the store about $1,800 during the past year.

Helen feels that something must be done to improve attendance. She had considered the adoption of a new set of stiff penalties which would be strictly enforced, but she wondered whether this would bring lasting improvement. She also feared that such stiff penalties might result in damaged morale and be difficult to enforce.

Helen recently attended a meeting of the local retailers' association at which a management consultant spoke on improving motivation through a technique called positive reinforcement. He described the way a store manager in another city had improved attendance dramatically by giving those employees who were neither absent nor late for a full week a ticket that placed them in a weekly drawing for a choice of prizes. A weekly prize might include a choice of a check for $15, a portable radio, or a pair of tickets on the fifty-yard line at a professional football game in town. There was one weekly prize for each twenty eligible employees. Employees with a perfect attendance record for a full six months became eligible for a drawing for a $100 prize.

Helen wondered whether such a technique would work at Beacon. She was also concerned about how she could maximize the effectiveness of doing this and what problems she might encounter.

QUESTIONS

1. Evaluate punishment as a means of motivating employees at Beacon Furniture to be late and absent less often.

2. Evaluate positive reinforcement as a means of improving attendance. Would a drawing, such as that suggested in this case, improve attendance? Why, or why not?

3. What other rewards might Helen utilize to improve attendance?

III

Informational Skills

5

COMMUNICATIONS

LEARNING OBJECTIVES

This chapter discusses communications in organizations. After you have read this chapter, you will

1. Know why supervisors communicate
2. Know how ideas and information are transmitted from one person to another
3. Know the meaning of <u>perception</u> and how perception affects communication
4. Know why communications break down
5. Know which conditions make for effective communications
6. Know why formal and informal channels of communication exist in organizations
7. Know how to make communications work for you

Statements such as the following are commonplace in organizations:

But I thought you said I should . . .

I don't believe the president's announcement that this plant will be moved to the Texas location.

Why didn't you listen when Mrs. Rogers said she wasn't satisfied with our service?

As I see it, the policy manual says that I'm entitled to accumulate my sick leave.

Each of these statements indicates that a breakdown has occurred in communications. As a consequence, someone misunderstood an instruction, a president's message was discounted, a valued customer was lost, and an employee disputed the supervisor's interpretation of company sick-leave policy. Good interpersonal communication is difficult to achieve, but it is critical for efficient management.

Interpersonal communication is the process of transmitting information from one person to another. Communication is involved in all exchanges between people. It can be official or unofficial; it can follow formal or nonformal channels; it can take place through verbal, nonverbal, or written media; it can be face to face or take place by means of the telephone, radio, or television.

Communication is the transfer of meaning between people. The purpose of communication is to influence others through the transmission of messages and meaning. To influence them it is necessary to obtain, first, their attention; second, their understanding; third, their acceptance; and, finally, their action. In organizations it enables the members to coordinate their activities in joint pursuit of a common goal. It is the "glue" that holds an organization together. Organizations can exist only if members communicate with one another.

The cost of effective communication is high. It is expensive in time, in understanding, and in emotional energy. It is difficult to achieve because understanding requires more than a grasp of logical facts. Words alone can do only a small part of the job in building understanding.

The ability to communicate effectively is one of the most important of all supervising skills. But it is also one of the most difficult to learn and utilize. This is so for several reasons: First, supervisors are accustomed to telling and commanding, rather than listening and collaborating; second, they are more accustomed to working with ideas than with feelings; third, they are active people and feel that time is a scarce resource; and, finally, their position and power inhibit a free exchange of facts and feelings, especially feelings, between them and their subordinates. Supervisors expect to issue orders and give instructions; they are less likely to expect that it is important for them to be sensitive to the feelings of their subordinates.

The development of mutual understanding is especially difficult for authoritarian supervisors who tend to think of communication as a one-way process. They frequently fail to encourage or permit open communication from subordinates. Furthermore, much misunderstanding occurs because these supervisors forget that subordinates always make some sort of response, in feeling and/or words, when a communication reaches them. This response is always important, and both sensitivity to it and the ability to interpret it are important supervisory skills.

COMMUNICATION OBJECTIVES

Communications are initiated for a variety of reasons. One study of the communication activities of both managers and nonmanagers indicated that they communicated with others in their organizations for the same reasons, and that they spent about the same percentage of their communication time in about the same manner. Table 5-1 indicates that they received and sent communications for five different reasons.

Table 5-1 Communications Frequency Classified by Purpose and Position

Purpose	Position	Percentage of Total Communications
Information	Manager	53.5
	Nonmanager	54.2
Instruction	Manager	22.4
	Nonmanager	21.3
Problem solving	Manager	11.1
	Nonmanager	12.5
Scuttlebutt	Manager	6.6
	Nonmanager	8.2
Approval	Manager	6.2
	Nonmanager	3.8

A. K. Wickesberg, "Communications Networks in the Business Organization Structure," *Academy of Management Journal,* 11 (1968), 255.

Seeking and sending information was the most important reason for communicating for both managers and nonmanagers, and seeking and giving approval was the least important. Managers and their subordinates spend their communication time in about the same manner, except that managers spend slightly less on nonbusiness matters and slightly more on giving approval.

THE COMMUNICATION PROCESS

Communication is a complex process because it is both abstract and subtle. The communication process is illustrated in Figure 5-1.

In the first step in the figure, one person, the <u>sender</u>, develops an idea, thought, or image which he or she decides to share with another person, the <u>receiver</u>.

In the second step, the sender <u>encodes</u>, or translates, this idea into a message appropriate for transmission. The sender employs various symbols that will convey meaning or intent to the receiver. Many messages are expressed in the form of language symbols, but symbols may also be nonverbal, such as facial and hand gestures and other "body language," sounds, or pictures.

In the third step, the sender selects a <u>channel</u>, or path, through which the message is physically transmitted. The channel may be interpersonal, which involves face-to-face exchange between sender and receiver; it may be nonpersonal, such as written exchanges between them; or it may be impersonal, such as a public address announcement in which a mutual exchange of ideas and feelings is very limited among the people involved.

As a message passes through the channel, it may encounter <u>noise</u> or interferences that block or distort the message. These interferences typically arise from the transmission of competing, ambiguous, or conflicting messages from the same or different senders.

In the fourth step, the message is <u>decoded</u> by the receiver. Decoding is the opposite of encoding; it is the translation of the message's symbols into an interpreted meaning. In other words, the symbols are processed back into ideas, thoughts, and images. The meaning conveyed will usually be different for the receiver from what was intended by the sender. The sender can never fully and correctly assess the state of mind of the receiver, nor can the sender know the meaning that the receiver will attach to the message.

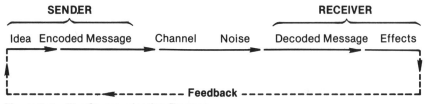

Figure 5-1   The Communication Process

Finally, the message produces <u>effects</u>, or changes, in the receiver. These effects will be changes in knowledge or information, changes in attitudes, or changes in behavior.

Feedback. The receiver of a message makes a response that is determined by the situation at that moment. The receiver's behavior and words provide the sender with information as to the receiver's interpretation of that message. For example, a smile, blushing, or a shrug of the shoulders all provide cues as to how the receiver feels about a message. Similarly, the receiver's verbal response or other behavior provides information concerning the impact of the message. This feedback enables the sender to send additional revised messages so that the communication objective can be attained.

Successful communication between people does not occur automatically. The basic problem is that the meaning that is actually received and acted upon by one person may not be what the other intended to send. The messages that pass between them can become distorted, and communications can break down for several reasons.

PERCEPTION

In the preceding section it was stated that a message is often interpreted differently from what the sender had intended. That is, the person receiving the message hears the sender's words and observes the sender's behavior and then attaches his or her own unique meaning to those words and behavior.

<u>Perception</u> refers to "the world as we see it." But the world that we see may be quite different from the world that really exists. What we see may not be what is in view; what we hear may not be what was said; what we feel may not be what was available to the touch. The glass may be "half full" or "half empty," depending upon how we feel about ourselves or the world at that time.

Words have different meanings depending upon the person's education, economic and social background, and expectations. Persons with very different backgrounds find it difficult to communicate. Words have different meanings; language style and accent arouse positive or negative feelings; gestures and posture carry their own special messages; and manner of dress calls to mind pleasant or unpleasant associations. Language is the system of symbols which we use to represent objects, facts, and feelings. A word's "meaning for me" may be quite different from its "meaning for you." Messages convey words; they do not convey meanings. The meanings are in people.

For example, the word *automation* refers to a type of technology in which a machine is continuously controlled by devices that automatically keep actual outputs consistent with the programmed output. This term tends to arouse strong feelings in many people. It calls to mind different feelings and associations in successful young managers than in middle-aged, blue-collar, semiskilled machine operators. The former see automation as a symbol of progress. Their associations include "higher profits," "better quality control," "lower labor costs." The semiskilled machine operators, however, see this new technology as a threat to their tenuous economic and social position. Their associations include "loss of income," "loss of status," "need to learn new skills." In short, mutual understanding occurs easiest among those who share the same general experiences.

Needs Influence Perceptions. We see, hear, and understand most readily that which will satisfy our needs; we also try to ignore that which is disturbing to us or which does not seem consistent with our past experience. In other words, we perceive selectively. We see and hear what we want to see and hear. If we cannot ignore it, we distort or interpret it to be consistent with what we need and expect.

WHY COMMUNICATIONS BREAK DOWN

Failure in communicating with another person is a problem for everyone. Knowledge of the common communication problems can help supervisors avoid some of them and minimize the frequency and effect of others. Perceptions have already been cited as a major cause of communication breakdowns. There are other causes, however.

Differences in Status and Power

Communication is easiest among persons of equal status and power. It is most difficult where status and power differentials are great. Power is the ability one person has to influence the behavior of another in an organization. The greater the power that a person perceives another to have over him or her, the greater the person's feelings of dependence. Communication occurs best in those situations where there is no difference in perceived power. Communication tends to be less open and less accurate where one person is capable of exercising great influence or control over the other.

Most organizations have a hierarchical structure in which those above have control over those below. In such organizations, the flow of communication downward tends to consist of instructions, directions, and orders.

The upward flow tends to consist of explanations, requests for help, and answers to questions. Upward communications are subject to distortion and filtering. Subordinates tend to report "good news" promptly and withhold or sugarcoat "bad news." Unfavorable information is usually reported promptly by a subordinate who fears that his or her boss will learn about it anyway from another source. In this case, prompt reporting enables the subordinate to transmit the information in the most favorable manner, and at the same time it offers an interpretation and explanation. The net result is that superiors tend to receive highly inaccurate information about the actual accomplishments of their subordinates. Subordinates tend to distort information in ways that will make it more likely that they will receive rewards or less likely that they will be subjected to punishments.

Lack of Credibility

Superiors despair of the "credibility gap," which often prevents them from enjoying open and accurate communication with subordinates. At the same time, subordinates complain that their superiors lack credibility. The source of the message must be perceived to be honest and trustworthy. It is therefore important for superiors not to make promises they cannot keep, to violate confidences, or to be insensitive to the values, needs, or expectations of persons with whom they are communicating.

Conflicting Goals

Persons with conflicting values, goals, or expectations find it difficult to communicate. For example, supervisors will find it difficult to communicate their point of view concerning labor unions to nonmanagement people who are suspicious of management's motives.

Stereotyping

Our worlds are extremely complex. We constantly receive a multitude of data from our environment. We see, hear, smell, touch, taste, and otherwise sense countless bits of information, which must first be assigned a priority of importance and then be interpreted, organized, and integrated into past experience. The amount of information is so large that we tend to form impressions and draw conclusions based upon only a small sample of all the information that may be available to us. Furthermore, we find it necessary to categorize and simplify the data because our brains are able to process only a limited amount of information. We stereotype or classify people into groups by forming impressions or drawing conclusions developed through our limited experience. While stereotyping is inevitable, we often perceive people, objects, or events incorrectly as a consequence of it. For example, women are often stereotyped as "emotional" or "flighty," Germans as "methodical," college professors as "liberal." Stereotyping causes us to perceive a member of a group uncritically. Thus, stereotyping frequently interferes with communication.

Message Distortion

There are four major reasons for distortion in messages. The first is <u>communication overload</u>. Individuals have a limited capacity to absorb and process information. For example, it is not possible to consider "all possible alternatives" in arriving at a decision to a problem. A person is seldom able to analyze and decide upon more than a very few alternatives. An excessive amount of information can lead to overwork of supervisors, failure to weigh information adequately, and poor decision making.

To protect themselves against overload, supervisors employ a variety of screening techniques to help ensure that they will receive only the information they need. Thus they have secretaries who screen visitors and telephone messages, or they employ the "management by exception" principle. In this latter approach they confine their attention to significant deviations from standing plans, standards, and operating procedures.

Superiors sometimes attempt to avoid information overload by limiting their communications with subordinates. While frequent contacts between superior and subordinate may help the subordinate, such contacts may also lead to overwork, increased errors, and neglect of other responsibilities on the part of the superior. Unrestricted communications can become burdensome, although too often the problem is one of inadequate communication.

<u>Threat to status or ego</u> is a second major cause of message distortion and failure to communicate. Individuals do not want to be influenced against their will; however, the more one person reveals of himself or herself to another, the more vulnerable to attack that person is from the other. As a consequence, individuals reveal themselves to others only to the degree that they can be trusted.

People also protect their self-image; they present a "face" to others. Protecting or saving face is a major barrier to communication, since no one wishes to appear inadequate. This frequently becomes a barrier in conferences and meetings where some individuals remain silent because they have nothing to contribute.

<u>Faulty or ambiguous expectations</u> cause distortions by both the sender and the receiver. For example, a sender assumes that the receiver either

knows more or knows less than the person actually does. Such false assumptions result in a message that the receiver either is unable to understand because it is too difficult or is unwilling to understand because it is too elementary, and thus a threat to status or ego. Messages must be consistent with the status or self-image of the receiver. If they are not consistent, they may be unacceptable; if they are not acceptable, they will not be heard or they will be distorted so as to be consistent.

Finally, some <u>messages go astray</u> because of the numerous links in the communication channel or chain. The more the message is handled, the greater the opportunity for distortion.

CONDITIONS FOR EFFECTIVE COMMUNICATION

A free flow of information and the development of understanding between organizational members is usually sought but is seldom achieved. In fact, complete understanding is impossible. The many possibilities for communications breakdowns should not be discouraging, but rather they should alert us to the need to develop our interpersonal communication skills. Supervisors can take several measures that will assist them in communicating effectively.

Sensitivity to Others

We can never completely understand ourselves, much less completely understand others. This does not mean, however, that we should not try to understand, nor does it mean that we cannot do a rather good job of it. As in almost everything, the more we work at it, the greater will be our skill. It is important that supervisors be sensitive to the motives, perceptions, and expectations of their subordinates.

We refer to the need to be sensitive in various ways. For example, in written communications, we speak of the "need to read between the lines." In verbal communications, we refer both to the need to "listen" to what the other person is saying and feeling and to the need to understand "where the person is coming from."

Two-Way Communication

Some communications involve the transmission of information with no intent or desire to obtain feedback from those toward whom it is directed. Examples of one-way communication include a lecture, a bulletin board announcement, and a television commercial. Other communications include a provision for receiving feedback from recipients concerning their understanding of the content of the message or their feelings and ideas concerning the message. Examples of two-way communication include a problem-solving conference, a telephone conversation, and an appraisal interview between a supervisor and a subordinate.

Communications between supervisors and their subordinates are frequently one way—from the top downward. While one-way communications require less time, they tend to be less accurate. They lack provision for testing whether or not the other person received the message correctly. They also do not enable the supervisor to tap the subordinate's reservoir of knowledge and ideas.

Giving and Receiving Feedback. Everyone gives and receives feedback in the process of interacting with others. Typically this happens without our being aware of it. In face-to-face communication, we are constantly on the alert for cues that will indicate how our message is being received. Some of these cues are verbal, such as "I understand," and "Would you repeat that again?"; other cues are nonverbal, such as a negative nod of the head or a glazed look in the eye. For example, a supervisor delivering a safety lecture may observe that the group of new trainees seems disinterested, drowsy, or uncomfortable. If this manager is sensitive to the nonverbal feedback being provided by the group, he or she might respond by moving on to a new topic, opening a window, or taking a short break. A good supervisor is sensitive to the feedback received from others.

While it is important to give feedback and to be sensitive to the behavior of others, it is equally important that supervisors learn how to *seek feedback* from others. It is the person sending a message who has a communication objective. It is not good enough for the sender to hope that the other person will provide feedback indicating how the message was received. The sender can and should take measures that will help ensure feedback. One obvious method is to ask for it. For example, ask the simple question, "Do you understand?" or even better, "What do you understand?" Other methods of obtaining feedback include a complaint and grievance system, an appraisal interview, and a suggestion system and morale survey. It is important that the supervisor create a "climate" in which others feel safe and are not punished for giving negative feedback. It is particularly important that the supervisor not feel threatened and defensive about the feedback received from others.

Timing

The readiness to receive a message and the interpretation placed upon it are in part determined by the recipient's state of mind. For example, a person who is experiencing feelings of anger or fear will interpret a message of an impending cutback in production differently from an employee who feels secure and who is generally happy with his or her life situation. Timing the message appropriately will therefore be very important in determining how it will be received, interpreted, and acted upon.

Appropriate Channels and Media

Some messages are best transmitted face to face on a one-to-one basis. Others can be delivered in a conference or over the public address system. Still others might be communicated by means of the departmental bulletin boards, the company newspaper, or even local radio or television. A supervisor might rely upon the informal group leader to "pass the word around"; the union steward might be enlisted to inform union members; or the message might be transmitted through formal organization channels. Thus the variety of media and channels from which a manager might select to transmit a message is extensive. These media and channels should be appropriate to the content and purpose of the message, the persons toward whom the message is directed, the need for accurate feedback, and the general atmosphere surrounding the situation.

Verbal and Written Communication

Most of the supervisor's activities are best implemented through face-to-face discussions, and most supervisors seem to prefer it this way. Oral communication has several advantages over written media:

1. It is personal—the message can be tailored to the educational, social, and work experiences of the individual. The message will get across.
2. The leader receives immediate feedback as to how the recipient interprets and feels about the message.
3. The person receiving the message can immediately respond by indicating approval, asking questions, expressing feelings, entering objections, or offering suggestions.
4. The leader can test whether or not the message was understood by asking questions or asking the recipient to repeat the message.
5. It is a rapid, natural, and easy means of communication.

Two-way verbal channels include not only the one-to-one interview situation but also small-group meetings and problem-solving conferences. Sometimes lecturers attempt to introduce a measure of feedback from their audience by asking for questions and comments from the floor. Not all verbal communication is two way. For example, announcements over the public address system or over the local radio or television station are strictly one way unless feedback is initiated from listeners or viewers.

Written communications are most effective where standardized information is disseminated, a permanent record is required, or feedback is not essential. Organizations rely heavily upon written communications to transmit information. These media include company newspapers, policy handbooks, procedures manuals, and job descriptions.

Organizations sometimes seek written feedback from employees through such devices as suggestion systems and employee question boxes. The employee opinion survey also constitutes an excellent means for obtaining information from employees concerning their attitudes toward the company, their supervisors, and their work.

FORMAL AND NONFORMAL CHANNELS

An organization chart represents the system of status and functional relationships as designed by management. It also describes the system of communication within the organization. Communications are supposed to follow the formal lines of authority from one level to another. However, much of the important communication within organizations does not utilize or follow the formal structure and channels. Individuals interact in order to perform their work, but they also interact because they seek friends and need companionship. They form groups based upon common interests and mutual needs for assistance and comfort. They also develop loyalties to one another, which extend beyond what is required to get out their work. Occasionally, formal communication channels are short-circuited because of the perceptions that people have concerning the amount of power or influence possessed by another person. For example, a supervisor who is perceived to have little influence with subordinates may be bypassed and ignored in favor of a person perceived to be more powerful, such as a union steward.

Communications flow horizontally across the organization as well as upward and downward. Managers communicate with their peers, including a large number of staff specialists, such as personnel, quality control, and maintenance. In fact, horizontal communication flows are more frequent than vertical flows.

Nonformal communications exist in every organization. They indicate that the formal structure and the formal communication channels are inadequate for satisfying fully the informational, friendship, and other needs of employees. The grapevine is an important nonformal communication channel found in every organization.

The Grapevine. Information continuously travels along the friendship and interaction networks in organizations. This grapevine meets the needs of people to be "in the know" and keep abreast of what is happening.

It provides an opportunity for self-expression among the more imaginative and insecure employees. Important news travels like wildfire throughout an organization; it bypasses formal channels, and it sometimes violates policies and rules of confidentiality. Information travels so fast over the grapevine that it often arrives far in advance of the formal communication. It is an effective channel because it is personal, verbal, and flexible. It permits feedback and helps to explain, interpret, and elaborate upon formal communication.

Managers sometimes avoid and discount the grapevine instead of using it. It is unrealistic to expect that rumors and gossip, as well as important information about what is happening, can be stamped out. The grapevine sometimes carries misinformation which must be corrected; it sometimes carries important information from unlikely and otherwise unavailable sources; it often provides valuable clues concerning the state of morale, attitudes, and feelings; it even provides the manager with an opportunity to transmit information quietly and "unofficially." The "news leak" for which the political arena is so famous is widely used in other types of organizations.

Improving other forms of communication provides the best way to minimize the need for the grapevine. The grapevine rarely causes trouble where facts are readily available. Rumors and gossip thrive in an atmosphere of official secrecy.

HOW TO MAKE COMMUNICATION WORK FOR YOU

Effective communication does not just happen. The implementation of this process requires planning and skill. The following measures will greatly enhance its efficiency and accuracy:

1. Determine the purpose of the communication
   a. What circumstances have given rise to the need to communicate?
   b. What is the idea to be communicated? What do I intend to say or write?
   c. Is the purpose to inform? Stimulate thought? Persuade? Change attitude or behavior? Seek feedback?
2. Identify your audience
   a. Who is supposed to receive the message?
3. Design the message
   a. Is it appropriate for the audience? Will it be understood? Will it be acceptable?
   b. Is it consistent with the purpose?
   c. Is it clear?
   d. Will it command attention?

4. Select the appropriate medium and channel
   a. Is the medium appropriate for the message and audience?
   b. Is the channel appropriate for the message and audience?
5. Anticipate distortions
   a. How and where might the message undergo changes?
   b. How can these changes be prevented or minimized?
6. Check for results
   a. Did I receive the desired feedback?
   b. Was the idea received and understood as intended?
   c. How do I follow up, if necessary?

SUMMARY

Communication is the transfer of meaning between people. In organizations, the purpose of most communications is to influence others. Communication enables members of an organization to coordinate their knowledge, skills, and activities in joint pursuit of common goals.

The ability to communicate is one of the supervisor's most important skills.

In the communication process, a sender with an idea encodes it into a message and transmits it by the appropriate channels and medium to a receiver. The receiver decodes the message into an idea which typically does not completely match the intended idea of the sender. The sender verifies the impact of his or her message by eliciting feedback from the receiver.

Perception refers to "the world as we see it." It affects how we interpret what we see, hear, and feel. Needs influence perception.

Communications sometimes break down because of differences in status and power between people, lack of credibility, conflict of goals, stereotyping, and message distortion.

Sensitivity to others, the use of two-way communications, appropriate timing, and the use of appropriate media and channels contribute to effective communication in organizations.

Verbal communication is often superior to the written, principally because of the prompt verbal and nonverbal feedback that occurs. Nonformal channels of communication are important and managers should make use of them.

Managers can improve their communication skills by adopting a problem-solving technique that includes (1) determining the purpose of the communication, (2) identifying the audience, (3) designing an appropriate message, (4) selecting an appropriate channel and medium, (5) anticipating distortions, and (6) checking for results.

DISCUSSION QUESTIONS

1. What is meant by *communication*?

2. Why do managers communicate?

3. Describe the process of transferring an idea or thought from one person to another.

4. What is meant by *feedback*? Why is feedback important? Give examples of both verbal and nonverbal feedback.

5. What is *perception*? Why is perception important in communications? How do our needs influence how we perceive the world around us? Can you give examples of both accurate and faulty perception?

6. Why do communications break down?

7. What is meant by *stereotyping*? Give examples.

8. What are the conditions for obtaining effective communication?

9. When is it preferable to use verbal communication over written communication? When is it preferable to use written communication? Why?

10. Why do nonformal communication channels develop in organizations? Are nonformal channels undesirable?

11. What is meant by "the grapevine"? How would you minimize the effectiveness of the grapevine?

12. How can you make communication work for you?

CASE 5-1.   Frank J. Olinger, Controller

AJAX, INC.
1918 McDonald Ave.

October 4, 19XX

Dean Herbert J. Hayes
School of Business
Southwestern University

Dear Dean Hayes:

Last year the university very generously and kindly presented me with a certificate calling attention to the fact that I had taught fifteen years as a member of the faculty of the School of Continuing Education. Dean Georgia McDonald of that school presided at the ceremony.

I sat next to Vice-President Vincent Spangler at the small dinner celebrating the occasion. During the course of the evening, I asked Dr. Spangler what the university's position was on using people without advanced degrees to teach courses in its evening classes (I have a baccalaureate degree in business administration). I asked the question because I am a member of the board of directors of a small liberal arts college. I know that prestigious universities require that a very high percentage of the faculty possess doctorates. Dr. Spangler stated that experience that people like me bring to a university outweighs the lack of an advanced degree.

I received quite a shock the other day when a student who sought to sign up for my course couldn't find it in the catalog and telephoned me for help. I was very much embarrassed to find that my course had apparently been dropped from the catalog, and that I undoubtedly had been dropped from the faculty. I have been quite concerned that nobody thought my position worthy of a phone call or a postcard telling me in advance of this change. It is certainly the university's business to hire the type of faculty it wants. But if this is the manner in which it conducts its business, I can understand why it has problems.

Incidentally, I have recruited and hired college students for Ajax for the past twenty years. I have repeatedly heard the criticism that college graduates tend to be steeped in theory but have no feel for the "real" world. I have also heard it said that much of this theoretical outlook stems from the fact that the instructors who teach them are steeped in academia and have no concept as to what goes on in business. There must be some place for the practical viewpoint in a school like Southwestern.

One last thought. A teacher always likes to hear that his students have made use of what he has taught. I frequently meet former students who say, "What you taught me about financial management is one of the most practical things that I learned at the university." The word has apparently gotten around that mine was an interesting and useful course. In fact, I had earlier telephoned Dean McDonald requesting that registration be limited to thirty-five. Last year I had forty-eight students.

In summary, I am not trying to tell the university how it should conduct its affairs. I guess that I am more than a little upset at the way the university treats people.

Best wishes for success at whatever is going on.

Very truly yours,

Frank J. Olinger
Controller

cc: Vice-President V. O. Spangler
Dean Georgia McDonald

QUESTIONS

1. What prompted Mr. Olinger to write this letter?
2. What do you hear him saying to Dean Hayes? (It is suggested that you study each sentence for the meaning it conveys.)
3. How do you think Mr. Olinger felt as he wrote this letter?
4. If you were Dean Hayes, how would you answer this letter?
5. If you were Vice-President Spangler, what would you do upon receipt of the copy of this letter? If you were Dean McDonald, what would you do?
6. What would have been the most effective means of communicating this message to Dean Hayes (letter, telephone call, face-to-face meeting)? Why?

6

FACE-TO-FACE COMMUNICATION

LEARNING OBJECTIVES

This chapter discusses verbal communication in organizations. After you have read this chapter, you will

1. Know the definition of the term interview
2. Understand why it is important that supervisors develop their interviewing skills
3. Know the meaning of listening and why it is important that supervisors learn how to listen
4. Know how to plan for an interview, and understand the importance of setting objectives
5. Know the rules for effective interviewing
6. Know how to conduct an interview

The manager's world is a verbal one. One study revealed that top-level managers spend 78 percent of their time in face-to-face interaction;[1] another study placed the figure at 80 percent for middle managers;[2] and a third found that first-line production supervisors spend 50 to 80 percent of their time in this manner.[3] Thus it is apparent that face-to-face communication constitutes a critical component of every manager's job. The breadth of a manager's contacts is considerable. Although managers spend much of their time with subordinates, typically three-fourths or more of their working hours are spent with staff and service groups and especially with other managers whose cooperation and assistance they need.

WHAT IS AN INTERVIEW?

An interview is a conversation between two people to exchange information that each will use to achieve a particular objective. Interviews are typically face-to-face conversations, although the definition includes telephone and other similar conversations. While we usually think of an interview as a formal scheduled meeting such as an employment interview, the authors' discussion of the term includes almost every personal contact that a supervisor has with others in the organization. Furthermore, an interview includes not only verbal exchange between the parties but also nonverbal behavior, such as smiling, frowning, and shouting. This definition is very broad. Everyone engages in interviewing. Sometimes we interview; sometimes we are interviewed. In this sense, an interview may be defined as a conversation with a purpose.

THE SUPERVISOR'S DAY: INTERVIEWING OR BEING INTERVIEWED

Supervisors are in constant contact with others in the organization. Their interpersonal relations can be divided into three main categories: informal contacts, scheduled interviews and meetings, and counseling interviews.

---

[1]Henry Mintzberg, *The Nature of Managerial Work* (Harper and Row: New York, 1973), pp. 38–44.
[2]Leonard R. Sayles, *Managerial Behavior* (New York: McGraw-Hill, 1964), pp. 33–45.
[3]Robert H. Guest, "Of Time and the Foreman," *Personnel*, 32 (1956), 478–86.

Informal Contacts

Supervisors are active people. Typically they constantly move about and talk with those whom they supervise or with whom they must coordinate. They make many casual contacts that are not an integral part of the daily work routine. For example, the supervisor meets employees when they report for work, on the parking lot, and during lunch and break periods. They talk and much is communicated, some of it unwittingly and unconsciously, on all these occasions. Everyone is always "on stage" in an organization. Since supervisors have power and influence, subordinates pay particular attention to what they say and do and look for cues which they hope will tell them what the boss is thinking and expects from them. How the superior behaves and what is said "communicates" much to others.

Making work assignments and delegating responsibility are tasks inherent in every supervisor's job. The manner in which the assignment is made influences the acceptance of the task. The supervisor who barks "Unload that truck" will arouse different feelings and probably elicit different behavior from subordinates than will the supervisor who states, "Let's unload this truck now—we have a rush shipment due at any minute."

The manner in which a work assignment is made is also situational. For example, a supervisor would make a work assignment to an experienced and trusted employee quite differently from that to an inexperienced and untested employee. Finally, making work assignments provides the supervisor with an opportunity to get to know the subordinate better, find out how the subordinate is getting along, or indicate interest in that individual as an unique and respected person. For example, in the course of giving one of the data processors a new assignment, the supervisor of a data-processing department might inquire, "How has the new billing procedure been working out for you?" or "Do you have any suggestions as to how we might reduce the idle time on the new LT100?"

The supervisor's on-the-job training activities constitute important occasions for informal interpersonal contacts with subordinates. Much of what people learn about their work they learn from their supervisors. Every coaching situation should be treated as an interviewing contact. Supervisors should, of course, have a good idea as to the training needs of each individual. But they should also be sensitive to what things they may say or do that will "turn the subordinates on, or off" in the process of attempting to influence or help the person.

The supervisor should also be sensitive to the feedback he or she receives from the individual. These contacts provide information about the employee's perceptions concerning how well the job is progressing, how he or she is developing, and how he or she feels about the job. For example, the following statements tell the supervisor much about how these employees perceive themselves: "No matter how hard I try, my typing speed stays at thirty-five words per minute"; "I feel very good about learning that new computer program"; "I wish there were more opportunity to learn how to sell."

Supervisors have a responsibility for orienting new employees. Some of this occurs in the personnel departments of larger organizations, but most of this must occur on the job. It is an important activity because new employees typically feel insecure. They often feel lonely, isolated, and friendless; they find the environment strange. Supervisors should be sensitive to these feelings because the impressions and attitudes developed at this time tend to be deep and durable.

A supervisor's friendliness and interest set a good example for others in the established work group. Stopping by the workplace, inquiring about progress, and offering to be helpful indicate genuine interest and concern.

Scheduled Interviews and Meetings

There are five major types of scheduled interviews: (1) selection, transfer, and promotion interviews; (2) appraisal interviews; (3) complaint and grievance interviews; (4) disciplinary interviews; and (5) exit interviews. While each type is somewhat different from the others, they have much in common. In each the supervisor must determine the purpose of the interview and the objective he or she hopes to achieve. In each it is essential that the supervisor establish a supportive and friendly climate in which the interviewee can feel respected and accepted as a unique person.

In all these interview situations, it is important that there be a genuine exchange of information about attitudes, values, perceptions, motivations, and expectations. For example, we customarily think of an employment interview as a situation in which the personnel interviewer or supervisor "orchestrates" the interview so that he or she can determine whether or not the applicant is the right person for that organization, for that supervisor, and for that job.

But what is the applicant doing while the supervisor is attempting to obtain information about his or her suitability for the organization? The applicant is trying to determine whether or not this is the right organization, the right boss, and the right job for him or her. In short, both parties to the interview should be satisfied that their questions have been answered by the time it is completed. Ideally, the relationship between the parties should be that of interviewer-interviewer, rather than that of interviewer-interviewee!

Finally, the supervisor in each of these interviews should stimulate the individual to talk while he or she listens to learn about employee motivations, attitudes, perceptions, and expectations, as well as about the facts of the situation.

Counseling Interviews

Subordinates frequently turn to their supervisors for help when they experience serious difficulties. The problem may arise out of either an on-the-job or an off-the-job situation. For example, an employee may be experiencing serious emotional stress arising out of a marital, health, or financial crisis; or an employee may be experiencing serious frustration because of failure to receive a much desired promotion, inability to master a new job, or interpersonal difficulties with a fellow employee. Under these circumstances a subordinate or peer may come to the supervisor expressing considerable fear, anxiety, or hostility. The purpose of the counseling interview is, first, to help the person obtain relief from the immediate situation in order that he or she might start functioning again; second, to locate and try to solve the problem; and third, to correct the underlying difficulty so that it will not arise again. In other words, the purpose of the interview is to help a disturbed person make a better adjustment to the job and life.

Counseling is one of the most difficult tasks that supervisors will be called upon to perform. Supervisors occupy positions of power, authority, and influence. The more they are respected and trusted for their interest and concern for people, the more frequently they will be sought out by those in need of help.

Sometimes the employee's problem requires expertise not possessed by the supervisor. For example, supervisors are usually not competent to counsel an individual suffering from a mental disorder, nor are they qualified to provide legal or medical advice. It is important that a supervisor be a good listener and encourage the troubled person to obtain help from a doctor, clergyman, psychologist, or some other professional, as appropriate to the situation.

THE ART AND SKILL OF LISTENING

The method of conducting a formal interview, making a job assignment, or coaching an employee is influenced to a considerable extent by the purpose of that interview. It is also influenced by people's need to participate in solving their own problems and in making their own decisions. Equally important, the supervisor usually learns much more by listening than by talking!

Listening means more than hearing. It means understanding. Understanding comes from being sensitive to feelings as well as facts, being alert to what is not expressed as well as to what is expressed, and using all of a person's senses to interpret "what is going on" in the interview.

We are able to note only a sample of all the observable information available to us. Selection of the data depends on the supervisor's interests, attitudes, skills, and values. It is almost impossible to take note of behavior without adding a personal element of interpretation. The supervisor may even select or modify information obtained during the interview so that it will support the conclusion he or she wishes to draw of the other person.

For example, if a supervisor likes an employee's cooperative and helpful attitude, the supervisor will tend to give that employee a higher rating for quantity and quality of work. Supervisors must also be aware of the possibility that their values, beliefs, and past experiences may bias their interpretation of a situation. For example, an employee who believes that a woman's place is in the home and that supervisory positions should rightfully go to men will tend to attach different meanings to the managerial behaviors of a woman as opposed to those of a man. The employee will tend to be especially sensitive to the manner in which the female supervisor gives orders and instructions. A style that would be considered decisive and authoritative in the man might be considered bossy and pushy in the woman.

Communications are further complicated by people's inability to always say what they mean or act as they feel. They do not say, for example, "Now I'm going to tell you about a very great fear I have, but I am going to disguise it behind a factual statement because I find it too threatening to express openly." A supervisor should be sensitive to the need to try to distinguish fact from feeling.

EXAMPLE

An employee who had been offered a promotion replied, "I don't want the job because I don't want the headaches that go with it." His supervisor decided not to accept this statement without further probing. She encouraged the young man to talk about it. In the course of the conversation he revealed that he was genuinely afraid to accept the promotion, fearing failure in the new job. Initially, he could not bring himself to "level" with his supervisor. In fact, the employee was not fully aware of his reasons for refusing the promotion until after he had been helped to talk it out. His supervisor, by listening to what the young man was *really* saying, was able to help him understand that he had the necessary skills and ability for succeeding at the job. As a result, the employee applied for the position—and subsequently became an excellent supervisor.

Listening is best accomplished by an interviewer who has a deep respect and liking for people. This respect and liking is translated into interaction in an interview situation by an attitude of acceptance. Acceptance does not mean agreement. It means that we try to understand what the other person is telling us. It also means that we do not judge that person as being right or wrong, or in any other way, but rather we judge him or her as being someone with unique abilities, attitudes, interests, and expectations. We indicate acceptance by conveying that we want to hear what the other person has to say about a situation.

EXAMPLE

An employee, Joe Banks, was involved in a fight with a fellow employee, Randy Hurst, in the company cafeteria. Interviews with several witnesses to the altercation revealed that Joe and Randy had a heated verbal exchange concerning Randy's dating Joe's girlfriend. They stated that in the course of the argument Joe lost his temper and swung at Randy, knocking him down and breaking a table and a chair. Randy swung back and the fight continued until broken up by company guards.

During the interview Joe told his supervisor that Randy had not only dated his girl but had also taunted him about it that morning in the office. Joe said that he was angry with Randy then, and that he still felt that way.

Although the supervisor realized that Joe had lost his temper, he was careful to maintain an acceptant attitude and not make moral judgments or take sides either in speech or in manner. He wanted to give Joe an opportunity to get the matter off his chest and to learn as much as possible about both the facts of the situation as seen by Joe and his feelings about it.

Joe's supervisor was a good listener. He gave Joe full opportunity to tell his version of the incident. He maintained an acceptant attitude, which enabled the employee to express his feelings openly and explain his behavior. Had the supervisor moralized or passed judgment upon Joe's behavior, Joe would not have been so open and honest in the interview.

After exploring a variety of alternatives permitted by company policy, including possible discharge, both agreed that Joe should accept a transfer to a similar job in another of the company's plants in the city. While discharge would have been the quick and simple solution, it would have been more costly to both the company and the employee. The supervisor's interest in Joe and his interviewing skill enabled him to avoid the loss of an otherwise excellent employee. He also enabled Joe to learn from his mistake and become an even better employee.

SETTING OBJECTIVES

The supervisor's first step in undertaking an interview is to determine the objective or purpose of the interview. The second step is developing a plan as to how the objective will be reached. Supervisors frequently fail to identify the purpose of the interview. They do so either because they feel that verbal interaction is so volatile and situational that planning ahead is of no value or because they believe that they can muddle through without advance planning. Thus the first step in planning an interview is to ask, What do I hope to accomplish in this interview? The question is as appropriate in making a job assignment as in conducting an employment interview.

Given the subject matter of many interviews, the circumstances under which they often occur, and the lack of knowledge about human behavior, it is often difficult to predict their outcome accurately. The supervisor must be flexible when approaching the interview and must be prepared to modify the objectives of the interview as a result of what occurs during it.

EXAMPLE

A data-processing supervisor, who undertook to teach a data-processing clerk how to program a new problem, found it necessary to change the purpose of the meeting when it was discovered that the employee had not as yet mastered the basic steps in programming problems on the company's equipment.

Thus, while it is necessary to plan ahead and to determine objectives, it is also necessary to be flexible to the needs of the situation.

GENERAL RULES FOR EFFECTIVE INTERVIEWING

Almost every interview is unique, yet there are certain rules that will help to ensure a successful outcome. The authors have already mentioned the importance of (1) being a good listener and (2) establishing objectives and having a plan. The following list includes other rules that a supervisor should observe.

1. *Create a climate of trust and confidence.* The person being interviewed should feel that he or she will be treated fairly and honestly. People deal openly with each other only to the extent that they trust each other. The more we reveal of ourselves to others, the more vulnerable we are to attack from them. The supervisor is in a position of authority over his or her subordinates. Therefore the subordinates will discuss themselves and their situation only to the extent that they feel safe to do so. For example, it requires a very supportive supervisor and considerable courage on the part of a subordinate to discuss such problems as alcoholism, mismanagement of personal finances, and fear of accepting a promotion or of inadequate job performance.

2. *Avoid demanding and judgmental statements.* Some statements arouse resistance and resentment in the other person. They also place the manager in a position from which it is difficult to retreat or to move.

EXAMPLE

"You must not attend that meeting." (absolute)

"It is not right for you to attend that meeting." (judgmental)

"Do not attend that meeting." (demanding)

It would be better to say:

"I wish that you would not attend the meeting. I understand that it is open only to members."

Similarly, statements that indicate evaluation, manipulation, or superiority arouse feelings of defensiveness. For example:

"That wasn't very smart." (evaluation)

"You didn't really believe that I'd fall for that story, did you?" (superiority)

"How about giving me *all* the facts?" (manipulation)

Statements that indicate tentativeness, equality, empathy, and support produce feelings of trust, openness, and confidence. Better responses would have included:

"Do you see any alternatives to what you did?"

"You say that your failure to report the accident resulted in the revocation of your driver's license."

"I'm having difficulty in following the sequence of events, as you report them."

3. *Be problem-oriented.* While maintaining a friendly, warm, and supportive climate, the discussion should be directed toward the issues. It should not be directed toward the worth of the individual, and it should not become a degrading experience.

Do not argue. When people argue, they each indicate that the other person's statements are not worthy of serious consideration. Arguing is also a strategy for pressuring the other person to think or behave as someone else wishes. "Don't think or behave as you do, but think or behave as I tell you." This tactic produces resistance on the part of the other person and can damage an interview relationship.

4. *Paraphrase.* Communication errors will be reduced if each of the parties clearly understands what the other has said. If each person paraphrases what he or she has just heard, communication errors will be minimized. For example, "I understand you to say that ...," or "Your position on this issue is ...," or "In other words, you feel ..." Paraphrasing enables the parties to make certain that each has a correct understanding of what the other has said; and if the feedback received by the first person indicates that the second person interpreted the message incorrectly, the first person has the opportunity to clarify or correct the message.

5. *Encourage an open expression of feelings.* This requires a certain amount of mutual trust, a condition that should exist among members who anticipate a continuing relationship in an organization.

It is sometimes psychologically threatening to express one's feelings. On the other hand, since feelings are tentative and real, they are subject to change. For example, "Shut up and let me talk" is quite different from "You have spoken for the last ten minutes, I feel left out of the discussion," or "I feel angry because I can't state my case."

The use of "I" plus an affective verb (such as like, love, fear, wish, want, need) provides an excellent method for expressing feelings.

EXAMPLE

a. "Move the glass; it is going to fall."

"I am afraid the glass is going to fall."

The latter statement tells where I am in this situation. It assumes that once you know the situation, you will take the appropriate action.

b. "You are a likeable person."

"I like you."

The latter statement is warm, supportive, and relative and denotes commitment. The former is cold and distancing.

c. Employee (to personnel director): "I hate my boss, John; he's a high-handed, arbitrary SOB."

Personnel Director: "From what you say, I get the feeling that you are terribly unhappy working under him. What's the problem?"

Examples of poor responses by the personnel director include:

(1) "You shouldn't say that."

(2) "You don't mean that."

(3) "I am sorry to learn that you feel that way; you would feel much better if you didn't think that way."

(4) "You will feel much better tomorrow."

(5) "What did you do to cause your superior to behave that way toward you?"

6. *Do not take sides or make moral judgments.* It is important that the supervisor maintain an acceptant, helpful, and supportive interview climate. If the supervisor indicates disapproval either through verbal or nonverbal means, the subordinate will sense that the conversation could be potentially damaging to his or her future relationships with this supervisor. Sensing this danger, most subordinates will change the topic of conversation, possibly at the very point where the supervisor would wish to continue it.

7. *Be wary about giving advice.* Subordinates feel that a person in a supervisory position is equipped to give expert advice and that, if they ask for it, it will be forthcoming. But there are several limitations, even dangers, in being too free with advice. First, solutions offered by the supervisor tend to produce resistance and stifle expression. While many people ask for advice, they also resist accepting it when offered. Second, advice often fails to fit the values, perceptions, and motivation needs of the subordinate. A course of action recommended for one person may be entirely consistent with his or her values, personality, motivation, and past experience, but entirely inconsistent with those of another. It is a very humbling experience for physicians, teachers, or supervisors to discover how frequently their expert advice is not followed.

Finally, some people ask for advice who really do not need it. Others seek advice because they either prefer to be dependent or are afraid to make decisions. Supervisors want their subordinates to be self-reliant, autonomous, problem-solving individuals; however, providing them with easy answers tends to keep them just the opposite—dependent and immature. Adults develop the ability to exercise good judgment, solve problems, and make decisions through a lifetime of experience in which they first learned to solve little problems as infants. Supervisors, by creating an environment in which subordinates are stimulated to solve their own problems, can help them grow and develop their abilities.

While advice should be offered sparingly, at times it is helpful to give it. It can serve as an indication of interest and willingness to be supportive and helpful. Furthermore, the supervisor may have information, experience, and insights that can help the employee "move off dead center." Such information and insights can usually be supplied without commanding that this advice be followed; they become only additional courses of action to be considered in making a decision.

8. *Be wary of making promises.* Do not make promises you do not have authority to keep or do not intend to keep. Supervisors sometimes make promises in an endeavor either to be helpful or to terminate a long or difficult interview. Sometimes these promises are only thinly disguised.

EXAMPLE

A supervisor, after being challenged by an employee who was passed over for a promotion, assured the employee that he would "receive full consideration" when the next opening occurred. About six months later, when the employee was passed over again, he said, among other things, "But you promised me the job." In fact, the supervisor had only affirmed his intent to give all candidates full and fair consideration.

When the employee, during the first meeting, interpreted the supervisor's statement optimistically and left the office, the supervisor did nothing to clarify it. In fact, he had hoped that the employee might feel reassured and leave so that he could turn his attention to other "more important" immediate departmental problems.

9. *Maintain privacy and do not violate confidences.* Some interview situations require privacy. The office is only one place to obtain it; others include a walk around the block, going to lunch, or meeting before or after work hours.

Maintaining confidentiality can be a problem for supervisors. When a person goes to a physician, a lawyer, or a clergyman, the confidential nature of the relationship is well established. It is less well established in organizations, even when the individual is talking with a member of the personnel department. In addition, supervisors sometimes have a responsibility for maintaining the confidentiality of the employee that is in conflict with their responsibility for making information available to the organzation.

10. *Use "responses" that stimulate the other person to talk and help move the interview toward its objective.* These include the following:

a. Structuring statements, which may be used to explain the purpose of the interview and to provide direction:

    (1) "I would like to hear your ideas on the new agenda for the meeting."

    (2) "I would like to discuss the accident with you."

b. Statements indicating approval, which indicate warmth and support:

    (1) "That sounds reasonable."

c. Statements that require assumption of responsibility:

    (1) "I would like to know *your* opinion about that."

    (2) "What would *you* recommend that we do?"

d. Neutral statements, which stimulate the person to talk but do not structure the content of the interview and which do not indicate the interviewer's opinion or feelings:

    (1) "How are you getting along?"

    (2) "Do you want to tell me more about that?"

    (3) "Do you see any disadvantage in that?"

e. Acceptant responses, which, in effect, say "I understand":

    (1) "Yes" or "no" (as appropriate)

    (2) "Go on"

    (3) "Uh-huh"

Any of these responses may be accompanied by a slow forward-backward nod of the head. Sometimes this nonverbal cue can effectively be used alone.

f. Restatement of content or feeling. This response is a summary of what the person has said and it is "reflected" back to that person. For example, an employee pounds a fist on the supervisor's desk and shouts, "I do excellent work; I help others; I like my job; I like the company. What do I have to do to get ahead around here?" The supervisor might tell the employee, "No one comes into my office and shouts and pounds on my desk like that." This would probably cut the employee off, but it would also prevent further open discussion of the problem.

    An alternate response by the supervisor might be, "As I understand what you are saying, you don't feel that promotions are made fairly in our department, is that correct?" This response will invariably stimulate the person to continue to blow off steam until the strong feelings are released and then subside.

    The latter response recognizes the importance of releasing strong feelings and of learning as much as possible about "where the employee is coming from."

    While a restatement of content or feeling may be viewed as a special type of paraphrase, it is much more. Both the purpose and the effect are different. The purpose is to stimulate continued talking about what the person has been talking about and to release feelings. The effect is to "clear the air" so that the two parties can communicate person to person without pent-up fears or hostilities getting in the way. Paraphrasing may seem stilted, but skilled interviewers have found that it works.

g. Silence is an important method of stimulating a person to continue talking. If the interviewer remains silent and looks at the interviewer pleasantly and expectantly, the latter will be under some pressure to continue. Also, silence provides an opportunity for the interviewee to organize his or her thoughts in order to continue. Sometimes interviewers rush in prematurely to fill a pause in the conversation, and they lose an opportunity to obtain valuable information or insights. On the other hand, it requires considerable sensitivity to recognize an "embarrassed silence" and pick up the initiative by moving the interview to a new topic.

AN INTERVIEWING MODEL

We earlier indicated that communication takes place in all interaction situations and that these interactions give rise to a wide variety of interview situations. While each situation is unique, the authors have developed a model that will enable supervisors to prepare for and conduct all three types of interview situations previously discussed: informal contacts, scheduled interviews and meetings, and counseling interviews. It is particularly helpful in enabling them to employ the general rules for effective interviewing.

The Interview Model

Step 1. Establish a working relationship. This is sometimes known as "breaking the ice," establishing rapport, or putting the person at ease. In some instances it is a very brief episode at the start of the interview: in other instances it may require considerable time.

Step 2. Learn the perceptions, motivations, and expectations of the employee. This includes getting the employee to talk about the situation from his or her point of view, where appropriate.
　　It is important that the interviewer get the other person to speak first. The interviewer not only gets an opportunity to check the facts he or she has against the facts the other person has but also gets an opportunity to see the world as the other person sees it. For example, in an appraisal interview, the interviewer might say, "I would like to know how you have gotten along during the past year." As appropriate, the interviewer might later ask, "Could you tell me more about ..." or "What has gone well?" or "Have you encountered any difficulties?"
　　It is during this part of the interview that the supervisor's interviewing skills will be most seriously challenged. The temptation to lecture, chastize, commend, or moralize must be resisted. Most of the emphasis should be placed upon listening and upon helping the employee talk.

Step 3. Communicate the needs and expectations of the organization. More specifically, the supervisor communicates personal needs and expectations and the "ground rules" under which personnel management decisions are made. This is a major step in interviews, for it provides the employee with the data needed for understanding the situation.
　　Note that in steps 2 and 3 the supervisor and the subordinate have an opportunity to communicate their values, needs, feelings, and perceptions.

Step 4. Develop understanding. Developing understanding is applicable to the supervisor and the subordinate alike. After each has the opportunity to learn the needs, perceptions, and expectations of the other, they are in a position to identify their areas of both agreement and disagreement concerning the situation. They have the opportunity to examine and discuss any new information they may uncover in the course of their discussion. Each is able to modify previously held perceptions and feelings as warranted by the new information.

Step 5. Develop a plan for the future. The supervisor and the subordinate are now in a position to discuss and develop a plan and course of action upon which it is hoped they can agree.

Not all interviews achieve their objectives. Sometimes objectives must be changed. On occasion, the interview may be terminated sooner than planned; the only agreement or plan agreed upon may be to meet again at some definite time in the future!

The application of this interview model will be somewhat different for each type of interview, but it is equally applicable in employment, appraisal, counseling, or work assignment interviews.

SUMMARY

Supervisors spend much of their time in face-to-face contact with others in their organization. Almost all of these contacts consist of interviewing situations. Interviewing is defined as any conversation with a purpose. These exchanges occur in informal contacts, in scheduled interviews, and in counseling situations.

Listening was emphasized as a major skill. It requires that the supervisor develop considerable sensitivity to the subtleties of both verbal and nonverbal communication. The need to define objectives before undertaking an interview was also stressed.

The authors presented several rules for conducting interviews: (1) create a climate of trust and confidence; (2) avoid judgmental, absolutistic, and demanding statements; (3) be problem-oriented; (4) paraphrase; (5) encourage an open expression of feelings; (6) do not take sides or make moral judgments; (7) give advice sparingly; (8) do not make promises you cannot keep; and (9) maintain privacy.

The authors also identified several types of "responses" that stimulate the other person to talk.

While each interview situation is unique, the authors suggest a five-step model that can be adopted to almost any interview situation: (1) develop rapport; (2) learn the perceptions, motivations, and expectations of the other person; (3) communicate organizational policies, practices, needs, and expectations; (4) develop mutual understanding; and (5) plan for the future.

DISCUSSION QUESTIONS

1. What is meant by the term *interview?*
2. What kinds of interviewing situations occur on the job? Give examples of each.
3. What is meant by the term *listening?*
4. Why is it important to establish an objective before undertaking an interview?
5. What are the general rules for effective listening? Give examples of both good and bad interviewing technique for each of these rules.
6. Describe the interview model suggested by the authors.

CASE 6-1.   Robinson's Department Store

Shortly after graduating from high school, Mary Roberts went to work in the receiving department of Robinson's Department Store as a marking clerk. Her job consisted mainly of preparing price tickets, according to detailed instructions received from her supervisor, and attaching them to merchandise before it was moved to the selling floor. She liked her associates in the department and enjoyed the casual and informal manner in which everyone dressed. However, the work was quite routine and she soon felt that it lacked challenge. Besides, she had always associated retail stores with selling, and meeting people. Through a friend in the store she learned of an opening as a salesclerk in women's sportswear. She applied for the job, and after an interview she was offered the position. She received a brief orientation, which included instructions on how to make a sale and on various policies relating to absence, sick leave, and employee discounts on purchases in the store.

Robinson's considered itself the "quality" store in town. It was somewhat conservative, although it was also a style leader in the area.

Mary was very excited about her new job and devoted much time to selecting the outfit she would wear that first day.

You are the manager of the women's sportswear department. It is 10:15 A.M. You have entered the department to pick up some fabric samples to show at an important meeting of all merchandising officers and department heads. This meeting has been called by the president, George Robinson.

As you make a quick observation of selling activity in your department, you spot your new employee, Mary Roberts, waiting on one of the store's best clients—and Mary is not only busily chewing gum but, even worse, she is obviously not wearing a bra. Both practices are strictly forbidden at Robinson's.

QUESTIONS

1. Do you speak with Mary now, or later?

2. If you decide to speak with Mary now, act out the meeting with one person playing the part of the department manager and another the part of Mary.

3. If you decide to speak with Mary later, act out the meeting with one person playing each of the parts as in Question 2.

4. Why did you decide to speak with Mary now or later, as the case may be? In talking with her, what objectives did you have in mind?

CASE 6-2. The Designer's Dilemma

Joan Thomas is in charge of design at Timely Togs, a small manufacturer of women's sportswear. At the age of twenty-six, Joan is already established in the industry as one of the most talented new designers of women's casual wear. She finds the work both stimulating and challenging. As she puts it, "There is always the excitement associated with being just one step ahead of the market, as well as the apprehension that I may be 'so far out' that the public will not accept my work." She does not find the technical part of her job nearly so difficult as the human part, however. In fact, George Randall, president of the company, is one of her principal problems.

Randall hired Joan away from a competitor two years ago after discovering that it would cost him about 50 percent more to hire a man of comparable talent. All his previous designers have been men. He likes Joan's work, however. In fact, as a result of her designs, the past year was the best in the company's history. In spite of her success, he still cannot quite believe that Joan, a woman, can be that good. While she is friendly and easy to work with, he finds it difficult to accept her in such a responsible position. He likes her creativity and he respects her sound judgment, but the combination is something he hasn't expected in a woman.

Joan has found it very difficult to communicate with Randall. He seems distant and aloof with her at the office. On the other hand, she has found him friendly and easy to talk to at social functions. She has noted that he tends to exclude her from important meetings involving other executives of the company, all of whom are men. This has created problems because these executives discuss many matters that require coordination with her department. For example, last week they discussed the possibility of using a new fabric in the fall line of women's blouses. Such a decision could not be made without her participation, since the fabric is in itself an important design ingredient.

Joan plans to attend the spring market exhibit in New York next week. Designers like to attend this function because it provides them with an opportunity to meet other designers and to compare each other's work. It is also on this occasion that manufacturers display their new lines and take orders from retailers for subsequent delivery. She spoke with Randall about going to New York, but he was not very enthusiastic about it. He told her that three other company representatives would already be there, and that she was needed to assist in the start-up of production on a new line of slacks. (High-speed production techniques frequently require slight last-minute design changes.) After much persuasion he finally decided that she could also go to New York.

Joan feels that her relationship with the president is interfering with the optimal use of her talents by the company. She also is concerned about her ability to develop professionally under these circumstances.

QUESTIONS

1. Why is the president treating Joan Thomas in this manner?
2. What would you do if you were Joan?
3. Assume that Joan has decided to discuss this matter with Randall. Act out the meeting, with one person playing the part of Joan and another playing the part of Randall.

IV

Organizational Skills

7

SUPERVISORY GOAL SETTING AND PLANNING

LEARNING OBJECTIVES

This chapter discusses the goal-setting and planning process. After you have read this chapter, you will

1. Be familiar with the traditional goal-setting concepts
2. Understand how individual goals can be attained through management-by-objectives programs
3. Understand the components of the planning process
4. Know which factors determine the effectiveness of the planning process

GOAL SETTING

Goal-oriented behavior is emphasized in contemporary organizations. Many top-level managers adopt the philosophy that administrators at all levels in an organization should consciously establish goals and then direct their efforts toward accomplishing the objectives they have specified. Studies have demonstrated the influence of organizational goal setting on leadership, motivation, and task accomplishment.

At both the individual and the organizational levels, goals refer to a desired future state of affairs. This future orientation helps both the organization and the individual to focus on the end states that they desire as well as the means for obtaining these outcomes. Specifically, by becoming goal oriented, we are able to concentrate our energies and activities on those things that are most likely to create desired results. Without such a future orientation, our present activities could turn out to be inconsistent or in conflict with one another. Thus we set goals and develop plans to direct our behavior in ways that help us obtain the objectives we desire.

Goals serve organizational purposes in other ways by providing a frame of reference for assessing supervisory and managerial performance. For example, a goal can serve as a performance standard when such measures as current production or sales volume are compared with desired standards. Also, goals can be used to justify supervisory activity. For example, a supervisor may defend a particular decision (such as reduction of overtime employment) against criticism by referring to a profitability goal that is held by the work unit.

Although wide agreement exists as to the overall importance of goal setting, it has been reported that many organizations fail to develop goals that are clearly communicated to employees. The significance of this finding is that even though most organizations embrace the idea or concept of goal setting, in many cases organizational members are not aware of the major goals or purposes being pursued by their organization. To help organizations and individuals be more effective in their goal-setting efforts, this chapter discusses various findings and practical techniques for implementing goal setting in organizations. Effective planning is also discussed as a means of obtaining desired goals.

Traditional Goal-Setting Concepts

There are three dimensions to the goal-setting process: priority, time, and structure. Goal priority means that some goals are more important than others. From this perspective, making a profit may be a more important goal for an organization than maintaining a positive image as a good citizen in the community.

The dimension of time in the setting of goals focuses on when an organization's activities are to be pursued (i.e., in the immediate future or long-term future). As a reflection of this time concern, we have defined immediate, or short-run, goals as those goals that are to be accomplished within the next period of reference (e.g., quarter, six months, or fiscal year). Intermediate goals are those that take longer than short-run goals but less than ten years to achieve. Long-run goals are those that take ten years or longer to achieve. The relationship between the priority of goals and the timing of goals is quite close. Goals identified as long-term goals tend to be the ones that the organization views as "crucial"; they tend to be associated with the long-term survival of the firm. Short-term goals, by contrast, frequently do not have the same impact.

The third dimension of goals is structure. This dimension acknowledges the organizational structure by assigning specific goals to the various departments, divisions, and so forth, of an organization. Thus we would expect the production department to have certain product output goals and at the same time the sales department would be assigned specific sales goals; both units would be given individual responsibility for attaining their respective goals. A problem associated with the structure of goals is the phenomenon called "suboptimization." The suboptimization problem occurs when various units within a single organization have conflicting goals, which results in one group reaching its goal at the expense of the overall organization's goal.

EXAMPLE

To increase profits the production department has been given a goal of reducing costs 12 percent by careful inventory control, and the sales department has been given a goal of increasing sales through quick delivery. The sales department may find that it is unable to meet promised shipping dates because the production department, in its effort to cut costs, has reduced inventory and run short of products for delivery. The resolution of this problem requires a careful balance of the goal requirements for each unit, by recognizing that the goals of neither unit can be totally reached at the same time.

Organizational and Individual Goals

Most business firms engage in profit seeking as a single and overriding goal. Unless the firm satisfies this goal, it cannot accomplish any other. Thus the goals that are pursued by the business organization must ultimately result in profits in exchange for the production of goods and services deemed desirable by the society. But, as we all know, profit seeking is not the only goal pursued by business organizations. The exact nature and mix of a firm's goals will depend to a great extent upon a manager's personal values as well as his or her technical capacity to deal effectively with problems.

A survey was made of over one thousand managers to obtain their opinions about the goals they viewed as important for their organization.[1] The following ranking of goals resulted from the survey:

1. Profit, efficiency, and productivity
2. Growth and stability
3. Employee welfare
4. General public, social, and community interests

This list of goals and order of priorities does not necessarily imply that public interest, for example, is of little or no importance to organizations. It does point out, though, what has been confirmed by other studies—that a major characteristic of successful profit-making firms is that they give their highest priority to customer-market, profitability-oriented objectives. However, it should be noted that in recent years, groups representing employee, government, consumer, and other interests have been trying to alter this priority system.

So far this chapter has focused on the goals pursued by the organization as a whole. But what of the individual? Of what importance are individual goals in attaining organizational goals? Early writers took the position that the members of an organization should subordinate their own personal desires to the goals and objectives of the organization as a whole. More recent discussions on this question have emphasized the degree of compatibility between the individual's and the organization's objectives. In other words, a person's motivation to work may be increased by a perception that work in the organization will lead to the attainment of personal objectives. As a by-product, the primary organizational goals may be achieved. From this perspective, it is in an employee's own best interest to pursue organizational objectives. The reverse is also true.

---

[1] George W. England, "Organizational Goals and Expected Behavior of American Managers," *Management Journal,* 10 (June 1967), 107–17.

Many managers understand that it is possible to integrate personal and organizational objectives. By communicating the compatibility of these objectives to subordinates, employee commitment to goal attainment can be increased. However, it was indicated earlier that many management groups fail to communicate specific organizational goals to each work unit and individual in the organization. This communication failure causes employees to feel that organizational objectives are fuzzy or that they do not know precisely what is expected of them. Moreover, genuine conflict can exist between personal and organizational goals. For example, conflict over the speed of the assembly line can expose differences in personal and organizational goals. Similar conflicts arise over who has power. These conflicts between personal and organizational goals are usually resolved by negotiation, clarification, avoidance or confrontation. At times, the conflict goes unresolved.

Even though a compatibility of objectives between individuals and the organization can exist, and employees develop the feeling that they do not have to subordinate their own personal goals to those of the larger organization, increased motivational benefits will not be forthcoming until each group and individual in the organization understand exactly what is expected of them.

Implementation of Goals: MBO

One method of increasing the practical implementation of organizational and individual goals is the process known as "management by objectives," or MBO. Using MBO, a superior and a subordinate in an organization sit down and jointly define common goals to be pursued. The MBO process includes a determination of (1) a statement of work goals and how these goals will be measured, (2) provision for a review of the objectives that have been completed, and (3) a statement specifying the time frame within which goals will be attained. The emphasis in MBO is on "outcomes" or results rather than on effort or inputs. The superior-subordinate goal-setting session in an MBO program should take place at all levels in the organization, beginning with managers at the top of the organizational hierarchy.

Several benefits can be derived from the management-by-objectives approach. First, top management commits itself publicly to specific and identifiable goals within a certain time frame. It is likely that top management will increase its own efforts to achieve these announced goals because they have been made public. Second, these goals are communicated down the organizational hierarchy to each manager and supervisor so that, by the end of the process, everyone in the organization is aware of the immediate objectives. Third, by coordinating the immediate objectives of each work unit, it is possible to reduce the suboptimization that can occur when different work units pursue divergent or conflicting goals. In summary, the MBO process proclaims where the organization is going; later it permits the subordinates, as well as top management, to determine whether or not they have arrived.

Management by objectives, however, is not a panacea—there are some pitfalls to the approach. Three of the major criticisms of MBO are the following: First, management-by-objectives programs result in enormous amounts of paperwork. This occurs because superiors and their subordinates must record their agreement regarding objectives to be pursued. Moreover, to ensure that suboptimization will not be a major problem in the organization, it is necessary to review the subordinates' objectives to ensure that there will be compatibility between individuals and work units. The process of record keeping and verification of objectives results in very substantial paperwork. Second, because of the flow of paperwork, many subordinates and their managers fall into the bureaucratic trap of "form over function." By this we mean that many managers and subordinates concern themselves mainly with filling out the MBO forms. Thus many managers are as concerned about getting the MBO forms completed as they are with the content of the objectives agreed upon. Third, the emphasis in an MBO program is on results, or "outputs," and it is possible that events outside the control of the particular manager or employee can affect the attainment of the objectives. For example, a goal or objective that appeared reasonable in January may be virtually impossible to attain by May because market events or factors outside the control of the employee have changed. In such a situation, motivation can be expected to decrease; the positive motivational attributes of MBO become undermined.

In general, the identification of organization goals and the translation of these goals into individual objectives is positive and useful. But as stated above, the mere fact that goals are identified does not ensure that they will be met. Similarly, merely launching an MBO program does not necessarily mean that employees will be more productive or more motivated to do their work. As with many programs, the problems with management by objectives seem to be associated more with the implementation of the concept than with the idea itself. Despite the difficulties, the MBO concept is one that tends to fulfill the requirements of making goals clear and providing for the measurement of goal attainment—both concepts are necessary for effective goal setting.

Thus far, this chapter has focused on the establishment of goals and objectives. The following sections focus on the planning process, or the means and strategies by which goals and objectives are attained.

PLANNING AND THE PLANNING PROCESS

Planning other people's work is a major characteristic of the supervisory job. Planning is so integral to the supervisor's job that it is doubtful that a supervisor is truly a supervisor unless he or she engages in at least a limited degree of planning. Moreover, research studies have shown that a principal factor in the success of various supervisors is their ability to plan. Because of this, it is difficult to overestimate the importance of planning. Without plans, a supervisor is much like a ship without a rudder, which drifts from place to place with no particular destination. A plan reflects an attempt to control one's environment and reduce the degree to which chance, guesswork, and uncertainty affect the job. Therefore it should be noted that planning is not merely an organizational nicety; instead, it is essential to effective supervisory success.

Research studies have shown that in most industries (i.e., metalworking, drug, and chemical and food), a company that has a formal planning process outperforms other companies that do not have such a formal program. In general, results have shown that planning increases managerial effectiveness, and it does this at all levels. Most simply, planning at the individual, departmental, or organizational level improves performance.

Planning is defined as a process of determining methods to attain identified goals. Thus plans are means by which goals are attained. In this process, goal setting precedes planning. Furthermore, a plan is not really a plan if it consists only of an objective or goal—it is merely a dream. The steps in the planning process are presented in the following sections. They are logical, simple, and easily mastered.

Specify the Goal or Objective

We have seen that planning is the implementation of a strategy to attain a goal. Integral to the planning process, therefore, is the need to clearly state the objective or goal to be attained. As mentioned earlier, a goal or objective at the individual or organizational level is something that fulfills the needs of the employee and/or the organization. Examples of organizational goals include a 15 percent return on investment, 10 percent sales increase, 90 percent use of production capacity, and so forth.

Gather and Evaluate Relevant Data

Having available as much information as possible is crucial in the planning process. To develop a good plan, it is important to have accurate information that can be interpreted correctly. Examples of relevant infor-

119

mation for planning include current product demand, production costs, inflation rate, foreign competition, taxes, consumer disposable income.

One must "get the facts straight" in order to develop a good working plan. Several research studies have shown that a supervisor who "takes time to plan," by searching for important information, is more successful and develops higher-quality decisions and plans. Specifically, by allocating a sufficient amount of time to search for significant facts and to understand the potential opportunities associated with a problem, a supervisor can improve the quality of the decision. The likelihood of making a creative and high-quality decision increases as (1) information is gathered systematically, (2) judgment is postponed concerning the implications of that information, and (3) time is increased to develop the alternatives, ideas, or solutions.

Determine the Individuals Involved

A vital component of the planning process is the designation of the individuals to be involved (e.g., board of directors, department managers, secretarial pool, etc.). It is important to determine who will develop the plan, who will implement the plan, and who will authorize and approve the plan. Determining who will be involved is a vital component of the planning process because these people have an impact upon the kind of plan that will be developed and whether or not it can be approved. This is the stage in which the plan is finalized.

Evaluate and Test the Plan

At this point in the planning process, the plan has been formulated. It is now necessary to determine the plan's effectiveness in moving toward organizational goals. Someone must now determine whether or not the plan will be evaluated or tested directly by comparing it with other plans or with prior experience. An alternative is to implement the plan on a limited or conditional basis.

In summary, the planning process involves specifying the goals and objectives, gathering the necessary facts and information, identifying and involving the necessary people, and, finally, evaluating and testing the plan. Although the supervisor may not have been aware of it, these are the steps that he or she has always followed in developing an effective plan.

Added Factors in Effective Planning

Several additional factors can make plans more effective. One of these is planning flexibility—the plan itself must be subject to change as conditions require. There is no such thing as planning "once and for all." A second factor in effective planning involves time considerations. Seldom is there enough time available to develop a plan that is faultless. Supervisors who have a need to develop "perfect" plans may actually find this personal trait to be counterproductive because they take so much time to develop the plan that they miss the opportunity to take action. The general rule should be to develop the best plan possible within the time available.

An additional aspect of time consideration deals with the notion of deadlines. It is essential to specify the length of time it will take to complete the plan and reach the goal to make the plan operational. The addition of deadlines and schedules adds impetus to getting the plan off the ground and gives meaning to the activity to be undertaken.

EXAMPLE

A supervisor who only tells a subordinate that he or she will "get a promotion" has made a statement that has little significance unless the time frame is specified. Getting a promotion within the next six months encourages the person to begin working toward accomplishing the goal. It also helps to measure success in the pursuit of the goal, because after six months a person can check to see whether or not the goal has been attained.

The final time concern is the planning horizon. All planning involves some degree of future thinking. Depending upon the plan, the planning horizon may be as short as a few days or as long as a few years. Those plans that deal with more immediate concerns tend to be short-range plans. Those plans that focus on the longer-term goals of the organization are, by their very nature, long-range plans. Within the planning process, the supervisor should ensure that short-range plans will serve as steps to achieving long-range plans. In effect, a series of short-range plans becomes a long-range plan.

SUMMARY

In this chapter we have explored the value and characteristics of, and approaches to, organizational goal setting. One widely adopted goal-setting and planning mechanism is management-by-objectives. The advantages and limitations of MBO were discussed. The latter sections of the chapter focused on the planning process. The steps in effective planning include specifying the goal, gathering relevant information, determining the people involved in executing the plan, and evaluating and testing the plan.

The goal-setting and planning process is one that determines how the organization is structured to accomplish the specified goals. The next chapter explores the concepts of organizational structure and design.

DISCUSSION QUESTIONS

1. What purpose do goals serve in organizations?

2. Identify and describe the three traditional goal-setting concepts.

3. What is *suboptimization*? Give an example of suboptimization from your own experience.

4. Why is it important that organizations make their goals known to all members?

5. Describe management-by-objectives. What advantages does MBO have for the manager and the organization? Describe some of the problems associated with MBO programs.

6. Describe the relationship between *planning* and *goal setting*.

7. Identify and describe the four steps in the planning process.

8. Evaluate the following statements: "If a manager will take the appropriate time and follow the correct procedures, planning can be done once and for all," and "If more time is taken in planning it right, then we shouldn't have to go back and do it over again."

9. Develop personal goals and plans for yourself for the next six months.

10. What goals and plans do you have regarding your exposure to this book? This course?

CASE 7-1. Jasper Water Company

CURRENT SITUATION

For the past three days you have been sick and at home. This is Saturday, July 15, and you have just arrived at the office. The time is 8:30 A.M.; you have to leave to catch a plane for Chicago at 9:35 A.M. A special committee meeting is scheduled for 4:00 P.M. in Chicago, and it necessitates your early departure. You will be out of the office until next Friday, July 21.

The following materials were left for you by your secretary. You should go through them and indicate in writing whatever action you think is appropriate. You can write your responses on the correspondence if you wish. Use your own experience as the basis for your actions as you take on the role of Ronald Pierce.

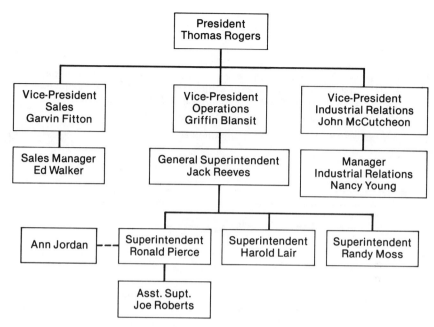

Figure 7-1   Jasper Water Co. Organization Chart

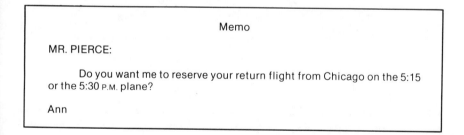

Memo

MR. PIERCE:

     Do you want me to reserve your return flight from Chicago on the 5:15 or the 5:30 P.M. plane?

Ann

From the desk of: GRIFFIN BLANSIT

Ron:

     Please attend an emergency meeting in my office at 8:00 A.M. Monday.

G.B.

Memo

July 14

MR. PIERCE:

After inspecting the building this morning, the city fire marshal reported that you are violating a fire ordinance by keeping an accumulation of oily rags in your stationery storeroom. I told Joe about this twice in the last month.

When are you going to do something about it?

Fred Forester
Building Supt.

From the desk of: GRIFFIN BLANSIT

July 13

Ron:

Please give me a report on Friday morning, July 21, on how many employees have been absent this month.

G.B.

From the desk of: JOHN McCUTCHEON

Ron:

Please make up your recommendations for the proposals we should make to the union in contract negotiations which start August 7.

J.M.

July 14

Mr. Ronald Pierce:

Because of a sudden switch in schedule, I am now free to attend that Illinois University program the week of the 17th, after all. George told me you would be the one to check to see if they can still take me. If so, please make the necessary registration, room reservations, etc.

The program is: *Safety and the Supervisor* (in the Conference Center on the campus, July 17–21).

Ed Walker

124

July 12

Ron:

I've been trying to get the feel of this job of being a new foreman, but I'm not quite clear on where my authority begins and ends. We've run into a few situations where some kind of written detailed statements of our responsibilities would have been useful.

The job descriptions in the manual are so vague that I don't get much practical help from them.

I would appreciate something more definite about what you expect from me on this job.

Alan Berndt
Foreman

R.P.

Here is the letter you asked me to write for your signature.

Ann, July 14

July 14

Dear Mrs. Jones:

Replying to your complaint of May 16, in which you said that your bill was out of line, I do not understand it. I checked everything personally, and I can assure you that everything was OK.

It is up to you to pay, now. We have done our part, and you must do yours.

Sincerely,

July 12

Ron:

You will recall that during last summer we had considerable difficulty with the lawn watering system at the house of Mr. John Miller.

I understand the Millers are out of town now but are returning Friday. Will you please go out Monday with a serviceman and see if we can't get that thing working right before they return. (Mr. Miller is Mr. Rogers's next-door neighbor.)

Griffin Blansit

July 14

Mr. Pierce:

    I have handled all the correspondence I could and left you only the letter I didn't know what to do with. All of your other appointments have been postponed until Tuesday, July 25, or Wednesday, July 26.

    Since you will be out of town next week, I would like to take the last three and one-half days off. If this is OK, I'll work all day Monday and Tuesday morning.

    I know you won't mind. You have always been so fair.

    Have a nice trip.

Ann

July 14

Ron:

    One of your presupervisory trainees—Jim Reilly—was involved in another argument on the job this morning. This is the second time in the past two months. I have felt for some time that Jim was not cut out for this training but have been willing to go along on your high recommendation of him.

    We are meeting at 11:00 A.M. on Monday (the 17th) to take some kind of disciplinary action. Would you like to sit in on the meeting? (You're the one guy who seems to be able to get through to him.)

Jack Reeves

QUESTIONS

    1. What priorities should you set among the issues raised by these memos?

    2. What matters can be delegated?

    3. Do you need to follow up any matters? Which ones?

8

ORGANIZING THE WORK

LEARNING OBJECTIVES

This chapter discusses how work and organizations are structured to accomplish desired goals. After you have read this chapter, you will

1. Understand why bureaucracies have both strengths and limitations
2. Be familiar with the classical concepts of labor specialization, unity of command, and decentralization
3. Know what the span of control is and the factors that determine it
4. Understand line and staff organizational structure and why tension exists between line and staff members
5. Know how organizational design contributes to organizational effectiveness

An organization is one of the most important and influential inventions of mankind. It consists of a relatively stable grouping of people and work relationships which are combined to accomplish more than any *single* individual could ever accomplish alone. In this way, organizations permit a combination of many persons' skills to attain mutually desirable goals.

Without organizations our modern economic system would obviously be nonexistent, and our very survival as individuals would be threatened. Fortunately, we have the use of organizations; and, from the supervisor's point of view, they provide a tool that permits the supervisor to designate *who* does *what*. This chapter considers various ideas that are relevant to the successful attainment of common goals and discusses effective ways in which employees and other resources may be grouped together to accomplish the work of the organization.

BUREAUCRACY

The term bureaucracy has different meanings for different people. Usually the term has negative connotations, but it was originally used to describe an attempt at increasing the efficiency, fairness, and performance of work organizations. The concepts associated with bureaucracy have been adopted to the extent that all organizations are now somewhat bureaucratic—they have rules, policies, chains of command, and so forth. Although some problems with bureaucracies have been identified and will be discussed in the following pages, a bureaucracy is not necessarily ineffective.

Among the first and most influential of the writers on bureaucracy was Max Weber, who criticized the practice of favoritism and the organizational equivalent of the divine right of kings which prevailed during his day. Weber outlined the following aspects of the effective bureaucratic organization:

1. Tasks are divided into specialized jobs.

2. Extensive sets of rules are developed to assure consistent treatment of employees and coordination of tasks.

3. Each person is responsible to a supervisor which creates a chain of command.

4. Formal relationships are fostered so that favoritism is reduced and efficiency increases.

5. Advancement is based upon technical competence, not personal relationships.

In Weber's view, a bureaucracy was superior to any other organization type. Thus the more closely an organization adhered to these concepts, the more it approached the "ideal."

Limitations of Bureaucracy. Most persons, however, have observed organizations that employ bureaucratic concepts but fail, for various reasons, to be "ideal" or particularly efficient. We are all familiar with the problem of "red tape," which develops when rules or procedures become valued in their own right. Another problem in bureaucratic organizations, which was discussed in the preceding chapter, is suboptimization.

EXAMPLE

An effort at cost reduction by a manufacturing unit can result in decreased product quality or ability to meet delivery schedules. While cost control could fit the unit's immediate goal, the larger organization could suffer.

Thus suboptimization may become a major problem when members of an organization subunit place the welfare of their unit over that of the larger organization.

The reliance on rules and procedures to establish minimum performance levels often serves to signal the expected or acceptable level of performance. As a result, a minimum performance standard becomes viewed as a maximum—there is little incentive to exceed the minimum established level.

EXAMPLE

If a minimum acceptable production rate of forty units per hour is announced, employees may accept this level as the desired level of output, even though an output of fifty or sixty units per hour is attainable.

These observations of bureaucratic organization structures demonstrate that the daily operation of most organizations produces some unexpected results. But although problems exist, the rational or bureaucratic approach to organizing the work efforts of people has proved very useful; it has resulted in resolving several fundamental organizational questions. Specifically, it has provided information that is relevant to determining (1) what the nature and content of a job should be, (2) how authority should be distributed, (3) how jobs should be grouped or clustered together, and (4) what the maximum size of a task group should be. The concepts of labor specialization, unity of command, decentralization, departmentalization, span of control, and line and staff address these questions.

Specialization of Labor

One of the most vital concepts in our modern industrial life involves specialization of labor. The basic idea underlying this concept is that if complex jobs are divided into narrower and narrower activities or duties, at some point the individual worker changes from a "jack of all trades" to an "expert" at a very specific and narrow task. Then, by combining the efforts of several of these "experts," the output of the overall group can exceed that of any single individual operating alone; and this may be done while maintaining acceptable quality. The implementation of this concept results in reducing the time available to complete one job cycle and in reducing the overall control an individual worker has in planning or controlling assigned duties. The organization chart shown in Figure 8-1 indicates that specialization of labor occurs both vertically (by level) and horizontally (by task function). Vertical specialization occurs as the level of the organizational hierarchy moves from high to low. Each lower level includes more persons who perform fewer but more detailed tasks. Horizontal specialization occurs as general task categories such as marketing or manufacturing are delegated to different groups of persons. Each group becomes a specialist at performing the assigned task. In general, specialization of labor results in reduced autonomy and increased productivity. It should be noted, however, that there is a point beyond which increased specialization can result in costs that outweigh increased output.

EXAMPLE

In an office it would make little sense to have one person file yellow copies and have a second person place blue copies in the same files.

Unity of Command

The unity-of-command concept focuses on authority relationships within the organization. Primarily, unity of command means that it is appropriate to have only a single supervisor for every worker. Stated differently, every subordinate should report to only one supervisor. By arranging the authority relationships in this fashion, potential conflict is reduced for a subordinate who could receive conflicting directives if he or she reported to two supervisors.

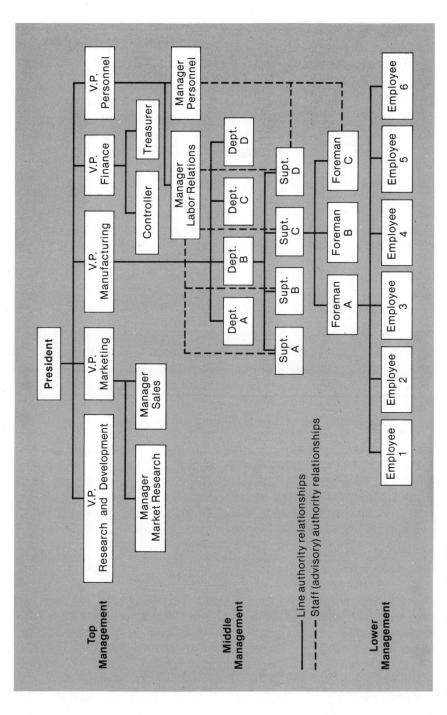

Figure 8-1 Organization Chart

Top Management

- President
- V.P. Research and Development
- V.P. Marketing
- V.P. Manufacturing
- V.P. Finance
- V.P. Personnel

Middle Management

- Manager Market Research
- Manager Sales
- Controller
- Treasurer
- Manager Labor Relations
- Manager Personnel
- Dept. A
- Dept. B
- Dept. C
- Dept. D
- Supt. A
- Supt. B
- Supt. C
- Supt. D

Lower Management

- Foreman A
- Foreman B
- Foreman C
- Employee 1
- Employee 2
- Employee 3
- Employee 4
- Employee 5
- Employee 6

——— Line authority relationships
- - - - Staff (advisory) authority relationships

Decentralization of Authority and Duties

As a supervisor's responsibilities increase, there arrives a point at which he or she is unable to accomplish all assignments while working alone. At this point, delegation of responsibility and authority becomes crucial. By giving a subordinate or group of subordinates responsibilities and the authority to accomplish these responsibilities, the supervisor decentralizes authority.

Decentralization of authority essentially means that decision making is delegated to that point in the organization (usually lower in the hierarchy) at which the problem exists. Using this procedure, the supervisor with the greatest amount of immediate and relevant information makes a decision about the problem at hand. Unfortunately, there is some controversy among scholars as to the degree of desirable decentralization. Supporters of the decentralization concept say that decentralization encourages the development of supervisors. Also, in a decentralized authority situation a subordinate is given increased freedom to make decisions; therefore, subordinates are able to participate more fully in the accomplishment of organizational goals. This can have motivational value. (See Chapter 10 for a discussion of the developmental consequences of participation by employees.)

The potential benefits of decentralized authority do not come without cost. Some of the problems involved in increasing decentralization are as follows: (1) subordinates may make costly errors while developing their decision-making skills; (2) the development of excellent supervisory decision-making ability may require expensive formal training; and (3) the sharing or delegating of authority by supervisors may run counter to traditional expectations or the personality needs of the supervisor. Specifically, a supervisor may enjoy his or her authority and may be hesitant to share any of it with others. This is particularly true when the delegated responsibility is crucial to the organization and when organizational leaders have a low tolerance for errors. In these situations, a supervisor frequently feels that since he or she will be held responsible for the outcome of the decision, no one else should make it.

Span of Control

The concept of span of control refers to the number of subordinates a supervisor can effectively manage; it refers to the maximum number of subordinates that report to a single supervisor. Logic suggests that there is a limit to the number of subordinates a person can effectively supervise. From a practical point of view, it would be useful to be able to specify the maximum number of subordinates that could be effectively supervised at any given time.

To determine an optimal span of control, a study at Lockheed Aircraft Corporation has provided useful information. Researchers at Lockheed, after years of experience and analysis of work groups in that organization, developed a ranking of factors that helps determine the appropriate span of control for a particular work group. The resulting six factors, indicated in Table 8-1, are arranged in general order of their importance to span of control (first order of importance is ranked "1," second order of importance "2," third order of importance is ranked "3").

Table 8-1. Factors of Determining Span of Control at Lockheed Aircraft Corporation

---

1. a. How much direction and control is required by subordinates (i.e., instructions, guidance, follow-up)?
2. a. How complex are the job duties (i.e., simple task versus very technical or skilled task)?
   b. What is the required coordination among workers and work units (i.e., work independently or must efforts be integrated)?
   c. How much planning is required to complete the work (i.e., materials, people, and equipment scheduling)?
3. a. How similar is the work being performed (i.e., all employees with same tasks or many different tasks being accomplished at once)?
   b. What is the geographical closeness or proximity of work stations to each other (i.e., are workers spread out or are they in one location)?

Adopted from Harold Stieglitz, "Optimizing Span of Control," *Management Record*, September, 1962, p. 27, © 1962 National Industrial Conference Board.

From Table 8-1 it can be seen that to determine the maximum span of control, a supervisor should focus first on the direction and control required by subordinates. The second consideration should be directed toward the complexity of duties and needed planning and coordination for successful work performance. The final consideration encompasses work similarity and geographical dispersion, but these latter factors have decreasing impact on the span of control.

In addition to the Lockheed findings, the National Conference Board adds the following considerations in determining the optimal span of control: (1) the competence of the supervisor and the subordinates; (2) the extent to which the supervisor must carry on nonmanagerial work; (3) the incidence of new problems in the supervisor's work unit; and (4) the extent of standardized procedures within the organization.

While the Lockheed and National Conference Board findings may be useful in determining the maximum span of control for a given level of supervision, once the maximum number has been reached it becomes necessary to add supervisors and group workers together on the same organizational level. The grouping of people who are doing similar work results in departmentalization.

Departmentalization

There are many methods of grouping, or departmentalizing, the work effort. Among the usual types of groupings are departmentalization according to output, or product; kind of work, or function; where the work is being done, or the territory; and for whom the product is being produced, or client.

Examples of the various departmentalization types include the Pontiac Division of General Motors as a representative of product departmentalization. Organizing according to function results in groupings of workers with similar responsibilities and skills (e.g., marketing or accounting or data processing). Departmentalization that reflects geographical location would reflect where the work is being done (e.g., production in a regional plant, sales personnel grouped by section of the country). Finally, an organization may departmentalize according to the customers to be serviced (e.g., sales force that distinguishes between commercial sales and residential sales, or between wholesale and retail sales).

In selecting among these various types of departmentalization, an organization should adopt the type of grouping that meets the needs of the market environment at a minimum of cost. It should be noted that departmentalization by territory, by customer, and by product tends to result in substantial duplication of effort and resources; however, in many instances this duplication may be well justified by customer demands. By contrast, departmentalization by function tends to reduce duplication of effort, but it increases the necessity for coordination; moreover, worker interdependence is increased, which makes decision making more complicated. In certain ways these observations are similar to those mentioned in the earlier discussion of the delegation of authority.

Line and Staff

As organizations grow, various persons and groups within the organization are given responsibility for particular tasks. Some units are concerned with producing a particular good or service that is the major output of the organization; other units provide vital but more specialized services to help the persons concerned with the primary output to perform their function more effectively. Those individuals involved in producing the primary output of the organization are considered line personnel, while those individuals involved in advising or providing assistance to line personnel are considered <u>staff</u> personnel. The basic difference between line personnel and staff personnel lies in the nature of their activities and the authority inter-relationship that exists.

Line groups have direct or command authority, while staff groups have advisory authority. In Figure 8-1 the line authority was indicated by solid lines, and the staff authority was indicated by dashed lines. Staff members have authority to the degree that their knowledge, skill, or service is needed by line personnel.

EXAMPLE

A production manager who has a problem of replacing a retired employee may use the staff expertise or services of the personnel department in finding a suitable replacement. Although the line manager is potentially capable of selecting a replacement without outside assistance, the utilization of the personnel department to screen, test, and recommend several potentially acceptable candidates is of material benefit to the line manager. As a result, the recommendations of the personnel department tend to have substantial influence over the decisions of the line manager.

In complex modern organizations, the distinction between line and staff can become blurred. The line and staff relationship is affected by one who knows what must be done, how to bring resources to bear on the task, and so forth. For example, an airplane pilot exercises control over the plane in the air, but the meteorologist has more weather information than the pilot. The meteorologist can exercise control over the pilot because the meteorologist has important and relevant information.

Line and staff conflict. Several factors can cause conflict between line and staff members. To begin with, staff personnel must be capable of providing expert knowledge and assistance to line personnel. As a consequence, staff members tend to be more highly educated than are line members. Other personal attributes of staff members are that they tend to be younger, dress more fashionably, have distinctive recreational concerns, and identify their success substantially with excellence and advancement in their chosen profession. By contrast, line members tend to be somewhat older, have less formal education, and measure their success by advancement within the organization.

An added source of tension for staff members is the general impression that in order to be successful in their job, they must be more cooperative and adaptable to the needs of the line than the reverse. Among some staff members, this may result in a sense of frustration and occasional feelings of inferiority. Moreover, in providing service to line members, the staff member frequently must show them how to improve their job performance but not "show them up." The result of embarrassing line managers can be a lack of cooperation between line and staff members; this can cause the staff unit to go unused. In this regard, it is important to recognize that a staff unit must provide assistance to the line to justify its existence. Finally, it should be noted that the conflict described here is not relegated exclusively to the formal line and staff arrangements. It can exist between any units or persons where the assistance is required by one party but not the other.

Although these tensions exist, over the years the line and staff arrangement has proved to be one of the more effective organizational types. It has the advantage of combining the specialty knowledge of certain individuals (staff) with the need of persons who are responsible for organizational outputs (line).

ORGANIZATIONAL DESIGN

Most work organizations have a structure that is arranged in a hierarchy. This hierarchy arrangement is primarily the result of factors that were discussed above under the headings of span of control and departmentalization. Specifically, to maintain control over various subordinates when the span of control has been exceeded, a manager may assign other individuals to supervise the work of two subgroups of subordinates. This results in an additional level in the organizational hierarchy. Following this logic, one can see that the narrower the span of control, the more levels there tend to be in a particular organization. Also, so long as the span of control remains constant, an increase in the number of employees causes an increase in the number of levels of management. (See Figure 8-1 for a diagram of these concepts.)

Although the traditional hierarchy is the most widely known and utilized form of organization, in recent years other forms of organizational structure have been devised. These variations in organizational structure have typically resulted from market and work environmental influences; that is, the task to be completed in a particular work environment revealed that the traditional hierarchy was unable to provide the needed flexibility or responsiveness. An example of a unique structural arrangement, which takes into account demands from the work environment, is the matrix organizational structure illustrated in Figure 8-2. This structure is particularly well suited to a single organization working on multiple projects simultaneously, and it has been adopted by many construction, architectural, and engineering firms.

In a matrix management organizational structure, various departments exist along functional lines (e.g., manufacturing, engineering, re-

Functional Area Manager / Project or Team Manager	Manufacturing	Engineering	Research and Development	Marketing
Project A				
Project B				
Project C				

Figure 8-2   Matrix Organizational Structure

search and development, etc.). To complete a specific project or task, various members of the functional units are assigned to a particular project. Under this arrangement, the unity-of-command principle may be violated because the subordinate is simultaneously a member of a functional unit and a member of a particular project team. Conflict may be generated when the manager of a functional unit makes demands that are incompatible with those of the project team manager. However, where technical complexity is involved and where projects have limited duration, a move to a type of matrix organizational structure appears to be almost inevitable. It would be too cumbersome to reorganize the complete organization each time a new project was started.

In conclusion, while most organizational structures are of the traditional hierarchical arrangement, this type of structure is not universally applicable. The task to be performed by the organization may require structures other than the classical hierarchy; matrix management is one such structure. Typically, the classical hierarchy is most appropriate in those environments that are more stable. By contrast, where environmental changes in markets, products, or technology are rapid and significant, more flexible and responsive organizational structures are required. For example, production departments in the container industry tend to have a more stable environment and a more highly developed hierarchical structure than do the research and development departments in the plastics or electronics industries.

SUGGESTIONS FOR ORGANIZATIONAL EFFECTIVENESS

The preceding discussion of organizational concepts should enable the supervisor to better understand organizational structure or design. The following suggestions can help the supervisor improve his or her effectiveness in utilizing these organizational concepts:

1. Don't exceed the effective span of control of subordinates who report to you. To determine the effective span of control or maximum span of control, utilize the rating criterion developed at Lockheed.

2. Don't violate the unity of command for your subordinates unless the organizational structure (e.g., matrix organization) requires it. Analyze and determine what you believe to be the best way to group the work activities. Don't put people with different responsibilities into the same reporting group.

3. Be aware that imprecise job definitions may lead to a lack of knowledge as to what one's job should be. When there is a gray area between job responsibilities, conflict is likely to result; also, duplication of effort is likely to result.

4. Utilize the appropriate organizational design for the work to be performed. If the work task is fairly repetitive or the demands placed on a work group are fairly predictable and standardized, the hierarchical arrangement provides the most desirable organizational structure within one department. In a more turbulent or changing environment, it would be necessary to develop a more flexible organizational structure.

SUMMARY

An organization permits the accomplishment of goals that normally are not attainable through individual efforts. This chapter discussed the concepts of work specialization, unity of command, delegation, span of control, departmentalization, organizational design, and line-staff relationships. The chapter concluded with a set of suggestions for the supervisor regarding the effective utilization of organizing concepts.

The preceding chapter discussed the establishment of organizational plans and goals. This chapter has focused on methods for combining the efforts of many individuals to accomplish those goals. The next chapter focuses on methods for acquiring personnel.

DISCUSSION QUESTIONS

1. Define *bureaucracy.*

2. Indicate how a minimum performance standard can come to be viewed as a maximum performance standard.

3. Define *specialization of labor.*

4. Define *unity of command.* Why is this concept important in organizations?

5. What are the benefits of decentralization of authority? Describe the costs of decentralized authority.

6. Define *span of control.* What guidelines were developed by the Lockheed study about span of control?

7. What is the source of line and staff authority?

8. What are the attributes of line personnel? What are the attributes of staff personnel? What are the sources of conflict between line and staff?

9. Differentiate between *hierarchial* and *matrix* organizational structures.

10. Discuss some of the anticipated problems that would result from using an inappropriate organizational structure.

11. Indicate a time when you were aware of organizational structure. What caused your awareness?

CASE 8-1.   Harrison Manufacturing Company

The Harrison Manufacturing Company makes die-cast aluminum products, such as outdoor barbeque cookers and parking meter housings. The president of the company, Thomas Harrison, Jr., recently took control of the organization upon the retirement of his father. He had felt for some time that the company needed reorganization among its fifty workers and staff of five secretaries. He decided to add the position of assistant to the president and advertised in the local newspaper for applicants. After much interviewing he selected Cynthia Greg, a recent graduate of the University of Georgia with a master's degree in Business Administration.

Mr. Harrison had informed Mrs. Greg that her duties would include assisting him on special projects and assignments in addition to supervising the secretarial staff. Historically, the president's secretary, Gladys McKnight, had supervised all the members of the secretarial staff. However, it had become increasingly apparent to Mr. Harrison that Mrs. McKnight was not a good manager of the staff; in addition, he suspected that she frequently initiated rumors that led to lowered morale among the secretaries and several of the firm's employees. For this reason, he wanted to eliminate her responsibilities as an office manager.

By coincidence, Mrs. Greg arrived for her first day of work on the very day that Mr. Harrison had to leave to attend a week-long convention of manufacturers. He was therefore only able to give her general instructions regarding the supervising of the office staff and the additional task of familiarizing herself with general office procedures during his absence. He also talked to Mrs. McKnight and told her that she would no longer have the office staff reporting to her but would instead serve only as his secretary in the future.

The next day, when Mrs. Greg asked Mrs. McKnight to type a report for her, Mrs. McKnight refused and said that she answered only to Mr. Harrison and that Mrs. Greg had authority only over the remaining secretaries. In addition, Mrs. McKnight said that Marie Larkin, a typist in the office, had always worked under her exclusive supervision and should continue to do so, since that arrangement had "worked well in the past."

The discussion between Mrs. McKnight and Mrs. Greg took place shortly before lunch. At 2:30 that afternoon, Mrs. McKnight told Marie Larkin that she was going home for the day because of personal problems. Later that night she telephoned Mr. Harrison at the convention, described the day's events from her viewpoint, and complained that she did "not understand the new structure."

QUESTIONS

1. What should be done now by Mr. Harrison? By Mrs. Greg?

2. What actions could have reduced the likelihood of this problem occurring?

3. What parallels exist between matrix management and the relationship between the new assistant and those managers who have been assigned a secretary?

CASE 8-2.   Automotive Electronics Incorporated

Established in the mid-1970s by an electronics engineer, Automotive Electronics Incorporated was in the business of producing CB radios for cars. The company, which had been organized during the height of the Citizens Band radio boom, encountered intense price competition in 1976, and quality control became a major issue because any quality control problems resulted in substantial losses on a unit that needed warranty repairs. Although the products made by Automotive Electronics were considered, by industry observers, to be quite well designed, the company had experienced a higher than average failure rate. This had had substantial negative effects on dealers, who hesitated to sell a product line that contained a large number of potentially defective units. There simply was not enough profit margin in the product to allow more than a minimal number of returns.

A review of the quality control problems disclosed that in a few cases the materials or components from suppliers had been faulty, and this had resulted in unit failures. However, the suppliers of these defective parts had been replaced, and the new sources of supply seemed to provide consistent and high-quality items. Most of the problems evidently stemmed from the new assembly techniques instituted in an attempt to cut costs to a minimum. To remedy these difficulties, the president of the company, Ted Sandits, hired a new quality control expert with experience in similar manufacturing problems.

The new quality control supervisor was introduced to the plant manager, John Haller, by the president. Mr. Sandits told John that the new man should help straighten out those production problems, but he gave John little direction as to whom the quality control supervisor was to report and what specific procedures were to be implemented for improvement of product quality. John decided that for the time being he would have this supervisor report directly to him.

During the following week, John was aware that the new quality control supervisor was exerting every effort to make a positive impact on product quality. Jack Nale reported to him that while the new man was knowledgeable, Larry Montgomery had complained that the new man was going down to the shop floor and "raising hell" with the operators about their carelessness. After receiving this information, John wondered whether he had a problem with organization or with personality.

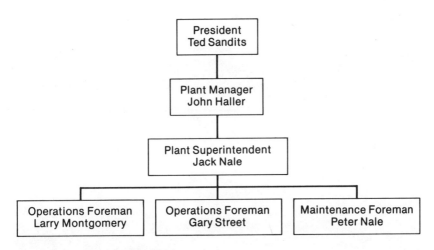

Figure 8-3   Organization Chart

QUESTIONS

1. What are the implications involved in having the quality control supervisor report directly to the plant manager?

2. What problems does the new quality control supervisor create by going down to the shop floor and dealing directly with the workers?

3. Can you foresee any problems with the father-son relationship between the plant superintendent and the maintenance foreman?

4. At what organizational level should the new quality control supervisor be located? What authority should he have?

5. Was the president's orientation of the new quality control supervisor adequate? What type of consultation should have occurred among the president, the plant manager, the quality control supervisor, and others?

9

STAFFING THE ORGANIZATION

LEARNING OBJECTIVES

This chapter discusses how the human resources in organizations are acquired and maintained. After you have read this chapter, you will

1. Know how to plan for employment needs
2. Be familiar with the various sources of employees
3. Know what role the application blank plays in selecting employees
4. Know how various types of interviews can affect the selection process
5. Be aware of the legal restrictions on using tests to select employees

Staffing is the process that ensures a continuous flow of qualified persons into an organization. Maintaining a flow of qualified people provides the starting point for building effectiveness in an organization. Effective staffing activity results in reduced training costs and time, reduced turnover, and increased productivity and improved morale for the organization.

The staffing process in organizations is threefold: employee planning, sources of personnel, and selection of personnel. This chapter examines these three phases of the staffing process, with particular attention being given to the third phase, selection.

PLANNING FOR EMPLOYMENT NEEDS

Employee planning, or manpower planning, is the vital activity of projecting the needs of an organization for various types of employees. It is important to plan for employment needs so that adequate numbers of qualified persons can be identified and secured. The basic activity in employee planning is forecasting the needed number of employees at various levels or jobs within the organization.

Adequate employment projections or forecasts can be made by tying the projections to such barometers as sales volume or increases in customers and taking into account the historical turnover and retirement experience of the organization.

EXAMPLE

A sales manager of an organization that expects a 15 percent increase in sales during the following year because of an expanded sales territory can reasonably anticipate adding sales personnel to the work force. The increase in member salespersons should approximate 15 percent of the current sales force plus those persons expected to leave the company due to turnover and retirement. Table 9–1 provides an analysis of the various sources and causes for losses of employees. In this analysis, the company should prepare to add approximately 16 percent to its employee sales force (see calculation in Table 9–1).

The planning that involves the hiring of additional employees can be done on either an informal or a formal basis. Typically, the larger organizations have a greater need for a formal planning process; some major companies, such as Du Pont, attempt to develop plans not only for the next year

Table 9-1. Example of Manpower Requirements in 1980
for Outside Sales Force

Change in personnel required as a result of change in sales	+ 15
Change in personnel required as a result of change in technology*	− 4
Change in personnel required as a result of change in public policy†	+ 2
Add number of employees who will leave the company‡	+ 6
Subtract number of employees available from other areas within company as a result of *normal* training, etc.	− 3
Number of additional employees who must be trained from within the organization or who must be hired from outside	+ 16

*Such as increased use of telephone sales, or providing each salesperson with automobile, or use of air travel.
†Shorter workweek.
‡Retire, die, move away, etc.

but for up to twenty years ahead. In larger organizations, such planning tends to be done by a personnel department that has had specific experience with this responsibility. When it is necessary for hundreds or even thousands of persons to be added to the payroll in a given year, the personnel department is forced to establish quite formal procedures for planning and selection activities.

Many large organizations keep detailed records of the various skills and other characteristics of employees at all levels of the organization. These records permit the detailed planning of an orderly movement of qualified employees through the organization. A key term here is qualified employees. It is not enough merely to have someone available to fill a specific position; it is necessary that the person be able to perform the required tasks.

EXAMPLE

Typically in the larger companies, records are kept of all the employees who currently hold a managerial position. A second set of records is available which contains names of employees who are able to take over the job of their supervisor at any given moment. In a third set of records are the names of employees who would be prepared and qualified to take over a position after a few months' notice.

Very elaborate manpower-planning procedures are practiced mainly at higher levels in the organization, but the principle of anticipating human resource needs is crucial to effective organizational performance in general. In the staffing process, planning for employment needs leads to the identification of sources of employees.

SOURCES OF EMPLOYEES

There are two major sources of employees: internal sources and external sources. Internal sources of employees consist of those persons who already are members of the organization and who would like to have the opportunity to fill a particular job opening. Of the several methods for filling job openings internally, the most widely used is the process of seniority. Using the seniority criterion, an employee who has been on the job the longest has the first opportunity to accept or decline a new job opening; this system rewards length of service. The advantages of the seniority system are that employees can easily understand it; it is traditional among union and many nonunion employees; and it is easy to calculate. It has the disadvantage of not using ability or performance as the selection criterion, and as a result the best performer may not get the job.

Job-bidding systems and talent searches constitute alternatives to the seniority system. An organization that utilizes job bidding usually publishes or posts various job openings for everyone to see. Interested employees can submit their "bid" for the job, and the person with the most appropriate qualifications is awarded the job. Among the disadvantages of this system are that employees may hesitate to bid on a job that requires a transfer for fear that such a bid will make a negative impression on their current supervisor. Also, peer pressure may cause some persons to refrain from bidding on a job if the organizational norm runs counter to it. An additional problem with this system stems from the fact that if relatively few persons bid on a job, the organization may be limited in its ability to select qualified persons. By contrast, the talent search is a more involved, but more worthwhile, effort—the qualifications of all the employees are cataloged and are used to identify persons for future job openings. When an opening arises, the "data bank" is used to identify persons who might fill the opening.

External sources of employees include not only those persons who have been referred to the organization by employment agencies, friends, unions, advertisements, colleges, and former employees but also walk-in applicants, and so forth. Although all of these sources are available, some are usually more desirable than others. Research has shown that turnover tends to be relatively high among persons who are referred by employment agencies or who respond to newspaper advertisements; employment agencies that prescreen applicants before referring them to a company have a better record of job retention than those that do not. Newspaper advertisements have the added disadvantage that the employer is not able to control the number of respondents; too many respondents may provide a work overload for the personnel department and create potential dissatisfaction among applicants who feel that they are not being given "appropriate" consideration. By contrast, turnover tends to be lower among former employees and walk-in applicants.

In those instances where the union has a hiring hall and the company needs workers who have specific skills, the union often serves as the major or even the only source of employees (e.g., maritime unions, construction and trade unions, and so forth).

The development and maintenance of both external and internal sources of employees is essential. Because a work history is available for current employees, internal sources of manpower tend to have an advantage in making good predictions of future job performance and of boosting morale. However, frequently the organization needs additional talent not available internally, and external sources must be tapped. In these instances the general reputation of the company is important. The stature of the company in the community also is affected by its public relations, institutional advertising, and reputation as a "good place to work." The selection of qualified persons from external sources of employees provides a significant challenge to the personnel department as well as the supervisor.

SELECTION

The selection process involves a match between the needs of a company and the needs of individuals. A company attempts to select those individuals who will perform designated tasks well, whereas individuals attempt to select those organizations that will provide them with career satisfaction. In a good selection process, both parties have their needs met.

Unfortunately, selection decisions frequently go wrong for the individual or the company, or both. Most errors in the selection process occur because the process is defined by both parties as being one of conflict. Conflict arises as the applicant attempts to give acceptable information, which may contain substantial distortion, in order to secure the job. At the same time, the organization attempts to appear attractive so that the applicant will accept an offered position; this may result in suppression or overlooking of the negative aspects of the organization. Thus a kind of "industrial seduction" occurs, which can lead to wrong selection decisions. Errors in selection lead to increased turnover and reduced productivity, both of which are expensive in financial and human terms.

Effective selection efforts begin with a detailed knowledge of the job to be filled. Without specific information regarding the kinds of tasks to be performed, it is difficult to make accurate selection decisions. Usually, the needed job information can be found in job descriptions and job specifications. Job descriptions provide a narrative summary of the activities and responsibilities to be performed on a particular job. Job specifications indicate the skills required to accomplish the job (see Figure 9–1 for an example of a job description and job specification). Armed with this information, a person from the organization (e.g., personnel department, manager, supervisor, etc.) can begin to assess the likely performance of various job applicants.

The determination of likely job success of any one individual results from gathering relevant information from various sources. The most widely used sources of this information are application blanks and references, personal interviews, and testing (including assessment centers).

Job Title: Machine Operator

General Duties: Sets up and operates drill press, lathe and saw to fabricate component parts

Supervision received: Carries out assignments from lead machinists and shop foreman

Supervision exercised: None

Major Duties	Time Devoted to Duty
1. Sets up and operates drill press and mills aircraft components	70 percent
2. Sets up and operates saws and lathes	15 percent
3. Reads blueprints and/or work order cards to determine job specifications	5 percent
4. Checks component specifications against fabricated parts	5 percent
5. Performs miscellaneous tasks: sharpens drills, cleans workplace, keeps records of production on a given shift	5 percent

Minimum Qualifications

1. Required knowledge, skills and abilities: knowledge of machine shop, mechanical ability, ability to read blueprints, and good eye-hand coordination.

2. Education: course in blueprint reading, high school mathematics

3. Experience: six months work in machine shop

4. Other: supply personal tools including: six-inch scale, one-inch and two-inch micrometer, dial calipers, and mechanics tool set.

Figure 9–1   Sample Job Description and Specification

Application Blanks

Application blanks are one of the most efficient ways of collecting standardized and verifiable information from job applicants. Application forms differ in their length and complexity. As in many other endeavors,

personal data

Please print:

Date _____

Name _____ Social Security No. _____
       (LAST)   (FIRST)   (MIDDLE)

Present Address _____
                (NUMBER AND STREET)   (CITY AND STATE)   (ZIP CODE)

Home Phone _____

Position Applied For _____

If your application is considered favorably, on what date would you be available for employment? _____ , 19 ___

Do you have any physical handicaps which would prevent you from performing specific kinds of work? Yes □   No □.

If yes, describe the handicap and explain the work limitations: _____

List all illnesses you have had in the last five years _____

How were you referred to us? _____

Do you have a relative presently employed at XYZ Corporation? Yes□ No□ If yes, what is name of relative? _____

education and training

NAME OF SCHOOL	LOCATION	FROM		TO		Graduate? (Yes or No)	Courses or Degree	Major
		Mo.	Yr.	Mo.	Yr.			
High School(s)								
College(s)								
Graduate School								
Business School								
Special Courses or Other Training								

If you plan to continue your education or training, explain: _____ When? _____

Please indicate below your office skills and check machines you can operate efficiently.

□ Typewriter { □ Electric _____ WPM   □ Adding Machine   □ Computer
               { □ Manual _____ WPM   □ Calculator   Model _____

Figure 9-1a   Application for Employment, XYZ Corporation

there is a tendency for the application form to grow more lengthy over the years as different questions are inserted to obtain desired information; frequently various questions on the application have little current usefulness. As a general principle, the information collected should be relevant to the actual position for which the person is being recruited.

employment record

Please account for all your employment beginning with your present or last employment and listing your complete employment record in reverse order.

Name of present or last employer			Type of Business	Telephone No.	May we contact?
Address of employer-Street and number			City	State	Zip Code

Date started	Starting salary	Title when you started	Supervisor's Name	Why did you leave?	
Date terminated	Ending salary	Present or last title	Supervisor's Title		

Brief description of responsibilities

Have you worked for the above employer under another name? Yes☐ No☐

If yes, what name?_____

Have you ever worked for XYZ Corporation before? Yes☐ No☐   If yes, when _____

If yes, please complete employment record below.

Please give any further information which may be helpful in considering your qualifications for the position to which you have applied. If necessary, attach additional sheets.

In case of emergency, notify (indicate name, relationship, address and nearest telephone number)

I understand that if employed, I am on a probationary basis for the first 60 days of continuous employment and that XYZ Corporation can terminate it any time within the period for any reason without advance notice or severance pay. I retain the same privilege.

I hereby certify that the answers given by me to the foregoing questions and statements made are true and correct, without reservations of any kind whatsoever and that no attempt has been made by me to conceal pertinent information. I also authorize my former employers, schools or anyone acting for them to give any information they may have regarding me. I hereby release them from all liability for issuing same. It is understood that all facts are open to investigation by XYZ Corporation and that if upon investigation, anything contained in this application is found to be false or misleading, I understand I will be subject to dismissal from employment at any time during the period of my employment and agree to hold XYZ Corporation and persons named herein blameless in that event.

If employment is obtained under this application, I will willingly comply with all orders, rules and regulations of this company.

_____   _____
Date   Signature

Figure 9-1b   Application for Employment *(cont.)*

Recently, analyses of application blank information have revealed that important selection concerns (e.g., performance) can be predicted by weighing certain items on the application blank more heavily than others.

EXAMPLE

> If it is found that on a particular job 70 percent of the married employees are high performers, whereas only 25 percent of the employees who are separated from their spouses are high performers, it makes sense to give some preference to married persons as opposed to those who are separated.

By analyzing each piece of information gathered on the application blank, weights or scores can be related to actual behavior on a job. A summary of the scores for all application blank responses can be developed to indicate future performance. It should be noted that it is necessary to conduct the weighting analysis for *each* job, since no universally applicable weights or categories have been found that apply to all jobs. Moreover, it is not clear to researchers exactly why a particular piece of information (e.g., marital status) may be highly related to performance on a particular job; nevertheless, this process shows promise.

One major problem can affect the usefulness of application blanks for the selection process. Much of the information that job applicants provide is not valid. As we mentioned earlier, the process of selection tends to be one in which distortions from the applicant can be expected. One study found that verification of application blank data revealed the following percentage of invalid responses:

Item	Percentage with Invalid Information
Age	10%
Marital status	15%
Education	21%
Age at disablement	33%
Job title	24%
Job duties	10%
Pay	22%
Length of employment	29%

From Goldstein, I.L., "The Application Blank: How Honest Are the Responses?" *Journal of Applied Psychology*, 55 (1971), 491–492.

Obviously, inaccuracies of this magnitude inhibit the effective use of application blanks.

As a supplement to the biographical data on the application blank, reference checks should be made. While these reference checks often involve writing, usually telephone inquiries are made. Most applicants attempt to provide only the names of those persons who can be expected to give very positive responses. Since most responses to recommendation inquiries are very positive, it is difficult to separate the truly high performer from the average or even the below-average performer. The following suggestion may help with the problems of detecting differences among highly recommended persons. If an employer receives *only* statements to the effect that the individual tends to be "cooperative" or is "considerate" or is "pleasant," the person writing the recommendation may have some reservations about that applicant. If, however, there are positive statements referring to an applicant's motivation, alertness, reliability and dependability, and/or intelligence, then it is more likely that the person making the recommendation has a higher regard for the ratee.

Because of the applicant's right to access of information in his or her personnel file and the legal responsibility that may be involved for inaccurate and damaging information, the use of the telephone is often more desirable than writing. If a written response is obtained, then the employer should make the contact rather than the applicant.

As a final note, it should be recognized that those recommendations from firms or relatives that have been suggested by the job applicant are probably not worth the effort and cost of mailing. On the other hand, former supervisors and others who have known the applicant may be able to provide quality information.

Interviews

The personal interview is one of the most pervasive of all selection techniques. This probably stems from the fact that most supervisors are quite uncomfortable when the company hires a subordinate with whom they have had no prior conversation. Interestingly, the weight given to impressions developed in the personal interview tends to be far greater than is justified by careful studies of their predictive ability. Stated differently, most interviewers think that they are quite capable of uncovering relevant and accurate information in the interview process. But this often does not seem to be the case. In Table 9–2 the relationship between interview rating and subsequent promotions reveals that substantial inaccuracy results from the personal interview. As shown in the table, interviewers are much better at predicting certain areas of future performance (i.e., mental ability, practical judgment, self-confidence) than other areas (i.e., technical competence, character). It has been demonstrated that a single interviewer will maintain a fairly consistent evaluation of a particular applicant from one interview to the next;

there is much less consistency between two different interviewers who interview the same individual. The problem seems to be that different interviewers utilize different pieces of information to arrive at their conclusions.

Other problems in the interviewing process include the following. First, decisions tend to be made quite early in the interview. Within the first five to eight minutes, most interviewers decide whether or not a particular applicant shows promise. After that decision is made, it is quite difficult for the applicant to present information that will significantly alter the initial judgment.

Table 9-2. Correlations between Interview Rating and Promotion

Interview Item	Correlation
Personal impression	.13
Effectiveness with people	.04
Mental ability for problem solving	.23
Imagination	.27
Practical judgment	.37
Technical competence	− .10
Character and habits	− .12
Self-confidence, maturity, and emotional stability	.40
Potential as a clientele builder	.05
Promotion potential	.36
Employment recommendation	.28

Adapted with permission from John B. Miner, "Executive and Personnel Interviews as Predictors of Consulting Success," *Personnel Psychology,* 23 (1970), 534.

Second, negative information tends to be given excessive weight in the interview process. The interview, as well as other selection procedures, tends to be used to "deselect" individuals; negative information provides a basis for ruling out an applicant from further consideration. As a result, most interviewees try their best to determine what the interviewer wants to hear and give it to him or to her. This is consistent with the earlier discussion where an individual is caught between providing accurate information and providing information that will "land the job."

Third, many interviewers talk too much. They spend so much time giving responses or providing information to an applicant that they fail to gather appropriate information from the applicant to make sound judgments. The major reason for this type of error is inexperience and a lack of planning by the interviewer.

Fourth, various biases and errors exist within the interviewer, which can affect his or her perception of the applicant. A very common error in the interview processes (and in any evaluation effort) is known as the halo error. The halo error exists when a single attribute of an individual affects a judgment about other attributes.

An applicant who appears to be quite intelligent may create a favorable impression. The applicant may experience a halo error if the interviewer then views this person as likely to be dependable in job performance as well. The initial positive reaction may affect the judgment of the interviewer on an unrelated dimension.

Other rater errors include personal biases and stereotypes.

EXAMPLE

The stereotype that females should not engage in certain manual tasks, such as truck driving, can affect the judgment of the interviewer regarding an applicant's potential in performing that job.

With all of these problems and limitations in the interview process, what can be done to make a personal interview more reliable? The following suggestions can help distinguish successful from unsuccessful selection interviews:

1. Use a trained interviewer who is familiar with the job.

2. Before the interview begins, make certain that the interviewer has some indication of the information that should be considered favorable or unfavorable for the specific job being discussed.

3. Maintain a substantial degree of structure in the interview so that significant material can be gathered on a consistent basis.

4. The interview should be concerned mainly with gathering selection information rather than providing information to attract the applicant to the organization.

5. The data gathered from the personal interview should be considered as merely an additional source of information. These data should be combined with other data to make the final selection decision. The interview should *not* be the sole means of uncovering data, nor should it necessarily even be the most important.

6. Use more than one interviewer. This can be accomplished either as a panel in a single interview session or in a series of successive interviews. Later, combine evaluations from the various interviewers to determine the group view of the applicant.

For a further discussion of interviewing, see Chapters 5 and 6.

Types of Interviews. Employment interviews can be divided into one or more of the following categories: (1) patterned, or structured, interviews; (2) nondirective, or unstructured, interviews; and (3) stress interviews.

Patterned interviews follow a predetermined set of questions; this serves two purposes. First, by determining the questions in advance, the interviewer can make certain that inquiries are made into specific job-related aspects of the applicant. Second, the patterned interview permits the interviewer to ask the same questions of each applicant, and it thereby facilitates comparisons between applicants. This procedure reduces the likelihood that various interviewers will ask questions about different topics, which results in responses that are not comparable. The major disadvantage of the patterned interview is that it may restrict the exploration of what the interviewer may feel to be important areas about the candidate because the questions are developed in advance.

The nondirective, or unstructured, interview is much more flexible than the patterned, or structured, interview. It tends to be much more time consuming and free flowing than the patterned type; in an unstructured interview, the interviewer spends most of the time listening and encouraging further discussion by the job candidate. The interviewer tends to ask for clarification, for further elaboration, and for judgments about feelings and intent. This approach usually results in a rather complete picture of the applicant's preferences, concerns, beliefs, and family life. But this picture may have little relationship to actual job performance. Furthermore, the direction the interview takes is often determined to a great extent by the concerns of the applicant. As a result, this procedure may make it quite difficult to compare one applicant with another.

The stress interview was developed during World War II as a way of simulating anxiety-producing situations to be faced by foreign agents. The procedure is one in which an applicant faces an aggressive, anxiety-producing person who attempts to put that candidate on the defensive. The intent of the stress interview is to see how an individual reacts "under pressure." The use of this technique is appropriate only if the interview accurately simulates the type of pressures that exist on the job. It may be helpful in screening out persons who cannot work effectively in such an environment. The validity of the stress interview may be questioned if the job does not contain the stresses it simulates. Moreover, it frequently increases the negative feelings an applicant has about an organization. On balance, it seems to be unjustified as part of most normal interview procedures.

To summarize, the combination of several interviewers utilizing the structured interview seems to produce the most valid and reliable data. By conducting interviews either in a group or sequentially and pooling the judgments of all interviewers, the most accurate job-related picture of the several job applicants can be gained. A major disadvantage of this approach is that it is relatively expensive. It requires more than one interviewer; as a result, it frequently is utilized only in filling higher-level positions in an organization.

Testing

Numerous tests have been devised to measure various aspects of the individual. Psychological tests measure abilities such as intelligence, and psychomotor tests measure abilities relating to muscular action (e.g., finger dexterity). Personality tests measure such things as interest, perceptions, and beliefs. Skill and achievement tests measure such things as knowledge; the general health of the job applicant is determined by a physical examination.

Regardless of the type of test, two components of the test instrument itself must be acceptable if the instrument is to have any value in selections. First, the test must be reliable. That is, the test must measure consistently the dimension that it is designed to measure. For example, a reliable test of job skills should produce roughly the same score the first time it is taken by an applicant as it does two weeks later; the item it measures (e.g., job skill) should be measured consistently. Second, the test must be valid. A valid test is one that measures what it says it measures. For example, a test of intelligence that employs limited time to solve reading problems should measure mental acuity, not the person's ability to read (e.g., reading speed).

The issues surrounding the two concepts of validity and reliability have become particularly important as they relate to equal employment opportunity considerations. Specifically, employers have been permitted the right to use tests, but they are being required to establish the link between a particular test score and performance on a specific job. In other words, it must be shown that a test predicts future job performance if it is to be used as a selection tool. In a landmark case, *Griggs* vs. *Duke Power Company,* these issues were clarified when the Court held that the employer discriminated against blacks by requiring them to pass a standardized intelligence test *or* have a high-school education as a condition of employment. The Court held that this was inappropriate because

> ... (a) neither standard is shown to be significantly related to successful job performance, (b) both requirements operate to disqualify Negroes at a significantly higher rate than white applicants, and (c) the jobs in question formerly had been filled only by white employees as part of their long standing practice of giving preference to whites.

The result of this decision was to restrict the use of tests that have an appreciably greater effect on one group of individuals than on another in the general population. Moreover, a similar prohibition exists for those instances where it is not clear that the test or high-school diploma is necessary to job performance. In this specific case, the company could not show that it was essential to have a high-school diploma in order to be a custodian or a manual laborer. The effect of this decision was to require organizations to use tests more appropriately.

Since tests measure only part of the person, though they may do that quite well, it is obvious that they may not measure everything that is relevant to performance on a particular job. For example, a typing test may be a good measure of the ability to use a typewriter, but it is limited in predicting general secretarial skills other than typing. Thus the typing test accounts for only a portion of this job. An additional caution regarding tests and test scores should be noted. In many cases a test is given too much weight in the selection process because tests typically produce quantitative scores that give the supervisor a false sense of precision and accuracy. This problem is more likely to arise when the interview and application blanks are administered in a general, nonpurposeful manner. The test score could be the only standardized information available.

In summary, tests represent a refinement in selection procedures; they can play a major role in the selection process when a job requires abilities or skills that can be measured and which people possess in different quantities. Generally, tests have been reasonably successful in identifying what people "can do," but they have been much less successful in predicting what people "will do." Thus, even though a test may accurately predict a job applicant's abilities, that same test cannot actually determine whether or not the applicant will apply these abilities to high performance on the job.

Assessment Centers

An additional and promising procedure for testing potential applicants involves the assessment center. The assessment center utilizes a battery of simulations and a team of assessors, who make a group determination of an applicant's likely managerial performance. The assessment center is used most often in selecting persons for managerial positions.

One of the most popular simulations used in assessment centers is the "in-basket" problem. In this simulation, an applicant is provided with a series of letters and memos to which he or she is asked to respond (e.g., see the case following Chapter 7). The applicant is scored by trained observers according to how well he or she responds to the situations contained in the letters and memos. Another popular simulation used in the assessment center is the leaderless group discussion. In this simulation, several job applicants are grouped together and are asked to discuss a problem without designating a particular leader. The participants are evaluated as to their effectiveness in their group discussion. Both the in-basket and the leaderless group techniques have proved to have some validity in selecting managers and supervisors.

The problems with assessment centers are similar to those associated with paper-and-pencil tests. The assessment center is mainly limited to its ability to measure the "can do" aspects of the job. Nevertheless, the technique is useful because it has had considerable success in identifying those persons who will be able to perform well on the job if they choose to do so.

SUMMARY

An effective staffing effort is essential for continued high performance at the departmental and the organizational level. In general, the staffing process involves the effective use of human resources to accomplish organizational needs. The staffing process includes planning for the human needs of the organization, maintaining sources of employees, and selecting those employees best suited to organizational needs. Thus the staffing process becomes a starting point for building quality into an organization. It is integral to increasing organizational effectiveness.

DISCUSSION QUESTIONS

1. What role does employee planning play in the staffing process?
2. Differentiate between *internal* and *external* sources of employees. How does a supervisor utilize internal sources of employees?
3. What are the disadvantages of newspaper advertisements as a means of identifying future employees?
4. What factors affect the ability of an organization to attract new employees?
5. What is "industrial seduction"? How does it affect the selection process?
6. Does an effective selection effort begin with knowledge of the candidate or the job? Explain.
7. Describe the kinds of information best gathered through an application blank. How does this information differ from that obtained in a personal interview?
8. How accurate or valid is information likely to be in the selection process? What steps can an employer take to ensure that information given by an applicant is valid?
9. How accurate are interviews as predictors of future performance on the job?
10. Describe some of the problems in the interview process. What steps can the interviewer take to reduce these problems?
11. What is a patterned, or structured, interview? How does it compare with a nondirective interview?
12. What is *test validity*? Describe *test reliability*. How are these two concepts employed in the prediction of future job performance?
13. What role does testing have in the selection process? Can a good test serve as a reasonable substitute for other selection methods? Explain.

14. Describe the "in-basket" problem and its role in an assessment center. Assessment centers are usually utilized to select employees for what type of jobs?

CASE 9-1.   Miller Manufacturing Company (A)

As a major midwestern manufacturer of automobile carburetors, Miller Manufacturing Company employed an average of six hundred people. Albert Carson, the personnel manager, had worked at Miller Manufacturing for the past seventeen years. He prided himself on his ability to conduct interviews effectively. When the new assistant personnel manager was hired, Mr. Carson took particular pleasure in "breaking in" the recent college graduate on the practical aspects of effective interviewing.

"I can size anyone up in ten minutes or less in an interview. My record shows how good I am at this, and I'll give you a few tips," Mr. Carson told his new assistant. "We don't use any written tests here because of EEO hassles with them. It's just as well because I didn't put much faith in what those tests showed anyway. As for personal interviews, we use several interviewers for important positions to get the effect of a group interview. Everyone asks the questions that they feel are important, and they report to me anything outstanding or particularly negative that turns up. My interview with a prospective employee is the one that usually counts the most, though. I'm looking for 'hard drivers' and people who I think will succeed around here. In just a few minutes, I can tell by the way they look at me, the kind of clothes they wear, and their general confidence in themselves whether or not they are likely to be good Miller Manufacturing employees. For example, you can tell a lot about a man by the kind of shoes he wears and how well they are polished. Also, I put a lot of stock in whether or not the applicants have finished the education they began whether it's high school, junior college, or a university. It shows that they can finish things and can stick to their tasks."

Mr. Carson continued, "The best techniques I've found to separate the poor applicants from those with real promise is to ask them how they would handle the following situation. I give them two alternatives to stop employees from arguing constantly with each other. First, the employees could be told either to work it out among themselves or to get a transfer out of the department. Second, the supervisor could sit down with the employees and work the difficulties out together. Whichever approach is taken, I tell them that they are wrong. If they select the first method, I tell them that their job is to develop and help employees to perform better. If they select the second, I tell them they have more important things to do than to work out personal problems between employees. By doing this, I see how applicants handle stress and see what they're made of. A good employee will stick by his guns and give me some good reasons why his approach should be followed. With all this information, I can usually make a good decision in a pretty short time. Also, I generally check with previous employers to see whether my impressions are similar to those of the applicant's former boss. I've found that I am seldom wrong."

QUESTIONS

1. Evaluate Mr. Carson's interview techniques.
2. Is it possible to do an adequate job of interviewing in so short a time? Discuss.
3. How useful was the stress aspect of the interview?
4. What recommendations, if any, would you make to Mr. Carson to improve his interviewing?

CASE 9-1. Miller Manufacturing Company (B)

Steve Ray was twenty-two years old when he applied for a position as a bookkeeper at Miller Manufacturing Company. He had held two bookkeeping jobs previously, and as a result he had had some experience with employment interviews. He wore a new suit which was neatly pressed, and he made every effort to express self-confidence in himself and his skills as an accountant.

In the interview with Mr. Carson, he displayed a high degree of ambition. Mr. Carson was impressed when Steve looked him right in the eye and said, "I plan to be the head of the accounting department in two years." Later when Mr. Carson asked him how he would stop employees from arguing among themselves, Steve said that he would use both of the techniques that Mr. Carson described. He would first sit them down to work out their problem together, and if that didn't work he would tell them to resolve it among themselves or get a transfer. Mr. Carson was very pleased with that response. One thing that Steve inquired about, though, bothered Mr. Carson. Steve's only questions about company policies or benefits were about the policy on sick pay and absenteeism. Mr. Carson did not know if that had any particular significance.

Steve had attended the local junior college and received his associate in arts degree there. He graduated with a 2.07 grade point average. He received C's and D's in his accounting courses.

Reference checks of his two previous employers were inconclusive. The most recent employer refused to comment on Steve's performance, and the other one said that Steve was somewhat immature but adequate as an employee.

After reviewing all the information, Mr. Carson decided that Steve's performance in the personal interview was so good that he should be employed. Mr. Carson felt that anyone with ambition and reasonable ability could perform the job after the initial training period. Steve began work the following Monday.

QUESTIONS

1. Why was Steve hired? How much weight should college grades and performance in previous jobs carry?
2. What added information could Mr. Carson have sought?
3. If you were advising Mr. Carson, what steps could the company now take to help ensure that Steve will become a productive employee?

10

DEVELOPING AND APPRAISING
THE PERFORMANCE OF EMPLOYEES

LEARNING OBJECTIVES

This chapter discusses both the developing and the appraising of subordinates' performance. After you have read this chapter, you will

1. Understand the scope of employee development and its relationship to performance appraisal
2. Understand how motivation, knowledge of results, organization of materials, and so forth, affect learning
3. Be familiar with various employee training methods
4. Know how to conduct a training program
5. Know which factors affect employee development efforts
6. Understand why the various performance appraisal systems have both strengths and limitations

Managerial talent has usually been in short supply. Our economy generally has been expanding for decades, and recently a drop in the number of persons who seek out top managerial responsibilities has been reported. Thus the need to develop managerial and supervisory talent among employees has become increasingly important. Recognizing that the development of employee potential is critical to long-run organizational effectiveness, good performance appraisals must be conducted in order to identify those areas in an employee's performance that need improvement. The relationship between employee development and performance appraisal is the major focus of this chapter.

EMPLOYEE DEVELOPMENT

In recent years, training and development has become available on a regular basis for almost all employees rather than being reserved for only the "chosen few." Training and development that has been historically conducted off-the-job, or outside of the company, is now usually conducted on the job during normal working hours. Fewer staff specialists and outsiders are used as trainers; frequently, management and employee development is conducted by line managers. Historically, businesses have focused on top-management problems, but more recently the emphasis has been on problems that face all employees or supervisors. In general, a shift has occurred from development of a *few* individuals to more general upgrading of skills and concepts for *most* employees, supervisors, and managers.

In a general way, all managers are responsible for developing their subordinates. Significantly, highly rated supervisors tend to have many good subordinates; by encouraging the development of subordinates, a supervisor increases the ability of his or her work unit to perform. The increased capability of subordinates has a positive effect on the overall unit for which the supervisor has responsibility.

Answers to four questions are very important in the development of employees: What do employees do? How do employees learn? How can we train them? and How do they perform? Previous chapters have focused on the nature of managerial and supervisory work, and they have therefore addressed the first question. For example, we have seen that a great deal of the supervisor's time is spent in solving unprogrammed problems. More information about specific job requirements can be obtained from a job analysis. This information can serve to uncover the requirements of a job. Such knowledge can be compared with job performance to identify needed training areas. In addition to individual needs, attention should be given to the needs of the organization and the effectiveness of various units in the firm. The questions regarding how employees learn and how they can be trained provide a major focus for the next two sections of this chapter. We will then present a method for systematic analysis of training and organizational conditions, which is designed to reduce ineffective development efforts. Following this, we will discuss performance appraisal and how employees perform.

HOW DO EMPLOYEES LEARN?

Effective learning involves several principles that are relevant to a supervisor in an industrial setting. A discussion of these principles follows.

Motivation

If training is to be effective, it must be seen by the recipient as meeting a need or being of some assistance. For example, an employee who aspires to be promoted can be expected to gain more from a training session than will a person who has little ambition and has been compelled to attend.

Knowledge of Results

Feedback that lets an employee know how well he or she has mastered a particular skill is useful because it indicates where the employee has done well and in what areas further efforts are required. Providing feedback can serve the function of reinforcing desired behaviors (see the discussion of behavior modification in Chapter 4). For example, persons trying to increase their typing skills are more likely to perform well if they are given specific information about their speed and errors instead of being told to merely "do their best."

Meaningful Organization of Materials

The presentation of concepts in a manner that is logical and relevant to the trainee is most likely to be effective. Those presentations that skip materials or are introduced in a confused manner have less impact. By contrast, learning is facilitated if materials are organized so that each experience builds upon the preceding one and if the trainee is helped to integrate these experiences into a usable pattern of skills.

Practice and Repetition

A training process that allows an individual to "try out" new ideas or skills can help the employee experience performing correctly. Moreover, the opportunity to try out these ideas or skills should be permitted to occur several times so that there is a repetition of the correct response. For example, rather than merely describing how a machine is operated, the employee should be given an opportunity to practice using the machine by operating it for several repetitions.

Distributed Learning

The amount of time devoted to a single session in the learning process can influence the effectiveness of the learning inputs. Whether or not the development technique should be concentrated in a few but long sessions or many but short sessions is a decision that the supervisor must make. Generally speaking, if one spreads out the training sessions into several shorter sessions, more rapid learning and more permanent learning will result. This is particularly true of very complex problems.

Whole versus Part Learning

The question of whether to convey the whole problem to an employee or break it down into parts is one that is associated with the distributed learning question addressed above. For example, a keypunch operator may begin learning the job by practicing moving individual fingers; the operator may then progress to moving all of the fingers. This is an example of part learning. In general, if a task can be broken down into smaller parts, it should probably be broken down to facilitate learning. Those tasks that do not lend themselves to being broken down should probably be taught as a unit.

Although the above principles focus on how people learn, they do not tell how to mount a program to train others. That is, they describe but do not prescribe. The following section discusses various methods for training employees and developing them effectively.

HOW CAN EMPLOYEES BE TRAINED?

Of the several different types of training methods available, the selection of the particular approach should take into account such things as the cost, the availability of time, the level of knowledge to be imparted, the number of people to be trained, and the background of the trainees. The three major training approaches are on-the-job training, job simulation, and classroom training.

On-the-job Training

Most training conducted in organizational settings consists of on-the-job training (OJT). Using this approach, an employee is expected to acquire adequate job performance by observing, practicing, and at times being coached by supervisors and fellow workers. A major advantage of OJT is that it is conducted by persons who know the job well—supervisors and co-workers. Also, on-the-job training is usually very acceptable to the employee because it is so obviously related to job requirements.

Unfortunately, what passes for on-the-job training is often a very haphazard and ill conceived attempt to permit a new employee to self-develop adequate job skills. Added problems are that OJT can disrupt the normal flow of work, and poor supervisory practices tend to be "passed on" to the employee. The end result is that an employee is put in the position of learning through trial and error rather than being trained through the active efforts of a supervisor.

Job Simulation

Job simulation is a type of classroom training in which employees receive instruction in the type of job-related activities they are expected to perform. Job simulation is very effective where job skills can be clearly identified and measured behaviorally (e.g., typists, checkout clerks, machine operators, etc.). Another major strength of job simulation is that it is efficient for training many individuals who are likely to hold similar jobs. Moreover, in work simulations it is likely that the training intent and content will be well conceived and the skills to be acquired can be measured. For example, the training of cashiers or checkout clerks at supermarkets or department stores can be effectively accomplished in a group setting where actual work activities are simulated on cash registers.

Classroom Training

There are many methods that can be utilized individually or in combination in a classroom setting. The most widely known classroom method is the lecture. Using this procedure, one individual makes a presentation to an audience in an effort to impart information to the larger group. The lecturer is expected to have mastered the topic and should be able to present his or her ideas in an interesting and meaningful way. Often members of the audience take notes to help them retain what the expert or lecturer has said. The lecture method is most effective in transferring facts and information to others; it may be used efficiently for building knowledge.

Case study approaches are used to simulate realistic problems that trainees may expect to face. Using the case study approach, trainees are asked to identify problems, to develop solutions to those problems, and to discuss the viability of both their analysis and their solution efforts. The case study approach is a skill-building approach and is most effective in improving trainees' analytic and decision-making abilities. It is not an efficient method for transferring raw data or information.

When there is a need to change the attitudes and behaviors of participants, such methods as role playing, demonstrations, or simulations are frequently effective. Using the role-playing method, participants act out a script or play a "part" that has been assigned to them by an instructor. They carry out the verbal or written instructions provided, and the remaining class members can act as observers who learn from the actions, statements, and behaviors that emerge from the role play.

In many ways the demonstration or simulation of a particular skill or interpersonal behavior is similar to that of role playing. That is, the demonstration or simulation of situations likely to be faced by employees not only serves as a model to aid understanding but also enables trainees to develop effective behaviors. In general, demonstration and simulation efforts are most effective in showing desirable methods of handling quite complex work situations, since a verbal description of effective job performance is often much more complicated than simply showing a subordinate "how to do it." Moreover, by involving the trainee in performing the task, his or her motivation is maintained. Finally, this kind of training usually takes place in an environment where errors are not costly in financial or human terms.

Programmed Instruction

Programmed instruction is a teaching technique in which the knowledge or skill to be mastered is broken down into very small units or steps. Each step is presented to the learner in a logical progression in the form of a question, statement, or picture. Each succeeding step builds upon the preceding one. When the trainee provides a correct answer or solution at one step, he or she proceeds to the next step. The learning program is designed so that the trainee receives immediate feedback on results of the completed work. This technique differs from the conventional forms of training in that trainees progress at their own pace without direct supervision from an instructor. This method has proved equally useful in teaching such diverse topics and skills as blueprint reading, keypunch and office machine operation, arithmetic, calculus, retail sales, and automobile mechanics.

JOB INSTRUCTOR TRAINING

The Job Instructor Training (JIT) procedure represents the systematic application of learning principles and teaching techniques to work situations. It was first developed during World War II to quickly train millions of people for industrial jobs. More than a million supervisors were given JIT instruction in how to train new employees. JIT continues to be the foremost procedure for training skilled, as well as unskilled workers for office, shop, sales, and technical positions.

Job Instructor Training is broken down into two parts: *Preparing to Teach* and *Teaching*.

1. Preparing to Teach.

    a. *Break down the job.* Prepare written job descriptions. Determine the operations to be performed. List the principal steps and sequence of operations. Identify any difficulties that may be anticipated. Key points, such as quality and quantity requirements, safety and health precautions, and factors requiring judgment and skill on the part of the worker should be noted.

    b. *Know the trainee.* The supervisor should have some knowledge of the worker before undertaking training. People differ in abilities, personalities, skills, and willingness to learn. In order to motivate the trainee, the supervisor must know his or her values, needs, and goals.

    c. *Have a timetable.* In establishing a timetable, the supervisor must determine what skills the trainee will be expected to develop and the date by which the trainee can reasonably be expected to acquire the desired level of performance. The timetable provides both the supervisor and the employee with a series of goals.

    d. *Have everything ready for teaching the job.* Have materials and equipment ready. Have the workplace arranged in the manner the trainee will be expected to maintain it. This is an important experience for the employee who learns during training not only the required job skills, but also attitudes toward such matters as good housekeeping, quality and quantity standards, and the supervisor's seriousness of purpose.

2. Teaching

    a. *Prepare the worker.* Put the worker at ease. Stimulate interest in learning by explaining the purpose and importance of the job, and its relationship to other jobs and the final product. Place the trainee in the proper position. (Some jobs can be taught more readily if the trainee sees it demonstrated exactly as it will be performed.)

    b. *Present the operation.* Explain, demonstrate, and question carefully and patiently. Stress key points identified in the job breakdown. Present no more than the trainee can learn at one time. Repeat the instruction as needed, but also make certain that the trainee understands *why*, as well as *how*.

    c. *Try out performance.* Determine job knowledge through performance. Have the trainee tell and show what has been learned, and explain key points. Correct errors, but avoid criticizing the individual. Compliment and encourage, as appropriate.

d. *Follow-up.* Have the trainee take over the job. Indicate where to go for help if questions or problems arise. Check frequently. Encourage additional questions. Check to determine understanding of the job and its relationship to other jobs. Taper off extra coaching. Finally, terminate follow-up when satisfied that no further coaching is needed.

Most of what people learn about their jobs they learn through their day to day interactions with their supervisor and fellow workers. The supervisor not only provides formal job training, such as described above, but also provides many other job experiences which enable employees to grow and develop at work. Employees who have the opportunity to accept temporary job assignments, work on special projects, and rotate to other jobs, acquire skills which qualify them for promotions at a later time. Job rotation is an important technique for increasing individual job skills and also for developing a more versatile and flexible work force. The supervisor is the key individual in determining the quality of the training function in an organization.

IMPLEMENTING EFFECTIVE EMPLOYEE DEVELOPMENT EFFORTS

The proper and effective implementation of employee development efforts must fit the situation. To be effective, the person developing the training program needs to know the training objectives and the organizational conditions. Specifically, it is important to know whether the training objective is to change knowledge, attitudes, abilities, or job performance. Additionally, it is important to know what the participant characteristics are, how much learning effort is necessary, and what the organizational and leadership climates are. Table 10-1 lists some of the conditions necessary for effective management development training. By analyzing organizational conditions and specifying development objectives, the basic conditions can be indicated in an abbreviated fashion. If all the conditions under each development objective are present, a supervisor increases the likelihood that the training and development effort will be effective and positive. Studies have shown that where the conditions listed in this table are present, important gains in knowledge, attitude, and behavior have resulted.

The table indicates that the conditions necessary for a change in knowledge or facts will differ from these necessary for a change in attitudes or in performance. Thus, specific objectives carry with them different prerequisite conditions for success. The whole process of development is extremely complex, but this complexity becomes manageable when we specify the purpose, the individual, and the environment. The factors identified in Table 10-1 help ensure that a good developmental "fit" can be obtained.

Table 10-1. Conditions Needed for Effective Management Development Training

| Conditions | Management Development Objectives | | | |
	Improved Knowledge	Improved Attitude	Improved Ability	Improved Performance
Employee characteristics	Sufficient motivation	Flexible attitudes on part of participants Agreement with spirit of the material to be learned	Non-conflicting habits or personality traits	
Learning effort	Direct method of instruction (programmed learning, lectures, films, readings, and so on) Competent instruction	Discussion of on-the-job applications and personal benefits	Practice of desired abilities Corrective training to correct undesirable habits and behavioral patterns	Opportunity for on-the-job practice of newly acquired skills
Leadership climate		Neutral or positive attitude of superior toward development	Superior's attitude and example consistent with desired improvement	Coaching, counseling, and periodic performance review by superior consistent with desired performance
Organizational climate		Goals, top management philosophy, and policies consistent with learning phase		Philosophy, practices and precedents of the policy-making executives consistent with desired manager performance

From *Managerial Process and Organizational Behavior* by Alan C. Filley and Robert J. House. Copyright © 1969 by Scott, Foresman and Company. Reprinted by permission.

HOW DO EMPLOYEES PERFORM?

To determine what training or development efforts are needed in organizations, an assessment must be made of the current performance levels of employees. This process is known as <u>performance appraisal</u>. The link between development of employees and performance appraisal is that a performance appraisal helps supervisors identify performance shortcomings; such shortcomings are indicators of development needs. Consequently, good development effort depends upon an accurate assessment of employee performance.

The basic objectives of performance appraisals are to (1) measure and document performance to meet legal requirements, (2) improve employees' performance by providing feedback, and (3) distribute monetary and nonmonetary rewards. From the supervisor's point of view, the issue is not *whether* to measure performance but *how* to measure it. Since we are being judged and are judging subordinates at all times, the major questions are, Which methods do we use? Which raters do we use? and What do we do with the results of the appraisal? This section identifies general approaches to performance appraisals so that accurate assessment of performance can be made and utilized to increase employee effectiveness.

In general, performance appraisals are based upon the following four steps: (1) a determination must be made about what the job is or what the employee does; (2) an idea or expectation of reasonable performance levels must be devised; (3) a measure of the actual performance must be made; and (4) a comparison between the expected performance level and the actual performance level must be completed. These four steps are incorporated into every sound performance appraisal system. Although there are several approaches to performance appraisal, these approaches generally constitute a trade between cost and convenience and accuracy; that is, the more accurate procedures generally are more time consuming and costly.

For the supervisor, perhaps one of the most difficult aspects of a performance appraisal is conducting the appraisal interview. Subordinates want to know which areas of their performance need improvement and which areas are satisfactory. If the supervisor does not have specific examples and specific suggestions, the subordinate may not be able to correct areas of perceived weakness.

Subordinates often feel threatened by performance appraisals and become defensive during the interview. We suggest that the supervisor practice the role of coach and try to find causes of poor performance and focus on ways to remove blocks that have resulted in the lowered performance. By emphasizing supportiveness and a problem orientation in an interview rather than evaluation or judgment, the relationship between the supervisor and a subordinate can be characterized by teamwork rather than by accusation or by finding fault.

Although there are several approaches to performance appraisal, we will focus on three representative systems: general methods, Behaviorally Anchored Rating Scales, and management by objectives.

General Performance Appraisal Systems

The two most widely used performance appraisal systems are the global rating scale and the dimensionalized rating scale. Figure 10–1 depicts a global rating scale. It can be seen from this scale that the total performance of an employee is indicated on a single dimension; the supervisor must combine all performance of an individual into a single point on the scale.

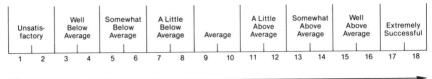

Figure 10-1   Global Evaluation

This type of performance appraisal has the advantages of being quick to administer, cheap to develop, and universal in its application to all jobs. Its disadvantages, though, outweigh its advantages because this scale is not good at providing feedback to employees about why they received the rating they did. Also, it is quite subject to rater errors because a supervisor may have a tendency to rate everyone high (leniency), low (strictness), or in the middle ranges (central tendency). Moreover, the form is quite susceptible to distortions caused by halo errors. A halo error occurs when the general rating is influenced by a more specific behavior or performance, such as when an employee is rated low on overall performance because he or she is frequently tardy but performs quite well when present. Finally, a supervisor may rate one employee as "well above average" because of accuracy on task assignments and another employee as "well above average" because of dependability in attendance and general attitude. Thus, two employees may get identical ratings for completely different reasons. The form does not make such distinctions clear (feedback).

One improvement over the global rating scale is the dimensionalized rating scale, which breaks the job down into various dimensions or components and rates each one of the dimensions separately. A dimensionalized rating form is illustrated in Figure 10–2. The figure shows that the various dimensions of the job provide the supervisor with the ability to indicate how performance is viewed on a number of scales rather than reducing it to a single dimension as in the global scale. This approach reduces many rater errors, and it increases performance feedback to an employee. Also, it is relatively quick and inexpensive to develop. Its major problem centers on the fact that a good or an average rating on this scale may not be consistent between raters. Specifically, performance that is rated "good" by one supervisor may only merit an "average" rating from a second supervisor. Thus the major problem with this approach is that there is no generally stated definition as to what good, excellent, average, or very poor performance is. Even with this caution, though, the dimensionalized rating scale is substantially superior to the global rating scale.

Job: Machinist Third Class Job Dimension	Excellent	Very good	Good	Slightly better than average	Average	Slightly less than average	Poor	Very poor	Unacceptable
1. Meets production standards									
2. Reads blueprints									
3. Checks fabrication quality									
4. Operation of drill press and mills									
5. Operation of saws and lathes									
6. Job attitude									

Figure 10-2   Dimensionalized Rating Form

Behavior-Based Systems

The Behaviorally Anchored Rating Scale (BARS) has several similarities to the dimensionalized rating scale. In a Behaviorally Anchored Rating Scale, job dimensions are identified. For each of these dimensions, various levels of performance are specified and can range from excellent to very poor or unacceptable. The major difference between Behaviorally Anchored Rating Scales and dimensionalized rating scales is that in a Behaviorally Anchored Rating Scale *each* of the performance levels is defined by a specific statement of observable work behavior or performance. This enables the supervisor to determine whether a particular performance level is average, above average, or below average. For example, in Figure 10-3 a Behaviorally Anchored Rating Scale encompasses the single dimension of "customer relations" for a hardware store cashier. On this one dimension, seven separate levels of performance are defined for the rater. To make a complete appraisal, additional dimensions and their definitions must be developed.

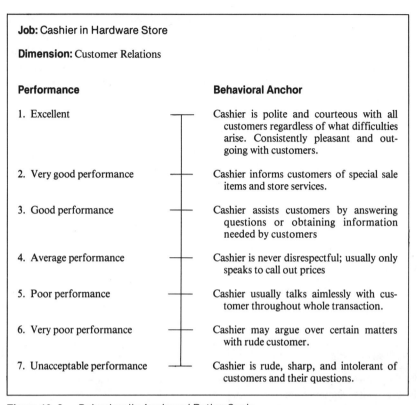

Job: Cashier in Hardware Store

Dimension: Customer Relations

Performance		**Behavioral Anchor**
1. Excellent		Cashier is polite and courteous with all customers regardless of what difficulties arise. Consistently pleasant and outgoing with customers.
2. Very good performance		Cashier informs customers of special sale items and store services.
3. Good performance		Cashier assists customers by answering questions or obtaining information needed by customers
4. Average performance		Cashier is never disrespectful; usually only speaks to call out prices
5. Poor performance		Cashier usually talks aimlessly with customer throughout whole transaction.
6. Very poor performance		Cashier may argue over certain matters with rude customer.
7. Unacceptable performance		Cashier is rude, sharp, and intolerant of customers and their questions.

Figure 10-3   Behaviorally Anchored Rating Scale

In the job of computer programmer, such dimensions as knowledge of machine capabilities and ability to develop efficient computer programs would probably become part of the total appraisal system.

Positive aspects of Behaviorally Anchored Rating Scales are that it tends to be accurate, provides good performance feedback to the employee, and cuts the rater errors of the supervisor. Its drawbacks include the necessity to develop a separate rating form for each job, and therefore this method tends to be more costly than others. Also, it requires observable behavior to measure—it has difficulty in measuring what are essentially mental tasks, such as decisions or the use of good judgment. Therefore its use is most appropriate in situations where there are several persons doing similar tasks of a physical nature. In general, Behaviorally Anchored Rating Scales tend to acknowledge employee effort or input into the job without holding the employee accountable for the results or effectiveness of performing the work.

Management by Objectives as a Performance Appraisal System

In contrast to the above methods, management by objectives (MBO) focuses on results or employee contributions. In the MBO process an employee sits down with his or her supervisor to decide upon the major objectives to be accomplished in a given time period. Second, the supervisor and the subordinate develop plans for how and when the objectives will be accomplished. Then they decide on the methods of measuring whether or not an objective has been met. The process is generally straightforward, and the theory is usually quite acceptable to most managers. In the MBO form shown in Figure 10-4, the objectives to be accomplished are specified, the current level of performance and the desired level of performance are indicated, the time frame for completion is specified, and the methods for

OBJECTIVES (What?)	LEVELS OF ACCOMPLISHMENT (How measure?)			TIME FRAME (When?)	METHODS (How?)
	Measure	Present Level	Desired Level		

Figure 10-4   Management-by-Objectives Form

accomplishing the goal are described. The general advantages of an MBO system are that it fosters teamwork, forces upper-level management to set specific goals for the organization, and permits creativity in accomplishing the employees' objectives. Since at each completed time period new objectives and thus a new performance appraisal system must be devised, one of the difficulties with management by objectives is the large amount of paperwork it requires. Also, MBO requires significant coordination among departments and employees so that they will all be working toward similar objectives. Moreover, certain employees who can obtain commitments from their superiors to achieve only easily attained goals have an advantage over employees who negotiate more difficult objectives. Finally, the focus is on accomplishing objectives, or results, rather than on effort or input; the failure of one person may affect the goal attainment of another. Animosity or bad feelings can result when one individual is prohibited from attaining a goal because of failure by a co-worker. These kinds of problems tend not to be so apparent in alternative appraisal systems. (For a further discussion of management by objectives along with its strengths and weaknesses, see Chapter 7.)

This discussion of performance appraisal and the preceding sections on employee development have indicated general ways of identifying employee needs and providing for better performance through the development of that employee.

SUMMARY

The development process is one in which all supervisors play significant roles. Supervisors are important in the development process because subordinates tend to use them as models. Employee development is vital because it helps the work unit perform at higher levels of competency. Much employee development is ineffective not only because it is haphazard but also because it is assumed that it is possible to train or develop persons to be whatever the supervisor or training department wishes. This last assumption simply is not true. However, by focusing on two facts, important training inputs can be accomplished. First, a good supervisor serves as an effective behavioral model for subordinates. In this respect, subsequent chapters are designed to help increase one's supervisor effectiveness. Second, by tailoring the training and development effort to "fit" the situation, an increase in training input can be expected.

This chapter has focused on (1) how people learn and how they can be trained or developed as individual supervisors, (2) the identification of employee needs through performance appraisals, and (3) the conditions necessary to develop employees when different development objectives and conditions are present.

DISCUSSION QUESTIONS

1. Differentiate between *management development* and *employee development*.

2. Discuss the principles of learning described in the chapter. How are they used in the classroom? In this text?

3. What is the most widely used training approach in industry? What training approach is most effective in conveying facts? In changing skills?

4. Describe job instruction training. What initial steps does JIT require of the instructor?

5. Discuss the various conditions that affect the successful implementation of training efforts. What relationship exists between these conditions and the trainer's development objectives?

6. What are three objectives of performance appraisals?

7. Compare and contrast the general performance appraisal systems with the behaviorally based systems. What factors would you consider in selecting one of these general approaches? Which system would you select for your performance appraisal? Why?

8. Describe how management by objectives can be used as a performance appraisal system. What are the critical components of an effective MBO performance appraisal system?

9. What is the relationship between *performance appraisal* and *employee development*? Discuss the implications of an inadequate performance appraisal system on your performance, personal development, and career.

CASE 10-1 Croom's Department Stores

Located in a large eastern seaboard city, Croom's Department Store consisted of a major department store in a downtown location with five suburban stores in outlying shopping centers. The company was known for its high style and quality merchandise. It presented a rather traditional image, and its management was organized in a rather traditional manner.

Because of the relatively high turnover among retail sales personnel, the company had a formal training department. A new training director had just been appointed. The new director, Jason Bonsteel, was hired from a department store chain in the West. His orientation and management style fit with Croom's Department Stores in that he had what everyone agreed was an "old school" orientation and was mainly concerned about training employees in improved operational efforts (e.g., inventory control, sales presentations, etc.).

Mr. Bonsteel's staff included one associate training director, Martha Heeber, and two assistant training directors. Prior to Mr. Bonsteel's arrival, Martha and her two assistants had discussed the general lack of training of department heads on such topics as leadership, human relations skills, and motivation. They felt that some of the high turnover the organization had experienced recently and the relatively low morale in departments, particularly in the suburban stores, could be improved if a substantial training effort could be devoted to developing leadership skills, human relations skills, and motivational understanding among the company's department heads.

Martha contacted a local university and worked on a program and its content with the professors in that institution. The resulting program outline was one that Martha was very excited and enthusiastic about. The exchange with the university faculty had improved what she felt were her good ideas. She felt very strongly that the organization department heads needed the kind of training and development that this presentation could offer.

Martha and her two assistants set up an appointment to talk to Mr. Bonsteel about the leadership development program. They made a formal presentation to Mr. Bonsteel in which they argued very strongly for the funds to present this new program to all department heads in the company. An outline of the proposed training and its objectives follows.

CROOM'S DEPARTMENT STORES DEVELOPMENT PROGRAM

Program Purpose:

To develop supervisory skills that enable a Department Manager to build teamwork and cooperation among employees; to aid Department Managers in establishing a work environment where people want to do the best job they can.

Specific Program Objectives:

1. To develop awareness of the Department Manager's own methods of relating to other people.
2. To define various styles of leadership, such as autocratic, democratic, and free-rein, and to establish when different approaches should be used.
3. To develop self-insight into the Department Manager's own style of leadership.
4. To define motivation; to discuss various reasons why people are motivated to work.
5. To describe and discuss various theories of motivation:
   a. Maslow's hierarchy of needs
   b. Herzberg's theory of job enrichment
   c. McGregor's Theory X and Theory Y
6. To discuss the implications of various motivational theories for the Department Manager as a supervisor.
7. To define positive and negative reinforcement; to discuss the timing and appropriateness of various types of rewards.
8. To identify those rewards (positive and negative) at Croom's Department Store that Department Managers can use.

9. To determine how the available rewards can effectively be applied at Croom's Department Stores.

10. To describe the communication process.

11. To discuss various dimensions of communication in terms of content, noise, communication network, and direction.

12. To identify factors that lead to successful communication; to identify causes of communication breakdown.

13. To relate communication theory to the Department Manager's job.

PROGRAM OUTLINE

	Introduction
	Program Purpose and Objectives
Seminar I	
1.	How You as a Department Manager Relate to Others
2.	Interpretation and Discussion of Questionnaire
3.	Factors Measured by FIRO-B Questionnaire
4.	Interpretation of FIRO-B Scores
5.	Application of These Concepts to Department Manager's Job
6.	Leadership Survey
7.	Leadership Styles
8.	How to Decide When to Use Each Method
9.	The Use of Authority
10.	Applying These Concepts to the Department Manager's Job
11.	Discussion of Case Study
Seminar II	
1.	Introduction by Discussion Leader
2.	What Motivates People to Work?
3.	What is Motivation?
4.	Maslow's Hierarchy of Needs
5.	Herzberg's Theory of Job Enrichment for Motivation
6.	Theory X and Theory Y
7.	Job Enrichment at Croom's Department Store
Seminar III	
1.	Rewards and Discipline
2.	Reinforcement Theory
3.	Application of Reinforcement Theory
4.	Discussion: The Rewards of Rewarding
5.	Discussion: The Correct Way of Correcting
6.	Applying Rewards at Croom's
Seminar IV	
1.	Importance of Effective Communications to Management
2.	The Communications Process
3.	What Are the Dimensions of Communications?
4.	What Factors Influence the Degree of Success at Each Stage of the Communication Process?
5.	Film "Avoiding Communication Breakdown"
6.	What Communication Problems Exist at Croom's?
	Program Evaluations

At the conclusion of their presentation, Mr. Bonsteel asked some questions that tended to focus on two areas. First, he questioned why it was necessary to hire outside persons to conduct the training program when the training department had an associate and two assistant directors who could do the training. He also wanted to know how the new program would be evaluated. Second, Mr. Bonsteel questioned the value of a training program in motivation and leadership skills. He felt that efforts focusing on the use of the new equipment or reduction in pilferage were justifiable, but that almost everyone who was a good supervisor already knew the basics of human relations. Martha responded to his first concern by saying that the university faculty would lend credibility to the course content. Even if the presentations were identical, she felt that the department heads would be more likely to take seriously information that came from a professor or expert in the field rather than from their own training staff. Her response to Mr. Bonsteel's second concern was simply that in her experience the department heads were *not* skilled in leadership, motivation, and human relations matters, and that since the company had never provided this kind of development for its employees, such a program would be worthwhile.

Mr. Bonsteel promised to let Martha know his decision at the beginning of the following week. As Martha left the meeting, she wondered about her future working relationship with Mr. Bonsteel, since it appeared that there was a fundamental difference in their approach to training and development. She was also troubled that he had not provided her with any help or guidance in performing her job during his five weeks with the company.

QUESTIONS

1. Evaluate the proposed training program as to its effect on both short-term profits and long-term profits.

2. How well does the proposed training meet the needs of Croom's department heads?

2. What factors should go into deciding whether to hire university faculty members as trainers?

4. Why was Mr. Bonsteel skeptical of human relations training?

5. How could the training be evaluated?

6. If you were Mr. Bonsteel, what would your decision be?

11

CONTROLLING FOR RESULTS

LEARNING OBJECTIVES

This chapter discusses the various control systems in organizations. After you have read this chapter, you will

1. Know how organizational rewards and rules control employee behavior
2. Understand how the personal needs and preferences of employees control employee behavior
3. Understand the consequences of imposing rules and controls on employees
4. Be familiar with a method for developing an effective control system by analyzing the organization

In an organizational setting, <u>control</u> is the process that ensures that both long-range and short-range organizational goals are being met. We have noted that goal setting is closely tied to the planning process and that organizational structure results from attempts to attain goals through the implementation of plans (see Chapter 7). It follows, then, that organizational control is tied to effective implementation of planning and organizing efforts. It has motivational implications also.

Organizations are made up of persons and units having a complex set of interwoven behaviors and relationships. As an organization grows, the coordination of these behaviors becomes exceedingly complicated and difficult. This helps explain why control mechanisms in large organizations tend to be more developed and formalized than they are in the smaller ones.

We encounter control mechanisms everywhere in organizations. For example, we use a variety of techniques for control: money/pay; budgets; quality standards; policies, procedures, and rules; time standards, schedules; production control schedules. In all of these cases, the major purpose of the control mechanism is to maintain momentum toward attainment of organizational and personal goals.

We typically think of the control process in terms of setting specific standards, checking the performance level, measuring performance against the standards, and taking corrective action. This approach reflects an <u>external</u> view of control in which a supervisor accepts the role of monitor or inspector. From such a perspective, the supervisor can appraise the situation and can initiate such control activities as reprimanding and recommending pay changes. The emphasis is on supervisory actions that are external to the employee.

A less obvious aspect of the control process is internal control. <u>Internal</u> control refers to an individual's self-control or self-motivation (e.g., pride in one's work), which leads to activities that are consistent with organizational goals (e.g., quality products). Douglas McGregor's Theory Y (see Chapter 3) incorporates this concept of self-control. Thus the overall control process consists not only of those supervisory activities that have a direct and generally immediate impact on individual performance (external control) but also of those supervisory activities that have an indirect impact on the motivation and self-control of subordinates (internal control). This chapter discusses both the external and internal control processes in organizations, and it explores many of the difficulties that various control systems create. Also, it describes a procedure that will enable supervisors to match their own behavioral styles to organizational needs in order to develop an effective control system.

EXTERNAL CONTROL SYSTEM

The external control system is based on the idea that people do things to obtain rewards or to avoid punishment. The external control system is effective to the degree that an employee modifies his or her behavior due to the offering or the withholding of pay, promotion, praise, interesting work, and so forth. To become effective, an external control system must make rewards dependent upon the performance of activities desired by the organization.

The implementation of an effective external control system involves six major attributes. First, the method of measuring performance should be complete, objective, and able to influence. Should the control system not measure the complete job, then those activities that go unmeasured will not be controlled. For example, an outside salesperson may be paid a commission on the products he or she sells. If no consequence results from failing to forward paperwork to the home office, then he or she will have little impetus to forward it. In addition, the means of measurement must be objective so that the employees will trust the results and not feel that the rater's bias has influenced the rating. Finally, the measures must be susceptible to employee influence so that changes in performance will be reflected. For example, in a department where the supervisor gives all employees acceptable performance ratings regardless of their actual performance, external controls have a diminished impact on performance.

Second, performance standards or goals should be set jointly with the employee and the supervisor. By engaging in a mutual goal-setting session, the employee and supervisor may have clearer ideas as to the desired outcome; they may also take into account practical problems and opportunities that may affect reaching the standard. Another major aspect of an effective goal-setting process is the development of moderately difficult goals. Research on goal setting has shown that establishing too difficult a goal for an employee usually results in a sense of personal helplessness; this leads to a reduction in goal attainment activity. Setting too easy a goal results in a lackadaisical attitude and encourages less than total commitment of effort to attaining the goal. By contrast, setting moderate-risk goals (i.e., fifty-fifty chance of success) seems to have a greater positive impact on goal attainment behavior. Thus, moderate-risk goals seem to be most appropriate for external control systems.

Third, if external control systems are to be effective, the persons who monitor job performance should include *both* the employee and a trusted other person. This permits the employee to obtain rapid feedback regarding job performance, and the employee's perceptions may be verified by a person who can be counted on to provide accurate judgments.

Fourth, information needed to meet desired standards should go to *both* the employee and his or her immediate supervisor. In this way the information is given to the persons who have the responsibility for meeting specific standards and who are able to change performance.

Fifth, to be effective, the information associated with external controls should be transmitted as quickly and frequently as fits the situation. Information that arrives too late for action or arrives only occasionally does not provide sufficient and reliable enough information to take meaningful corrective action.

Sixth, to be effective, the external rewards should be those things that are valued by the employee. Although some generalizations can be made, it is not possible to predict how strongly a person will value any particular reward. For example, a young employee may view increased responsibility as desirable, while an older employee may be more interested in ensuring a secure job position before retirement. Consequently, the effectiveness of the external control system will vary depending upon the personal value placed on various rewards.

There are other aspects involved in the effective utilization of external control. (1) Certain rewards have a greater effect on employees because in general they are viewed as more important. For example, pay is usually more important than status symbols. (2) A manager must consider the degree of flexibility available to vary the amount of any reward. (3) Visibility of the reward is significant because a more visible reward (i.e., office change) may affect the status and esteem needs of an individual; a low-visibility reward (i.e., retirement benefits) has little ability to meet such needs. (4) The frequency with which a reward may be administered is important because the employee must understand that there is a relationship between performance and the resulting reward; rewards that come too infrequently (e.g., promotions) can lose their potency. (5) Finally, one must consider the cost of providing various rewards. Financial costs meet real organizational constraints and are therefore not available in unlimited quantities.

Table 11-1 summarizes various external control outcomes with regard to importance, flexibility, visibility, frequency, and dollar cost. A review of the table indicates that none of the rewards listed rates high on every criterion, but pay is the one reward that possesses almost *all* of the desirable characteristics (except low cost). Promotion and dismissal are low in flexibility because these actions can only be taken infrequently. Praise and interesting work are generally important factors in the external control system,

Table 11-1. An Evaluation of Common Rewards as Motivators

Rewards	Importance	Flexibility in Amount	Visibility	Frequency	Dollar Cost
Pay	High	High	Potentially high	High	High
Promotion	High	Low	High	Low	High
Dismissal	High	Low	High	Low	High
Praise from supervisor	Moderate	High	Indeterminate	High	Low
Interesting work	High	Moderate	High	Moderate	Low
Tenure	Moderate	Low	High	Low	High
Status symbols	Moderate	High	High	Low	Moderate

Adapted from Edward Lawler and John Rhode, *Information and Control in Organizations* (Pacific Palisades, Calif.: Goodyear, 1976), p. 59.

but it is difficult to continually give people more and more interesting work to do. For example, on an assembly line the flexibility of assigning different work is limited; it is even more difficult to increase an inherent interest in the work if an employee desires more than task variety but is not qualified for supervisory responsibility. Finally, the value placed on praise and interesting work may vary greatly between individuals; this will affect the impact of these items on the external control system.

The external control system is therefore quite important in the overall control of employees, but to be effective the system must have several specific characteristics. Because of individual preferences, there seems to be no single reward that is a perfect external motivator; this is a limitation of these controls. Therefore, though external rewards are specifically designed by the organization to affect employee behaviors, they are only one part of the overall control process.

INTERNAL CONTROL SYSTEM

It is possible to design control systems that stimulate the internal needs of employees who have substantial "higher-order" needs (see Maslow's hierarchy in Chapter 3). These individual motives affect behavior and form the basis of a control mechanism for persons who desire responsibility, achievement, satisfaction, and self-actualization.

Evidence has shown that many people are influenced by work in which they gain a sense of internal satisfaction or reward. However, it also should be noted that some persons do not respond to internal rewards. As a result, to have an effective control system, organizations should probably provide a combination of both internal and external rewards.

Creating effective internal controls is often more difficult than developing an effective external control mechanism because activating the internal motives tends to be less a "commonsense" situation than providing the external motives. Internal controls reside within an employee and are not directly controlled by the organization. Nevertheless, an effective control system should take into account the employee's internal needs in the overall design of effective controls.

To maintain high internal controls, several conditions should be met. First, as with external controls, the measurement system should be complete and objective, and it should respond to changes in performance. The individual must perceive that there is a link between actions and results. Since internal rewards are self-rewards, measures that are not complete, or are felt to be biased, or are not able to be influenced tend to be discarded and have little effect on behavior.

Second, goals or standards should be set by the individual performing them, and they should be of moderate difficulty. To have a personal sense of satisfaction, it is important that the individual determine what the standard will be. For example, a supervisor who meets the deadline set by a superior is less likely to have a sense of satisfaction than if that deadline had been set personally. Moreover, as with external rewards, standards of performance that reflect moderate difficulty for the employee tend to have a greater positive impact on performance and satisfaction than do very easy or very difficult goals.

Third, either the employee or another creditable source could monitor job performance and results. Since these rewards are internal or self rewards, it is unnecessary for the supervisor to monitor the results directly.

Fourth, information should be provided immediately to the employee as feedback on a schedule that fits the appropriate time span of the task. For example, a foreman whose work unit completed a number of orders would experience strengthened internal motivation from knowing each day the number of orders completed; a delay of a month (e.g., monthly report) would reduce the daily sense of accomplishment to a once-per-month experience.

Fifth, high internal motivation is possible on jobs that give the employee a sense of autonomy; this usually results in a feeling of personal responsibility for accomplishing the task. In addition, internally motivating jobs tend to be viewed as worthwhile. Such jobs usually encompass a variety of tasks, and the person performing them does the whole job. By having responsibility for the whole job, the employee develops a feeling of "Look what I have done," or "Look at my job."

Finally, internally rewarding jobs tend to provide feedback about what has been accomplished. For example, a person assembling and testing an entire component, such as a small engine or pump, gets immediate feedback about what has been accomplished when the testing procedure begins and the performance of the component is determined (i.e., the engine meets or fails its specifications).

An organization that provides a climate that encourages the development of internal motivation is able to influence (i.e., control) the behavior of those employees who seek such satisfactions from their jobs. In this way, internal control mechanisms are somewhat indirect because the organization designs work and provides an environment that the individual finds rewarding; to maintain the satisfaction from this organizational situation, the employee modifies his or her behavior. This differs from external rewards, which the organization controls directly. Although the organization does not have direct control over internal rewards, it is a significant participant in the maintenance of this control system through job design, and so forth.

DIFFICULTIES WITH IMPLEMENTING CONTROL SYSTEMS

Although we have noted the importance of control systems in organizations, their implementation frequently creates problems. Generally, control systems are designed to make the organization operate more efficiently and become more responsive to demands from the external environment. However, in many cases the control system itself leads organizational members to act in ways that are contrary to the original intent.

Rigid Bureaucratic Behavior

One of the more common unanticipated consequences of control systems is the rigid bureaucratic behavior that results from the implementation of rules. One set of problems arises when a rule becomes valued for its own sake; that is, employees use the rule as a crutch or defense against accusations of inappropriate actions in performing the job. This can occur regardless of whether the utilized rule is the most appropriate way of dealing with the situation. For example, in a hospital emergency room, an employee could require that financial arrangements always be completed before medical attention is given to a serious disease or injury. Another set of problems arises when rules interfere with effective organizational performance as employees identify with the success of their smaller work unit or group at the expense of the larger organization. An emphasis on standards or rules in a single work unit can have the effect of focusing the employees' attention on the success of their own work unit; a feeling may emerge that other units or divisions within the organization are less important. At times these other units may even be seen as competitors. The result of such views can be the suboptimization of overall effort.

Inappropriate Behavior

A second category of unanticipated results from control systems involves the altering of behavior to fit control measures. Stated differently, employees become concerned with "looking good." Examples of such behavior are the maintenance of "just in case" files, and the decision to purchase unessential equipment to utilize remaining funds in a budget period merely to justify *future* budget requests. In these situations, behavior has been changed through the control process, but the change has been one that is contrary to the intentions of the budget maker.

Reporting Incorrect Information

Another type of difficulty resulting from control systems involves the reporting of incorrect data. Individuals or work units may report fallacious information about what *has been* or *can be* accomplished. When individuals or work units overestimate their needs, the planning process is undermined. In such situations the budgeting effort becomes a "game" in which units are expected to overestimate their needs, and the budget maker cuts the budget on the assumption that requests for resources have been inflated.

Resistance to Controls

Individuals' resistance to the control process may be due to three major reasons. First, a new and effective control system may change the relationship among employees by giving a new individual, in charge of gathering information, expertise and power that a former employee held.

Second, a new control system may measure people more thoroughly and accurately and thus be resisted because of the potential threat that such disclosure may bring. For example, performance reports that reveal that brief periods of high activity are separated by long periods of minimal effort can be more threatening than the report of total or average performance.

Third, by specifying rules and procedures, the control system may reduce the supervisor's discretion in solving certain problems. This can result in a decrease in the internal satisfaction with the task and can cause resistance to the new control system. For example, if a supervisor is required to deduct pay from employees who are tardy despite the performance of the individual or work group, the motivation to perform can be undermined.

This section has discussed difficulties associated with implementing new and effective control systems. These systems, though necessary, frequently cause unexpected and undesired results. Difficulties with control systems generally fall into two categories. First, the control system itself may be used as a defense from outside criticism by relying on available rules. Second, the control system may be viewed as an obstacle that may be overcome through distortion, cunning, or manipulation, such as the reporting of false data. It should be noted that these difficulties are more obvious when an inadequate control system exists or when it has been ineffectively implemented. The next section provides guidelines for developing effective organizational controls. By following these guidelines, the difficulties just discussed should be minimized.

HOW TO DEVELOP EFFECTIVE ORGANIZATIONAL CONTROLS

The preceding sections of this chapter have examined internal and external control systems. It remains for supervisors to determine whether one or both of these systems should be utilized. In several instances the two systems seem to be somewhat in conflict. For example, it is essential to provide accurate information to the employee for internal personal motivation, but substantial exaggeration of performance accomplishments could be expected in information that is used for reward motivation. Thus it is not easy to devise a system that involves both types of control. In several instances, moreover, these two types of control systems may not be necessary, since internal controls alone can produce both valid information and behavior that is very adequate.

The use of two systems is probably most appropriate for tasks that are simple, somewhat difficult to measure, and important to organizational effectiveness. To help the supervisor select between the two basic control systems, four major questions should be asked. Table 11-2 lists these four questions, and the answers given in the table can be used in analyzing the organizational climate and the individual supervisor's needs. These questions focus on supervisory style, organizational climate, accuracy of measures, and employee preferences. The decision tree in Figure 11-1 enables the supervisor to use the answers to the questions in Table 11-2 to designate the appropriate motivational and control strategy. The choice of strategies ranges from purely internal controls through modified strategies to purely external control strategies. In assessing the selection of control systems, the supervisor should consider the trade-offs between various strategies. Such a

Table 11-2. Questions a Supervisor Should Ask in Selecting a Control Strategy

1. In general, what kind of supervisory style do I have?
   a. *Participative:* I frequently consult my subordinates on decisions, encourage them to disagree with my opinion, share information with them, and let them make decisions whenever possible.
   b. *Directive:* I usually take most of the responsibility for and make most of the major decisions, pass on only the most necessary job-relevant information, and provide detailed and close direction for my subordinates.

2. In general, what kind of climate, structure, and reward system does my organization have?
   a. *Participative:* Employees at all levels of the organization are used to participate in decisions and influence the course of events. Supervisors are clearly rewarded for developing employees' skills and decision making capacity.
   b. *Non-participative:* Most important decisions are made by a few people at the top of the organization. Supervisors are not rewarded for developing employee competence or encouraging employees to participate in decision making.

3. How accurate and reliable are the measures of key areas of subordinate performance?
   a. *Accurate:* Measures are reliable, all major aspects of performance can be adequately measured, changes in measures accurately reflect changes in performance, measures cannot be easily sabotaged or faked by subordinates.
   b. *Inaccurate:* Not all important aspects of performance can be measured, measures often don't pick up on important changes in performance, good performance cannot be adequately defined in terms of the measures, measures can be easily sabotaged.

4. Do my subordinates desire to participate and respond well to opportunities to take responsibility for decision making and performance?
   a. *High desire to participate:* Employees are eager to participate in decisions, can make a contribution to decision making, and want to take more responsibility.
   b. *Low desire to participate:* Employees do not want to be involved in many decisions, don't want additional responsibility, and have little to contribute to decisions being made.

Adapted with permission from Cortlandt Cammann and David A. Nadler, "Fit Control Systems to Your Managerial Style," *Harvard Business Review*, January–February. 1976, p. 67, Copyright © 1975 by the President and Fellows of Harvard College; all rights reserved.

consideration should depend on the particular work situation facing a supervisor. For example, if there are few opportunities for distorting information and the cost of distortion is low, a tight or high control strategy may be appropriate. In most organizations, however, the potential cost of distorting information or playing "games" is very high, and emphasis on internal control strategies seems appropriate. A reliance on *only* external control

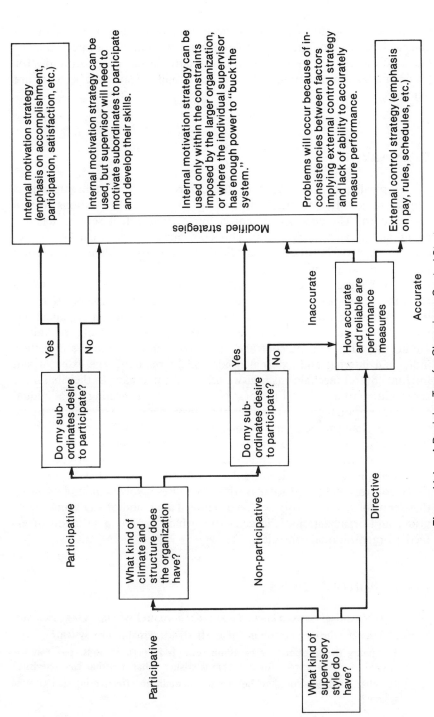

Figure 11-1 A Decision Tree for Choosing a Control Strategy

Internal motivation strategy (emphasis on accomplishment, participation, satisfaction, etc.)

Internal motivation strategy can be used, but supervisor will need to motivate subordinates to participate and develop their skills.

Internal motivation strategy can be used only within the constraints imposed by the larger organization, or where the individual supervisor has enough power to "buck the system."

Problems will occur because of inconsistencies between factors implying external control strategy and lack of ability to accurately measure performance.

External control strategy (emphasis on pay, rules, schedules, etc.)

Modified strategies

Yes

No

Do my subordinates desire to participate?

Participative

What kind of climate and structure does the organization have?

Participative

Yes

No

Do my subordinates desire to participate?

Non-participative

Inaccurate

How accurate and reliable are performance measures

Accurate

Directive

What kind of supervisory style do I have?

191

systems would be most feasible in those situations where tasks are simple and easily measured, and where there is a known standard of performance that is considered fair by all parties. In this latter instance, opportunities for producing false information and engaging in rigid bureaucratic behavior are minimized.

SUMMARY

Typically, considerations of the control function in organizations emphasize both the identification and the correction of deviations from a set standard. The concern for correction carries with it several negative connotations. The supervisor takes on a policing or correctional role. Moreover, this approach can cause very rigid responses to problems that require unique and thoughtful solutions.

The concept of organizational control that we have discussed differs from the simplistic, correctional approach and takes a more positive outlook. In this regard, it is important to note that behavior in organizations meets the desired standard, for the most part. Usually, control mechanisms are not negative. On the contrary, they assure most employees that their individual internal and external needs will be realized. The external and internal control mechanisms that we have presented have as their basis the coordination of activity within organizations and the meeting of individual and organizational goals. Stated simply, the proper design of organizational control mechanisms helps ensure that individual needs will be met. Thus it is in the individual's own interests to meet or exceed the standards.

To help the supervisor understand and implement more effective control mechanisms, we have identified sources and characteristics of organizational controls and noted some of the difficulties involved in implementing these control systems. Also, we have included a method of analyzing supervisory and organizational characteristics which permits a selection of effective organizational controls.

DISCUSSION QUESTIONS

1. Differentiate between *internal* and *external* control systems in organizations.
2. What are the major attributes of an effective external control system?
3. Among the attributes of common rewards in organizations, pay was the reward of choice except for one characteristic. What was that characteristic?
4. What conditions need to be met to maintain an effective internal control system?

5. What parallels exist between Herzberg's motivator-hygiene theory and internal and external control systems?

6. Indicate some of the problems associated with control systems. Give examples of personal experiences with control systems in organizations.

7. How do control systems result in increased rigid bureaucratic behavior? Give examples.

8. Give three reasons why employees may resist controls. Do you feel this resistance is justified?

9. Using the college classroom as an example, outline an effective control strategy using the questions in Table 11-2 and the decision tree in Figure 11-1. Would your analysis result in different conclusions in other work situations, such as a bank, the military, or field sales?

CASE 11-1.   Turnee Furniture Company

Located in a small midsouthern town, the Turnee Furniture Company employed 140 workers in the manufacturing of church furniture. The company prided itself on providing good quality at a moderate price. While several specialty items were manufactured, the basic product of the company was church pews made of hardwood veneers.

John Banks, the new assistant superintendent of manufacturing, was hired to help the manufacturing superintendent supervise the employees, the number of which had recently increased by 26 percent. John found that the company had no formal review of performance and few written policies. The company had been founded six years earlier by Ralph Turnee, and most procedures were governed by the informal understanding of acceptable company practice. Although it troubled John a bit that he had no guidelines for either the performance of employees or his supervisor's expectations of his performance, he decided to use the situation to his advantage. He was overheard saying at one point, "Forgiveness is easier to get than permission."

During the following weeks it came to Mr. Turnee's attention that John had made two decisions which obligated the company to some financial outlay. First, John had contacted a consulting firm in a nearby large city to provide safety training to plant foremen to comply with OSHA requirements. The training would cost $970 for three sessions. Second, John had ordered a new $1,150 hand-operated gluing machine for repair of faulty pew ends. The plant had recently experienced an increase in rejects of pew ends, and the new gluing machine was designed to repair minor faults in the veneer. When Mr. Turnee learned of these two incidents, he passed them off as necessary expenses for the company in complying with federal laws and in meeting better-quality expectations by customers.

QUESTIONS

1. Did the Turnee Furniture Company rely on an internal or an external control system?

2. Evaluate John Banks's view that "forgiveness is easier to get than permission."

3. What steps should be taken by the company regarding written policy statements?

4. Does the fact that John Banks was a new employee affect your recommendations for action? Why, or why not?

CASE 11-2.   The Elite Typewriter Company

The Elite Typewriter Company manufactured a very reliable and high quality office machine. This machine was distributed by the company through its own sales force, which was assigned to various territories throughout the United States. To attract an aggressive sales force, Elite advertised that it would pay a straight commission with no upward limit on the potential earnings of an employee. In practice, however, the sales territories were frequently "adjusted," with the usual effect that territories were reduced somewhat for salespeople with very high earnings.

Steve Henderson, an employee of Elite, had been with the company for two years. He had done quite well during his first year with the company and had earned $27,800 as a result of his commissions. He was a conscientious employee who planned his schedule in the evening after work for calls he would make the following day. One of the aspects of the job, however, left him baffled. Although he lived four miles from the Elite office, he was required to come to the office personally at 8:30 each morning before he set out to see his first client. The company expected him to make nine calls on the average each day and to submit a trip report on each call. Moreover, at the end of the day he was required to report back to the office before going home. This requirement prohibited him from going directly to a customer from his home in the morning or from returning directly home at the end of the day after seeing a customer.

Although the practice of requiring sales personnel to report in in the morning and to return to the office before leaving for home was a substantial annoyance, one additional practice of the company was personally offensive to Steve. At various times a company representative would telephone a customer for whom a sales trip report had been submitted the preceding day and ask whether or not Mr. Henderson had left his price book in that office. This call was placed under the guise that Henderson had lost his price book and that the secretary from the main office was trying to assist him in locating it. The real purpose, however, was to determine whether or not Henderson had actually called on the customer or had fabricated the visit in the trip report. This type of tactic was normal practice and was used for all salespersons.

QUESTIONS

1. From the company's perspective, what was the desired purpose of the control system?

2. How effective do you think this control system was?

3. What unexpected results might you predict as a result of this control system?

4. Can you suggest any improvements in Elite's control system of its sales force?

V

Decisional
and
Administrative Skills

12

SUPERVISORY DECISION MAKING

LEARNING OBJECTIVES

This chapter discusses various aspects of individual and group decision making. After you have read this chapter, you will

1. Be familiar with the rational decision-making procedure
2. Understand the modifications to the rational decision-making procedure, and know how to implement these modifications
3. Know the advantages of group decision making
4. Understand how to lead a group to make effective decisions

A supervisor spends a great part of the working day making decisions. Studies have revealed that top-management personnel make decisions on the average of every eight to ten minutes. The time span for decision making becomes shorter as one moves lower in the organizational hierarchy. For example, first-level supervisors have been found to make decisions on the average of every few seconds. These findings reveal that decision making comprises a major portion of the managerial job. Thus an understanding of improved decision-making and problem-solving methods is of primary importance to supervisors.

This chapter focuses on the decision-making and problem-solving process in an effort to provide the supervisor with a more complete understanding not only of the decisional process but of ways for improving effectiveness in decision making. The chapter includes a presentation of the classical decision-making model, as well as practical modifications and recommendations in using this model.

RATIONAL DECISION-MAKING MODEL

A rational analysis of the decision-making process reveals that five steps are involved. First, the decision maker must define the problem. Second, information must be gathered about the circumstances pertaining to the problem. Third, the anticipated consequences of alternative solutions must be determined. Fourth, the most promising alternative must be selected. Finally, any new problems that result from implementing the chosen alternative must be determined. These steps, or phases, are summarized in Table 12–1 and will be discussed in detail.

Table 12–1. Five Phases of Decision Making and Problem Solving

1. Define the problem
2. Gather information and develop alternatives
3. Determine the anticipated positive and negative consequences of each alternative
4. Select the alternative with the most positive (or least negative) consequences
5. Determine any new problems resulting from implementing the chosen alternative

---

Define the Problem

It has been said that there is nothing more useless than the right answer to the wrong problem. Since most people feel that they seldom make errors in pointing out problems, it is easy for these people to begin implementing solutions when, in fact, the problem definition is in error.

EXAMPLE

Assume that you are a supervisor and have two subordinates who continually argue and bicker; they just do not seem to be able to work together. You have noticed that they argue over job-related matters, and it appears that they have particular problems with accusing each other of intruding on the other's "territory." You could define this problem as one of a personality conflict between the two subordinates; that is, these personalities clash, and the employees don't get along together. A reasonable solution to this situation would be to separate the two subordinates so that they would not have personal contact. This could be done by physically locating their work stations at distant points from each other or by asking for a transfer of one of the subordinates. On the other hand, if it is found that the subordinates have an ill-defined concept of their functions, duties, or responsibilities, then it is possible that they are arguing over who has a particular responsibility. In this case the problem would *not* be one of personality conflict at all, and it would be inappropriate to transfer or separate these two persons. A more viable alternative would be to look at the job description to determine who was responsible for a particular task. Thus, in this example, the problem definition determines the appropriate supervisory response.

Gather Information and Develop Alternatives

After defining the problem, the decision maker should gather information and analyze the problem so that a broad number of alternatives or options can be developed. In analyzing the problem, or "getting the facts," the supervisor should guard against personal biases in which extra weight or consideration is given to information from a "favored" employee. That is, supervisors must guard against giving more credibility to information from someone who is held in high esteem in contrast to information from a lesser-esteemed colleague (someone the supervisor does not "like" as well).

After "getting the facts," the supervisor should enter the phase of decision making in which alternatives are developed. One of the more productive techniques for generating decisional alternatives is brainstorming. The term brainstorming refers to the principle of suspended judgment—we should turn on our judgmental mind at one time, and our creative mind at another time, rather than trying to think critically *and* imaginatively at the same time. One study showed that suspension of evaluation or judgment from the process of alternative development produced almost twice as many good ideas as compared with those obtained when judgment was allowed to jam the imagination. An additional finding has been that <u>quantity</u> leads to <u>quality</u> in idea production. Since twice the number of ideas are typically generated by the brainstorming technique, the process results in many more good ideas when compared with traditional methods.

The following suggestions can be of value in conducting an effective brainstorming session:

1. Choosing the Brainstorming Topic

   a. Break down complex problems into problems specific enough to be brainstormed. Instead of "How can we promote a new product?," use three separate problems:

   "How can we promote a new product

   (1) to the retailer?"
   (2) to the trade?"
   (3) to the consumer?"

   b. The basic aim of brainstorming is to pile up a <u>quantity</u> of alternative ideas. Therefore the problem must be one that lends itself to many possible answers.

   c. Do not try to brainstorm problems requiring value judgments, such as "What's the best time to start our new campaign?" Brainstorming cannot make a decision for you.

2. Rules for Brainstorm Sessions

   a. Criticism is ruled out. Judgment is suspended until a later screening or evaluation session.

   b. Freewheeling is welcomed. The wilder the ideas, the better. Even off-beat, impractical suggestions may "trigger" in other panel members practical suggestions that might not otherwise occur to them.

   c. Quantity is wanted. The greater the number of ideas, the greater the likelihood of winners.

   d. Combination and improvement are sought. In addition to contributing ideas of their own, panel members should decide how suggestions by others could be turned into better ideas, or how two or more ideas could be combined into a still better idea.

   e. Take action on the best ideas. Report to panel members what action is taken on ideas.

   f. Do not use brainstorming as a substitute for individual thinking. It is a supplement.

By applying the proven technique of brainstorming, the decision maker will have a broader range of high-quality alternatives to consider for implementation.

Determine the Anticipated Consequences

After the decision maker has generated a substantial number of alternatives, each alternative must be evaluated. This evaluation should include consideration of the risk, the timing, and the available resources to implement that alternative. The decision maker is usually looking for that alternative that will provide the best results with the least effort. It will now become apparent that many of the alternatives developed in the prior phases are clearly impractical and unworkable.

Select an Alternative

Selecting the "best" alternative is what most persons consider to be the "decision-making" process, but as we have seen, several steps precede this one. The decision maker now uses his or her personal judgment in selecting that alternative with the greatest positive or least negative anticipated consequences. Decision makers may rely on their own past experience, advice from other persons, or a mere hunch or intuition.

Selecting the "best" of the available alternatives requires the supervisor to consider many factors: (1) those things that need to be done in the short run (now) and in the long run, and the short- and long-run implications of each alternative; (2) the existing policy limits within which the decision can be made; (3) the history of the organization—its values, customs, and past practices; (4) the personalities of the people who will implement the decision and who will be affected by it; (5) the "stage of events" (to discuss "how we might have avoided this problem" is useful for the future but is of little help in deciding what must be done now—for example, once an accident has occurred, the manager must ask, "What must I do now?"); and (6) the "precedent setting" dimension (the manager must estimate the implications of each decision for the future, since every decision not only has a policy-setting effect but also affects the expectations of people as to how they will be supervised in the future).

In any event, an alternative must be selected and put into action. Interestingly, after selecting an alternative, many persons feel that the decision-making process has been completed, but this is only partially true.

Determine Any New Problems

After selecting an alternative to solve the immediate problem, a supervisor should appraise the results of that decision to determine whether any new problems have arisen. In short, the supervisor should ask, "How has the decision worked out? Has it completely solved the problem?" The answers to these two questions will help point out any new problems. Usually a particular solution will not solve the whole problem; it will leave a part of the problem unresolved or will create new problems in itself. This process may be visualized in Table 12-1 by drawing an arrow from the phase *"5"* (determining new problems) to the phase *"1"* (problem definition). In this way, a loop or decisional process may be visualized.

ADDITIONAL DIMENSIONS TO THE RATIONAL DECISION-MAKING MODEL

The preceding discussion has provided the reader with a traditional and rational decision-making model. Studies have revealed two modifications to this model, which increase its applicability to the managerial decision-making process. These modifications are (1) the satisficing concept and (2) decisional confirmation.

Satisficing Concept. Earlier in the chapter we asked the decision maker to determine *all* possible alternatives. In reality, a supervisor cannot know all the alternatives. Only a few alternatives can be evaluated because all supervisors are limited in their ability to gather and process information. This limitation causes supervisors to consider only a simplified version of the real situation. This has been labeled the "Administrative Man"[1] concept. (This is a different way of acknowledging the time and energy constraints discussed in other chapters.)

Stemming from the Administrative Man concept is another idea, which has been labeled "satisficing." According to this view, we do not know if all the alternatives have been considered, but we do know that we can choose the "best" among several given alternatives. Thus the supervisor searches for alternatives that are "good enough" to meet the requirements of the situation. That is, a supervisor will establish the level of quality needed to solve a problem and will look for alternatives only until he or she finds one that will solve that problem. Since supervisors operate under substantial time constraints, they are unable to continue a search for alternatives indefinitely. Thus supervisors satisfice rather than look for *the* absolute best alternative (optimize).

EXAMPLE

A supervisor may be required to increase departmental sales by 4 percent in the coming quarter. To deal with this problem, he or she will search for an alternative that will provide the necessary 4 percent sales increase. But since time is

[1]March J. G., and Simon, H. A., *Organizations,* Wiley, 1958, p. 140.

limited, little or no time and effort will be spent in searching for alternatives that may provide an even greater increase than 4 percent.

Thus the satisficing concept predicts that a supervisor will be satisfied to find a solution that meets the objectives (a 4 percent increase in sales). In this case the supervisor has searched for an alternative that will "get the job done." It takes too much time to pursue even "better" solutions.

Decisional Confirmation. As we have seen, decision makers search for alternatives when they are faced with problems for which they have no immediate solution. Research has revealed an interesting finding concerning the final selection of an alternative: A decision maker, early in the search process, develops a personal "favorite" alternative. (This alternative could be merely the alternative that had been selected when the decision maker faced a similar problem in the past.) In any event, this "favorite" alternative will tend to be one that is felt to have some real promise for solving the problem at hand. But rather than immediately selecting that alternative without considering other alternatives, the decision maker tends to "go through the motions" of the search process. New alternatives are compared with the first one, and very frequently the result of this effort is to reject any new alternatives in favor of the early "favorite" alternative. Interestingly, it has been found that if a decision maker is forced to announce a decision before feeling "ready," the decision (selected alternative) will tend to be the same as that selected when much more time is available, but the decision maker will feel less confidence in the "rushed" decision. In summary, then, decisional confirmation refers to the selection of an alternative that was an early favorite in the decision-making process.

EXAMPLE

Assume that a supervisor has a vacancy in the work unit. To fill that vacancy, it will be necessary to interview several job applicants. Suppose that the very first applicant sent to the supervisor for an interview by the personnel department appears to be in all ways capable and adequate for the job. If there were no real time demands to fill that job immediately, most supervisors would probably prefer to see additional job applicants. Even though the original applicant had no particular faults, the supervisor would like to see if possibly there would be an even better candidate available.

The process is one in which it is likely that each additional candidate will be compared with the original one. The new candidates are likely to be compared critically with the early predisposition, and the supervisor will be searching for reasons why the additional candidates are not as good as the first. In this way the decision maker confirms an earlier decision.

In conclusion, barriers to using the classical model suggest that limited time and energy result in a reduced search for alternatives—satisficing takes place. Moreover, among the limited alternatives generated, the decision maker tends to select an early favorite, resulting in decisional confirmation.

How to Implement These Modifications

How does a supervisor make the refinements or modifications in the rational decision model to improve the quality of decisions? There are several suggestions. First, to deal with the satisficing problem, a supervisor can set higher quality and performance goals than the minimum established by a superior.

EXAMPLE

Rather than setting a 4 percent goal for an increase in sales, the supervisor could set a 5 percent goal. By raising the minimum standard, the supervisor is increasing the minimal quality that will be accepted for the alternative.

To reduce the effects of decisional confirmation, a supervisor should quantify and weigh relevant criteria for a decision prior to reviewing alternative solutions. In this way the supervisor can look for the specific and major aspects of an alternative to help increase the objectivity of the decision rather than relying solely on subjective, emotional, and frequently inaccurate decisional criteria.

EXAMPLE

The decision to make a new capital expenditure could be broken down into critical criteria such as cost, delivery time, reliability, and acceptance of the product by employees. "Weights" could be associated with these components, and a total "score" could be derived for each supplier. Such a procedure would *help* minimize overweighting of less relevant factors as a "favorite" alternative is identified and selected.

Most supervisors are aware that important decisions are usually not made by an individual but rather by a group or a committee. Frequently the group or committee is used when individual decisions would be more appropriate, and vice versa. The discussions in earlier chapters of small-group behavior and selecting a leadership style are particularly relevant to group decision-making considerations.

DECISION MAKING IN GROUPS

Most supervisors are concerned with making decisions of high quality. Previous sections of this chapter have discussed methods for improving the decision-making skills of the individual supervisor. They have emphasized the development of relevant expertise in coping with problems faced by the supervisor. While the rational model of decision making concentrates on the supervisor as the appropriate focal point in making decisions, other more recent approaches have suggested that a group or participative mode holds much promise. The rational model is useful, however, whether used by an individual or by a group. The participative approach moves beyond a concern only for <u>high-quality</u> decisions and includes a second, <u>acceptability</u>.

A primary fact of contemporary organizational life is that there are few, if any, decisions whose proper execution is relevant or important *only* to the decision maker. The reality is that most supervisory decisions will be executed, at least in part, by other organizational members. This fact points out the second major aspect of supervisory decisions—the necessity of obtaining <u>acceptance</u> of the decision by others. Thus, both quality and acceptance are necessary for effective decision making. (The discussion in the leadership chapter is particularly relevant here.)

The quality and acceptance of group decisions refer to the task concerns and group maintenance concerns in a group setting. The leader of the group may be solely responsible for both task and group maintenance concerns, or the leader may have assistance in providing for these needs of a work group. In general, a leader of an effective group accepts full responsibility for the performance of the group, but the leader does not emphasize his or her status or "rank" because this can have unfortunate consequences for group maintenance.

The following suggestions are provided for effective maintenance leadership:

Listen well and patiently
Do not be impatient with group progress, particularly on difficult problems
Accept more blame than may be warranted for any failure or mistake
Give group members ample opportunity to express their thoughts
Be careful never to impose a decision upon the group
State contributions often in the form of questions or speculatively
Arrange for others to help perform leadership functions

To provide task leadership in a group, the following suggestions are helpful:

Have adequate competence to handle technical problems facing the group or see that
access to technical knowledge is provided

Build a keen sense of responsibility for achieving group goals

Discourage complacency and help members become aware of new possibilities and
goals

Serve as a source of enthusiasm for the significance of the mission of the group[2]

In addition to the issues of task and maintenance concerns in the decisional
process, a phenomenon known as "risky-shift" has emerged. This phenomenon has been observed among group members who make more risky
decisions in the group than as individuals. That is, individuals in a group of
persons who are making a decision tend not to take as great a risk on their
own as they will in a group. It is unclear why this takes place. Possibly it
occurs because the group can diffuse responsibility for its actions. But for
whatever reasons, groups tend to adopt more risky decisions than individuals.

EXAMPLE

The chairman of the board of a large petroleum company, in explaining the
critical role played by the board of directors, said that he could never sleep at
night if he were required to make a billion-dollar decision to exploit a new
technology or to develop a new oil field. The board, backed by the extensive
research and collaboration of various vice-presidents and specialists, will make
these risky decisions much more readily.

Group decision making takes more time. Because groups have several
members who have personality needs and who must share information, the
decision-making process of the group as a whole is more time consuming
than that of individuals working alone. As a result, it is more appropriate to
use groups for nonroutine and important decisional issues than for the more
mundane ones. This is also consistent with the idea of preserving the effectiveness of time, as discussed in a later chapter.[3]

In summary, groups and individuals in the decision-making process
have different characteristics. Groups *tend* to be accurate, make high-quality
decisions, and increase acceptance of the resulting decision—but there are
costs. The costs of group decision making are a tendency to increase risk
and time consumed. It is up to the supervisor to determine which approach
is preferable.

---

[2]Likert, R., *New Patterns of Management,* McGraw-Hill, 1961.

[3]See Chapters 2 and 18 on leadership and time management for further suggestions regarding
effective task leadership in groups.

SUMMARY

In describing the decisional process, we have analyzed traditional decision-making and problem-solving concepts. Recent theorists have contributed concepts (satisficing and decisional confirmation) that have revealed certain limitations to the rational approach. We have discussed suggestions to overcome these limitations; these suggestions have resulted in certain modifications to the original problem-solving approach.

Subsequent to the focus on individual decisions, there was a general discussion of group decision making. Task (quality), maintenance (acceptance), time, and risk characteristics of group decision making were considered. Thus this chapter has provided specific methods for improving supervisory decision-making skills for both individual and group decisions.

DISCUSSION QUESTIONS

1. Describe the five phases of decision making and problem solving. In which of these phases is your competence the strongest? Weakest?

2. What is *brainstorming*? How is it useful in the decision process?

3. What is *satisficing*? How can satisficing solutions be improved?

4. What aspect of the decisional process (i.e., search behavior, decision making, postdecisional process) does decisional confirmation most affect? Is decisional confirmation a rare phenomenon? Can you think of personal examples where you have confirmed a prior decision?

5. Describe the role that quality and acceptability play in group decisions.

6. Describe five things a supervisor can do to increase group maintenance.

7. What suggestions do you have for supervisors who wish to increase the task orientation of a group? What concepts from the chapters on leadership and time management are relevant here?

8. In group decision making, what is the "risky-shift" phenomenon?

9. Do studies show groups generally to be more accurate or less accurate in the quality of their decisions? What factors would lead you to select a group versus an individual in making decisions?

CASE 12-1. Anderson, Wiggins and Associates

Jeffrey Wiggins was a principal partner in the architectural firm of Anderson, Wiggins and Associates. George Anderson had retired three years earlier and, for practical purposes, Jeffrey had become the sole operating manager of the firm. The firm's personnel consisted of two senior architects, seven draftsmen, and three secretaries. The firm had recently outgrown its office space and new quarters were required. Jeffrey asked both of the senior architects to submit their suggestions for arranging the floor plan of the new quarters.

The men set about this task with much enthusiasm. This was an opportunity to design a floor plan that they would use rather than merely developing one for a client. In two different meetings, Jeffrey listened to their suggestions and viewed their plans and drawings. He told them that he would consider their inputs.

Three weeks after their final meeting Jeffrey revealed his own plan, which bore little if any resemblance to the plans prepared by his subordinates. Although both senior architects realized that Jeffrey had the final authority in making a decision, they were very disturbed that the plans to be implemented did not include any of their suggestions or contributions. One of them was heard to mutter, "Why did he waste our time with this if he didn't plan on using our ideas? Who is he kidding?"

QUESTIONS

1. What is the appropriate use of groups in the decisional processes?
2. Why do you think Jeffrey failed to implement the suggestions of the senior architects?
3. Can participation in decision making be used as a manipulation of subordinates to make them "feel involved"? Discuss.
4. What is the likely impact of this incident on future participation by these architects? What effect will this have on morale?
5. What should Jeffrey do now?

CASE 12-2.   Northwest Electric Company

The billing department of the Northwest Electric Company owned twenty-five computer terminals for its computerized billing system. As a new billing supervisor, Hank Martin was contacted by a representative of the Dependable Service Company, which wished to renew its maintenance contract on the office machines, including the computer terminals, in Mr. Martin's department. These terminals cost $523 each, and the maintenance contract cost $2,325 per year for all twenty-five machines. Mr. Martin decided to review the experience that his predecessor had had with breakdowns and repairs of this equipment, and he found that the average repair cost was approximately $145 per call and that there were rarely more than two machines down at any one time. On the average, there were four calls during a six-month period.

When the service company was discussing the contract for the computer terminals, its representative brought up the matter of renewal of the service contract for the typewriter used by Mr. Martin's secretary. This machine cost $550, and the contract was $45 per year. The records showed that the average repair cost was $37, and it took approximately one day for the repairman to come and make any necessary adjustments. As a result, Mr. Martin's secretary, who was paid $700 per month, would not be able to use the machine for a day. Mr. Martin promised the service company's representative that he would look into this matter and would make a decision within a few days.

QUESTIONS

1. Why were these service contracts made originally?

2. How can a supervisor catch this expense before it becomes excessive? How can the problem-solving approach be used?

3. What recommendations should this supervisor make for the computer terminal maintenance contract? For the typewriter maintenance contract?

13

POSITIVE DISCIPLINE

LEARNING OBJECTIVES

This chapter discusses discipline as a state of orderliness in which employees meet the standards of performance and conduct expected of them. After you have read this chapter, you will

1. Understand self-discipline
2. Know how to take disciplinary action
3. Know how to develop positive discipline in an organization

Policies, rules, and standards provide employees with guidelines as to how they are expected to behave on their jobs. When an employee fails to meet expectations, the supervisor attempts to bring the subordinate's behavior into line with what is desired. Discipline is usually associated with punishment and the exercise of power by the supervisor over the subordinate. However, discipline also has a positive meaning. Discipline means a state of orderliness in which employees meet the standards of performance and conduct necessary both for the organization to achieve its objectives and for employees to achieve theirs. Discipline is good when workers willingly meet or exceed standards, follow rules and regulations, and carry out instructions. Discipline is poor when employees fail to meet prescribed standards, refuse to follow rules, and require constant surveillance by their supervisors.

SELF-DISCIPLINE

Almost everyone follows reasonable policies, rules, and regulations. People have been trained from early childhood to accept orders from those legitimately entitled to give them, including parents, teachers, and supervisors. Rules are respected, not because punishment is feared but because it is widely believed that each person should carry a fair share of the work load and that what is worth doing is worth doing well. Most adults have learned through their early experiences as a member of a family and through their neighborhood groups and organizations that all organizations must impose limits upon the behavior of their members. They have also learned that cooperation typically brings greater rewards than conflict. Thus, if the employment relationship is good in other respects, most employees will exercise a great degree of self-discipline. They will respond to positive leadership, and their supervisors need not threaten or punish them. Most employees regard as reasonable such conditions as coming to work on time; following their supervisor's directions; not fighting, drinking, gambling, or stealing at work; and punching their own time cards. The foundation for good discipline lies in the commitment of employees to be productive and to support the standards and rules of the organization.

While employees have been socialized to follow reasonable rules and do what is right, supervisors also possess within their "motivational arsenal" the means for shaping the behavior of their subordinates. They can exercise considerable control over employee behavior through their power to reward desired behaviors and not to reward (extinguish) undesirable behaviors.

Group Discipline

Work groups set standards of the performance and conduct they expect from members. Wherever good teamwork exists, group discipline can supplement and reinforce self-discipline. For example, members of work groups expect their fellow workers to arrive on time and do their share of the work. Members of some work groups also informally agree to help a fellow worker whose job is going badly or who is experiencing temporary personal problems that hamper job performance. Workers who do not abide by their group's standards will be encouraged to conform. And those who continue to deviate greatly from the standards of performance and conduct that the group has established for itself may be ostracized or punished by the other members.

TAKING DISCIPLINARY ACTION

Some employees fail to abide by an organization's policies and rules and to meet standards of acceptable performance and behavior for a variety of reasons. Some are unable to meet desired performance standards because of lack of job skills, physical or mental inadequacies, or lack of interest in the job. These situations typically do not call for disciplinary action. Rather, they require that the supervisor work with the employee to take appropriate corrective action. Such action might take the form of training or retraining; transfer to a job that more nearly matches the skills, abilities, or interests of the employee; on-the-job counseling to change the employee's attitudes or to stimulate the employee to seek appropriate professional counseling; or, as a last resort, separating the employee from the organization (usually without prejudice).

There are also some employees who generally comply but whose behavior in a given situation will depend upon such factors as the amount of stress the individual experiences, the example set by the supervisor, the promptness and consistency with which the rule or standard is enforced, and the certainty and appropriateness of punishment. Finally, there is that unruly minority who have learned to satisfy their needs by antisocial methods. These individuals find it difficult to live within any set of laws, policies, or standards. While their number is very small, their behavior is very disruptive to the effective functioning of a work group.

Taking disciplinary action requires that supervisors exercise good judgment and considerable sensitivity so that they can motivate, rather than "demotivate." Punishment is a "last resort" technique for obtaining employee compliance. It seldom improves attitudes or stimulates enthusiasm and cheerful cooperation. If informal discussions with the employee do not produce the desired change in behavior and if rewarding other more desirable behavior does not eliminate the undesirable behavior, the supervisor has no alternative. Even though the supervisor may wish to help a problem employee, he or she may not have adequate time or the technical skills to provide the necessary counseling. Or the employee may refuse to seek professional counseling outside the organization.

A Problem-Solving Approach to Discipline

The first step in taking disciplinary action is to obtain all the pertinent facts. Supervisors must resist the temptation to act too hastily under the pressures and tensions that often accompany disciplinary situations. Obtaining the facts also includes looking for the reasons why the employee violated the rule or failed to meet a standard. In the process of obtaining the facts, supervisors should seek answers to the following questions:

1. Did the employee know the rules? Had he or she been forewarned of possible consequences of conduct and given a chance to improve?
2. Did the employee deliberately violate the rule?
3. Was the rule or order reasonably related to orderly, efficient, and safe operation of business?
4. How important or serious is this violation?
5. Is this employee a chronic violator or is this a rare instance?
6. What extenuating circumstances contributed to the situation?
7. What is the attitude of the employee?
8. What policies, rules, and past practices are applicable to the situation?
9. How have similar cases been treated in the past?

Arriving at a decision is the final step in the problem-solving approach. The penalty, if any, should consider both the past record of the individual and the seriousness of the offense. The decision should also spell out the immediate action to be taken and plan for longer run follow-up action. For example, a supervisor who issued a written warning to an employee for failure to meet production standards provided for taking immediate action. This supervisor also planned for longer-range action by providing this employee with additional job training and stimulating her job performance by reinforcing improved productivity through such rewards as praise and recognition.

Progressive Discipline

The principle of progressive discipline is well established in the American culture. First offenders receive less severe penalties than repeat offenders, and more serious offenses result in more severe penalties than lesser offenses. The concept of progressive discipline tends to be more formalized in blue-collar work groups than among office, technical, professional, and managerial groups. The progression typically starts with <u>informal discussions and counseling</u>, and proceeds through <u>oral warning</u>, <u>written warning</u>, <u>disciplinary layoff</u>, and, finally, <u>discharge</u>.

The expectation is that each disciplinary action will serve as a warning to the employee and that this warning, along with the discomfort that accompanies it, will produce a change in behavior. The disciplinary layoff is considered by managers to be a very serious warning. However, employees who chronically break rules often regard this action less seriously, and sometimes a two- or three-day layoff is even considered by some employees to be a welcome break from the job! The disciplinary layoff is seldom employed among white-collar groups. Instead, employees who do not respond to repeated informal discussions and counseling are discharged.

<u>Discharge</u> is a very serious form of disciplinary action and is considered corporate "capital punishment." In effect, the supervisor admits that not only is the employee's behavior unacceptable but it cannot be changed. Discharge is currently used less frequently than in the past. The expense of hiring and training a new employee makes the loss of an experienced person very costly for the company. Correction and rehabilitation are often less costly and disruptive than replacement. Discharge is a very severe form of punishment for an employee. Employment brings with it many rights and privileges, including paid vacations, retirement benefits, medical and life insurance, opportunities for promotion, and protection against layoff during cutbacks in production. These are all lost upon discharge.

<u>Demotion</u> to a lower-level or less-desirable job is an ineffective form of punishment, although it is used occasionally. A demotion is such a serious blow to the self-esteem of most individuals that they usually find it impossible to accept such a disciplinary transfer, especially within the same work group. When used, it is generally regarded as an invitation for the employee to quit rather than be discharged. Demotion has other disadvantages, too. It extends over a long period of time. The humiliation creates ill will, loss of motivation, and even loss of hope. The financial burden that results from loss of pay is often greater than the infraction justifies. Finally, it is a great waste of human resources to utilize a person at less than his or her highest skill.

Demotion should be distinguished from <u>remedial transfer</u>, the purpose of which is remedial rather than disciplinary. Employees are sometimes erroneously promoted to positions for which they are unqualified. Also, employees sometimes lose the ability to perform their jobs satisfactorily. In these instances a transfer to another job that the employee is able to perform is in the best interests of both the individual and the company.

Obtaining Acceptance of Disciplinary Action

Supervisors want their subordinates to trust them and to look to them as a source of help with both work-related problems and personal problems that affect job performance. Yet, taking disciplinary action tends to build a barrier between supervisor and subordinate. It reminds the employee that the supervisor maintains superior power in their relationship. It may also raise questions in the mind of the employee about the fairness and helpfulness of the supervisor. While taking disciplinary action inevitably places a strain upon the supervisor-subordinate relationship, it will be more acceptable if (1) punishment promptly follows the violation; (2) employees are advised in advance of the rules and of the consequences that will follow their violation; (3) discipline is enforced consistently; and (4) discipline is administered objectively.

Immediate Discipline. The more prompt the discipline, the more closely it will be associated with the infraction. If the association between the infraction and the punishment is strong, the individual will be less likely to repeat the offense in the future. A person who commits an offense expects to be punished, if apprehended. An individual is more acceptant of disciplinary action that occurs promptly than of that which occurs a long time later.

Prompt discipline does not mean that a person will be judged without thorough investigation. It does mean, though, that the supervisor should take notice of the violation as soon as possible and follow through with an investigation.

If the facts are not clear or if the appropriate course of action cannot be determined immediately, many companies provide for suspension of the employee pending final disposition of the case. This technique is also helpful when tempers run high and when a cooling-off period would enable the parties to determine facts better and arrive at a just decision. An employee who is suspended is required to cease work and to leave the company premises immediately. All other rights are retained by the employee under suspension until such time as the final decision is rendered. The decision may range from acquittal with restoration of all rights, including back pay, during the period of suspension to discharge and loss of all rights retroactive to the time of suspension. The advantage of a temporary suspension is that it enables the supervisor to take prompt action and at the same time provides an opportunity to make a full investigation and arrive at a fair decision.

Advance Warning. In order that employees may maintain self-discipline and accept punishment without resentment, both the individual who is being punished and the individual's fellow workers must look upon it as fair. Everyone must know what the rules require and what will happen if they are not followed. Unpredictable disciplinary action is almost always considered unfair. This means that (1) the rules must be known; (2) there must be a clear warning that a given infraction will result in discipline; and (3) there must be a clear warning of the amount and type of discipline that will be imposed for a given offense.

Organizations employ several techniques for communicating standards of performance and conduct to employees, including the following:

1. Explaining the standards of performance and conduct to new employees at the time of employment. This might be carried out in part by the personnel department, if the company has one. The supervisor should communicate the specific standards that he or she expects in the department and on the job.

2. Posting rules on the departmental bulletin board and publishing them in employee handbooks which are distributed to employees.

3. Notifying employees when rules are changed by calling a group meeting, notifying individuals informally, and posting changes on the bulletin board. Written notices of changes may also be included in the pay envelope.

4. Informing the work group and individuals informally about infractions of rules and the intent to tighten up enforcement.

All rules should be reduced to writing; however, misunderstanding is minimized when published rules are supplemented by oral communications.

Consistent Enforcement and Application of Rules. Consistency of enforcement and application means that disciplinary action will follow each infraction. Inconsistency may occur in three ways: (1) when a rule or standard is enforced at one time and ignored at another; (2) when a rule is enforced with a severe penalty on one occasion or against one individual; and with a lenient penalty on another occasion or against another individual; and (3) when one supervisor enforces or applies a rule differently from another supervisor.

Inconsistency diminishes employee respect for supervision. It also increases feelings of insecurity by creating a condition in which employees are unable to distinguish what is acceptable behavior from what is unacceptable. Thus it is often said that "everyone should be treated alike" or that "people should be treated equally." However, consistent application of rules is not the same as equal application. Equal application implies identical treatment, once the occurrence of an infraction has been established. Consistent application allows for mitigating circumstances.

Most organizations publish a list of rules to which employees are expected to conform. Some organizations also list the specific penalties that will accompany each type of infraction. These organizations state that a schedule of penalties reduces inconsistencies in taking disciplinary action. Other organizations prefer to allow considerable latitude in levying penalties in order that the supervisor can give adequate consideration to the unique circumstances pertaining to each case. For example, a rule may state that "theft of company property shall result in immediate discharge." This rule is completely inflexible. The theft of a pad of notepaper is considered to be as serious as the theft of an electric typewriter. If the company wishes to treat *every* theft in this manner, the rule is accurate and correct. However, supervisors may be reluctant to prosecute minor offenses because the rule is so harsh that it will be enforced only against major thefts. In such cases the rule is restricted in its ability to reduce minor thefts.

The circumstances under which a specific rule or standard may be violated are almost unlimited. No set of penalties in advance can spell out adequately how each set of circumstances should be treated. There are always "mitigating circumstances" which call for special consideration and which may result in a modified penalty. For example, a widow employed in the data-processing section of a hospital reported late three times within two weeks because her baby-sitter had failed to show up on time. Another employee in the department also reported late three times within two weeks because she had overslept. The supervisor considered the widow's lateness less serious than that of the other employee and took different action with respect to each. Whatever the appropriate disciplinary action may be in each instance, it is important that the two employees involved, as well as others in their work group, look upon the action as being fair and consistent. It is especially important that all members of the group feel that they would be treated similarly in the same situation.

Objectivity. Disciplinary action, from the start of the investigation to the fulfillment of the penalty, should be carried out in private and objectively. Friendships and personal feelings about the individual under review should be set aside. Furthermore, the disciplinary action should be directed toward the individual's behavior, rather than toward the self-worth of the individual. In other words, it should not be a "bawling out." Finally, taking disciplinary action is an important managerial responsibility. The supervisor should not feel guilty or apologetic about the action so long as the entire process has been carried out promptly, consistently, and objectively after having given the individual adequate warning.

RIGHT OF APPEAL

Americans place a high value upon the fair administration of justice. In unionized work groups, employees can appeal their cases through the grievance
procedure all the way to top management. If the case cannot be satisfactorily
resolved within the organization, it may be appealed to an independent
outside party for adjudication. Some nonunion organizations also permit
employees to appeal their cases to top management, and a few also provide
for review and adjudication by an outside party.

Some supervisors feel that the right of appeal lessens their authority.
While this may seem to be the case, supervisors who sincerely encourage
subordinates to appeal their disciplinary actions gain respect and confidence;
and, in the long run, these supervisors achieve increased influence with
subordinates.

POSITIVE DISCIPLINE

The goal of positive discipline is to motivate employees to meet or exceed
performance standards willingly, even enthusiastically. There are six important measures that will promote positive discipline among employees:

1. Establish reasonable standards of performance and make certain that they
are known to those concerned. Performance is often deficient because employees do not know what is expected of them or because they assume that
their work is satisfactory if not informed to the contrary. Establishing and
communicating standards go far toward implementing positive discipline.

2. Let employees know how they are doing. This is particularly important
where the standards are more qualitative than quantitative and where, therefore, employees find it difficult to evaluate their own performance. However,
recognition and praise of a job well done are important rewards which stimulate motivation even where employees know that they are meeting standards.
Where standards are not being met, the supervisor can usually improve performance (1) by helping the employee recognize this in a discussion of the
problem, (2) by helping the employee uncover the causes of inadequate performance, and (3) by working out a corrective program with the employee.

3. Reward desired performance. As discussed in Chapter 4, rewards may take
a wide variety of forms. They are most effective as motivators of desired
behavior if they are closely associated in the mind of the employee with the
behavior being rewarded.

4. Give employees the opportunity to participate. Most employees want to be
consulted in advance about the policies, rules, and standards that will affect
them. Participation tends to build commitment.

5. Set a good example. Many employees look to their supervisor to furnish the cue as to behavior and performance. Even though supervisors typically do not perform the same kind of work as their subordinates, their standards regarding such matters as quality and quantity of work, punctuality, housekeeping, and customer service serve as guides to workers.

6. Prompt corrective action. Inadequate performance or undesirable behavior that is allowed to continue tends to become habitual and more difficult to correct later. It also tends to become in the minds of employees the new standard which may take precedence over the prior standard.

SUMMARY

Discipline can be defined as a state of orderliness in which employees make a commitment to be productive and support the necessary rules of the organization in order that it might achieve its objectives. In its broadest sense, discipline results from training. Most adults have learned to meet reasonable standards of performance and conduct. They understand that all organizations must place restrictions upon individual freedom.

There are occasions when employees fail to abide by an organization's policies, rules, and standards. It becomes necessary to take disciplinary action if the supervisor is unable to change an employee's undesirable behavior through informal discussions and the use of rewards to encourage more desirable behavior. Taking disciplinary action involves the use of a problem-solving approach to discipline, progressive discipline, and obtaining acceptance of disciplinary action. Acceptance is very important in maintaining good discipline and is promoted by taking prompt action, communicating both the rules of the organization and the consequences of breaking them, and being consistent and objective in enforcing standards and rules.

Supervisors can promote positive discipline within their organizations by (1) establishing standards of performance and communicating them to their subordinates; (2) letting employees know how they measure up to the standards; (3) rewarding desired performance; (4) giving employees the opportunity to participate; (5) setting a good example; and (6) taking prompt corrective action.

DISCUSSION QUESTIONS

1. What is meant by the term *discipline*? Good discipline? Poor discipline?

2. What is self-discipline? How does a group affect the performance of its members? What are some of the expectations that groups have about their members? Are all groups alike in their expectations? Why?

3. Why do some employees fail to meet the standards of performance and conduct required by a company?

4. What is meant by a *problem-solving approach* to taking disciplinary action?

5. Discuss progressive discipline. Why is it often used? What are the steps commonly used in progressive discipline?

6. How might a company reduce resistance to discipline and minimize the negative feelings it might be expected to create?

7. How might supervisors promote positive discipline in their departments?

CASE 13-1.   The Disappointed Best Man

"Mary is my only sister, Mrs. Pope. What do you mean I can't take personal leave to be best man at her wedding?" X-ray technician, Joseph Mooney, asked angrily.

"Sorry, Joe, personal leave is not to be used for social activities. If I granted you this kind of leave, other people would be asking for time off for parties and games, and even trips to the beach," replied Marjorie Pope, assistant administrator of the Shelton Community Hospital.

"Being best man at my only sister's wedding is more than a social function; it's a family obligation. I can't even imagine not being there. You've got to be kidding!" interjected Mooney.

"No I'm not kidding. A wedding is a social affair where socializing, feasting, and renewing old acquaintances are the main activities."

The hospital included in its *Employee Handbook* a policy on personal leaves. The policy stated that employees may be granted "up to three days of leave during each year without loss of pay to attend to necessary matters of a personal nature that cannot be conducted outside the regular work day." The leave policy included a list of eight reasons that would not entitle employees to take personal leave. Rule number six stated that personal leave would not be granted for "attending fraternal, social, political, or similar functions."

Mooney followed the required procedure in applying for two days of personal leave. He stated that the purpose was to attend and participate in his sister's wedding.

QUESTIONS

1. Was Mooney seeking a leave to participate in a social function?

2. What would you do now if you were Mooney?

3. Discuss the case from the point of view of positive discipline.

4. If you were Mrs. Pope, how would you have handled this case? Give your reasoning.

CASE 13-2.   Ajax Engine Rebuilders

As Arnie Hill, foreman in the engine assembly department, checked the production records for the week, he noted that one of his assemblers, Bob Winslow, had again produced far below his other assemblers. Furthermore, he noted that Winslow's rejection rate continued to be high—higher than that of any of the five other employees on engine head subassembly. He was particularly concerned because Winslow had been a good worker prior to his five-month layoff because of a production cutback.

Winslow has been back at work for about six weeks. However, his productivity has been poor since returning to work. In fact, Hill has already spoken with him three times during the past four weeks, and last week he gave Winslow a written warning. The warning stated that the quality and quantity of his work was substandard and that he would be suspended or discharged if it did not improve.

During the last meeting, which resulted in the written warning, Hill pointed out to Winslow that he had been producing only three assemblies per hour, while the average output was eleven per hour. He also reminded Winslow that, while other assemblers had an average of two units per week that failed to pass inspection, Winslow had an average of five rejects per week.

At that meeting Winslow complained that the other workers were "speed demons." He argued that he should not receive a black mark because he could not match their output. He also told Hill that his health has been bad for some time. However, when Hill asked for a statement from his doctor, Winslow replied that such a request was a violation of his privacy. He refused to supply a doctor's statement.

Winslow had challenged the company's right to discipline him for poor production, since it had established no output or quality standards. He also said that no one had ever told him that he had to produce a specific number of assemblies each day.

Foreman Arnie Hill is wondering what he should do now.

QUESTIONS

1. Is the quality and quantity of Bob Winslow's work substandard? What is the basis of your decision? What significance do you attach to the company's failure to establish definite quality and production standards? Does the production and quality of the other employees' work provide Arnie Hill with an adequate basis for deciding that Winslow's productivity is substandard?

2. What warning has Hill given Winslow? Has it been adequate?

3. What significance do you attach to Winslow's long period of layoff?

4. What significance do you attach to Winslow's refusal to support his health claim by providing a doctor's statement?

5. If you were Arnie Hill, what would you do now?

14

MANAGING THE COMPENSATION SYSTEM

LEARNING OBJECTIVES

This chapter discusses wage and salary policies and techniques. After you have read this chapter, you will

1. Understand the supervisor's responsibility for administering wages and salaries
2. Know which compensation policies and techniques are used in maintaining an effective wage and salary structure in a work group
3. Know how a supervisor can help maintain a sound compensation structure in an organization

Compensation administration is one of a supervisor's most important, challenging, and interesting responsibilities. Compensation in its many forms usually makes up a large part of a firm's total costs; therefore, it must be administered properly if the firm wishes to be competitive. At the same time, compensation is concerned with the fundamental needs and goals of people. It constitutes the means by which they satisfy most of their basic physical and biological needs. It also constitutes the means by which they satisfy many of their social and self-esteem needs, such as recognition, achievement, and self-respect. Alleged compensation inequities are the most frequent source of grievances and low morale in organizations.

The term compensation refers to all forms of payment received by individuals as a result of employment. It includes money received directly in the form of hourly rates or piece rates; weekly, monthly, or annual salaries and commissions; cost-of-living adjustments; and compensation in the form of bonuses and awards for extra performance. It also includes various cash and noncash "fringe" benefits, such as vacations, year-end bonus, insurance, pensions, and company cafeteria. It does *not* include various nonfinancial rewards, such as Herzberg's "motivators."[1] The term wage and salary administration is frequently used interchangeably with compensation administration both here and in many other texts.

SUPERVISORY RESPONSIBILITY
FOR COMPENSATION ADMINISTRATION

Compensation administration is one of those important management functions that seems so complex that supervisors usually are content to leave it to specialists in the personnel department. Government regulations, union demands, and the changing expectations of employees all seem to make it incomprehensible. Then, too, the individual supervisor may have little discretion in many wage and salary matters because the rules governing pay are often fixed through collective bargaining; and company compensation policies and practices are frequently so routinized as to make pay decisions almost automatic.

However, it is important that managers at all levels understand not only the techniques but also the principles and purposes of compensation administration. Imagine, for example, the damage that can be caused by an

---

[1] See Chapter 4.

office supervisor who plays favorites in awarding pay increases. It is the supervisor who implements a compensation program. And the supervisor either handles this responsibility in such a manner that the company appears to employees to be a good place to work or the supervisor so mishandles it that the compensation system breaks down, and morale and productivity suffer.

OBJECTIVES OF A COMPENSATION PROGRAM

A well-designed and well-administered compensation program should be directed toward attaining the following objectives:

1. Attracting and retaining an adequate number of qualified employees to perform the work of the organization

2. Gaining employee acceptance of the fairness of the compensation system

3. Establishing a compensation system in which rates paid for each job will reflect its relative difficulty and worth when compared with other jobs in the firm

4. Compensating employees according to their individual performance

5. Determining the combination of cash wage payments and noncash wage supplements desired by employees so that the firm will receive the maximum amount of labor services for each dollar spent

Attracting and Retaining Employees

The general level of wages paid by a company strongly influences its ability to hire and retain employees. If the wage level of one company is too low in comparison with other companies in the local labor market, it becomes difficult for that company to recruit and hold qualified personnel. On the other hand, if its wages are too high, the company may find that its costs are higher than those of competing firms.

What Determines Wage and Salary Levels? Competition (the demand for and the supply of workers in a labor market) is the principal determinant of wages and salaries. A labor market may be limited to twenty to thirty miles around a plant or office, as in the case of clerical and semiskilled production workers; or it may extend over the entire country, as in the case of college graduates.

Other determinants include

1. Financial condition of the company, that is, its "ability to pay"

2. Cost of living

3. Federal, state, and local government regulations[2]
4. Presence or absence of labor unions
5. Type of industry with which the company is associated, and its geographical location

Ability to pay and cost of living are frequently mentioned as important determinants of wages. When the cost of living is rising, employees claim that they should receive wage increases in order to maintain their current standard of living; however, when the cost of living declines, they cease using the argument. If the cost of living declines, employers urge that wages be reduced or held constant. In a similar manner, if a firm's profits are large or if they increase, employees claim that these profits justify increasing their wages; however, if profits are small or if they decline, management argues for decreased or stabilized wage rates. Since both ability to pay and cost of living can be manipulated as wage determinants, supervisors should keep in mind that competition is the basic determinant of wages and salaries.

Wage and Salary Surveys. Each firm must determine whether it shall pay the market rate for labor services, or pay rates either higher or lower than market. Market rates for specific jobs are determined by wage and salary surveys conducted by leading firms, employers' associations, and government agencies in a community. Employers exchange information about a set of jobs common to all their firms in order to learn the competitive rates being paid in the local labor market for those jobs. Periodic surveys provide information that enables employers to set wage and salary rates in their organizations.

What is Fair Pay?

The determination of fairness is personal and subjective. Individuals each determine what is fair for them. While few people are able to explain what they mean by "fairness" as they see it, it is possible to infer what they mean from their behavior. Most employees want to be paid in such a way that the value of what they give to their organization is equal to the value of what they receive. They also look at what other workers in similar jobs are receiving from the organization and at what these other workers are also giving to it. If they conclude that what they are giving is of about equal value to what they are receiving *and* if they also conclude that other workers are not being treated better than they, they will conclude that they are being paid fairly.

---

[2]See Chapter 16.

How Employees Respond to Feelings of Unfairness. Employees each react differently when dissatisfied with their pay. Some give less to the organization by being absent or late more often than otherwise, or by producing less; some attempt to receive more by asking for an increase in pay, filing a grievance to obtain more pay, or joining a labor union to increase their bargaining power; some change their attitudes and become less cooperative; and others leave the organization. The number and types of ways in which people express their dissatisfaction are almost infinite, but all of them spell trouble for the supervisor.

Comparing Jobs within the Organization

A company's wages and salaries must be reviewed and revised from time to time to keep abreast of changing conditions in the labor market. A company's internal wage and salary structure must also be reviewed and adjusted in order to set and maintain job rates that reflect their relative worth to both management and employees. In the organization, wage rates represent not only earnings but also social distinction. If the rates do not correspond with the relative significance of the jobs as employees see them, employees will consider them inequitable.

Job Evaluation. Job evaluation is the process of determining the value of each job in relation to other jobs in the company. Each firm is somewhat different from every other firm because of its unique historical development, products, processes, personnel, and so forth. Since each firm is different from every other, some of the jobs are unique to that firm. Thus they have no market rate—a market rate can exist only if there are many competing buyers and sellers of a particular labor service. Job evaluation helps solve this problem by providing a procedure for determining the relative worth of each job in the organization. In short, job evaluation is the process of comparing jobs whose market rates are known with jobs that have no market rate. After comparing all these jobs, a monetary value is assigned to those jobs that have no market rates.[3]

The Supervisor's Role in Job Evaluation. Managers, including first-line supervisors, are actively involved in implementing a job evaluation plan. They review and approve the job descriptions and they participate in evaluating the jobs. They not only know more about the jobs than the staff specialists in the personnel department but also have the responsibility for making the program work.

---

[3]Job evaluation is usually administered by personnel specialists. For a brief, but simple, description of the technique, see Raymond L. Hilgert, Sterling H. Schoen, and Joseph W. Towle, *Human Resources Management, Policies and Cases,* 3rd ed. (Boston: Houghton Mifflin, 1978), pp. 277–88.

Performance Appraisal for Compensation Administration

Performance appraisal provides the means for measuring work effectiveness on most jobs.[4] It helps assure employees that they will be paid according to their individual contribution to the firm, and especially that extra performance will be rewarded. Companies usually attempt to base monetary rewards upon productivity because strong motivation to work occurs only if pay is related to performance.

A performance appraisal system designed for compensation administration should include the following attributes:

1. The appraisal system should identify and accurately measure those behaviors that are important to performing the job.
2. The necessary behaviors must be within the control of the employee.
3. The measures should be as objective as possible.
4. Employees must understand and trust the appraisal system.

Paying for Performance

Almost all organizations express a desire to reward employees on the basis of their contribution. However, they find it very difficult to satisfy the requirements and conditions for implementing this objective.

Requirements for Paying on the Basis of Performance. First, employees must want more money. While it is often stated that everyone wants more money, this is not always the case. Individuals differ in their need for money. In addition, the more of it they acquire, the less value they attach to it. And the desire to earn more money often conflicts with other important needs, such as socializing with other employees, taking time off from the job, and recreation. This conflict becomes serious when the desire for more pay by one employee conflicts with the desire on the part of other employees in the work group to stabilize output, avoid undue competition between members, and restrict output to some agreed-upon level.

Second, employees must believe that their increased effort will result in better performance. This is largely a matter of the proper selection and training of employees. That is, employees must possess the skills and abilities that will enable them to produce more if they work harder.

Third, employees must believe that better performance will lead to better pay. This will occur best in those situations where (1) individual effort is directly and entirely responsible for paid results, (2) the increased pay resulting from increased effort is substantial relative to pay without such effort, and (3) total pay is substantial. Examples include salespersons

---

[4] Also see Chapter 6.

who are paid entirely on the basis of the amount of their sales, such as insurance and automobile salespersons. Other examples would include coal miners who are paid on the basis of the number of tons of coal they produce in a day, and truck drivers who are paid according to the number of miles they travel in a day.

If employees observe that they are being paid on the basis of friendship or seniority rather than on the basis of productivity, their productivity will be adversely affected. They learn what the firm really pays for, and they behave accordingly.

Sometimes employees discover that they are not supposed to perform "too well." For example, if they double their output and this doubles their pay, they may discover that the firm will "restudy" the job in an effort to cut their pay. After one such experience, the group will restrict its output to that level that management will tolerate without cutting the rate.

Payment on the Basis of Performance or Time. The methods for paying employees fall into two broad categories: (1) payment on the basis of output—by the piece, or by the time required to complete a unit of work; and (2) payment on the basis of time worked—by the hour, day, week, month, or year. Payment on the basis of output is preferable when

1. Employees have control over output, and a direct relationship between effort and output exists
2. Units of output can be measured
3. Quality is not so important as quantity, or if quality is important, it can be readily measured and controlled
4. The job is standardized, the flow of work is regular, and delays are few or predictable
5. It is important that direct unit labor costs be accurately known before production is undertaken

Payment on the basis of time is preferable when

1. Employees have little or no control over output, and there is no direct relationship between employee effort and output
2. Units of output are difficult to distinguish and measure
3. Quality considerations are important and inspection is difficult
4. Delays are frequent, beyond the control of the individual, and unpredictable

Requirements of a Good Incentive System

Supervisors often look to an incentive system for a solution to their problem of low work performance. They hope that the opportunity for workers to earn a bonus for output over what is normally produced will overcome such problems as poor leadership or lack of interest on routine jobs. They invariably learn, however, that an incentive plan is no substitute for good supervision and a motivating job design. An incentive system requires, above all else, that workers trust their leaders. It also requires good two-way communication and full participation on the part of those affected. The following guiding principles are important for the successful design and administration of an incentive system:

1. Consultation with employees in advance of the installation of the incentive system. They should understand how the plan will work, why it is necessary, and how it will affect them. The plan must not only be technically fair, but employees must also believe that it is fair.

2. The incentive system must be simple and easy to understand. If employees do not understand the relationship between performance and pay, and how earnings are figured, the system loses much of its motivational impact.

3. Job performance standards must be determined accurately, preferably by motion and time studies. The jobs should first be analyzed in order to simplify and standardize job methods, equipment, and job conditions. They are then timed to establish the output standard on which incentive earnings are based.

Determining output standards involves several judgments: (a) the amount of work an "average" worker can complete in a given amount of time; (b) how the amount of work completed by the workers being timed compares with the amount expected of the average worker (this is usually called "effort rating"); and (c) the proper time allowance for personal needs, fatigue, and unavoidable delays. Since these are matters of judgment, they are also matters subject to dispute. The credibility of time study results depends heavily upon the accuracy and acceptability of these judgments.

The incentive rate per unit of output is determined by (a) the output standard as best determined by a time study; and (b) the rate that should be paid for the job as determined by job evaluation. For example, if the output standard is fifty units per hour and the job rate is $6.00 per hour, the incentive rate is $0.12 per piece ($6.00/50).

4. Piece rates must be guaranteed against change, except where there has been a clerical error in calculating them or where there has been a substantial change in methods, materials, or quality standards.

5. Employee complaints concerning any technical, human relations, or administrative problem should be promptly investigated and adjusted.

6. Other groups of employees who are supportive of those on an incentive wage plan should also be included in the system, if feasible. Such groups as maintenance workers, materials handlers, and housekeeping, inspection, and warehouse persons facilitate the achievement of bonuses.

Group Incentives. A group incentive plan is one that pays additional monetary rewards to a specific group of employees for producing more output than that normally expected of them. Such plans may be limited to only a few workers or may include large groups, such as entire departments or even the entire work force in a plant.

Group and plantwide incentives are used when

1. Not all employees can be included in an individual incentive plan because it may be too difficult and expensive to establish accurate job standards

2. It may be difficult to measure individual job performance

3. Cooperation among members of the group is essential

4. A "weak" incentive is more desirable than a strong one because of quality considerations, or because workers have only limited control over output

A group incentive places a high premium upon cooperation within the group. Regular members are motivated to train new workers, to help one another, and to share job secrets and shortcuts because the earnings of each individual depend upon the total output of the group.

Profit Sharing. Profit sharing is a type of group incentive under which employees are paid bonuses based on the profits of the company. The principal objective is to build among employees the same feeling of "ownership" and teamwork that they would have if they were in a business of their own. Management hopes that by participating in the good fortunes of the company, employees will produce more, waste less, and become good "salespersons" for the company. Profit sharing, and similar group incentives, not only emphasize the interdependency of people in an organization but also recognize the importance of both their social and their self-esteem needs.

Profit sharing has been successful in motivating employees to improve their productivity in those companies in which (1) profits are large and relatively stable, and (2) the company is willing to share these profits liberally with employees. On the other hand, the effectiveness of a profit-sharing plan is weakened when there is (1) a considerable time lag between the employee's effort and the reward received and (2) a lack of a direct relationship between effort and reward. For example, it is usually difficult for workers to see the relationship between effort expended in January and a bonus received three to twelve months later. In addition, profits are influenced by many factors besides employee performance—factors over which they have no control, such as management efficiency and competence, a rise or a drop in prices, and the actions of competitors.

Productivity Sharing. In order to relate monetary reward directly to employee performance, companies have adopted plans that reward increased effort and labor cost savings. The best known of these is the Scanlon

Plan developed by Joseph N. Scanlon in the early 1940s when he was president of a local branch of the United Steelworkers Union in a small Ohio steel company. He suggested the formation of joint labor-management committees to solicit suggestions for increasing efficiency, reducing waste, and lowering production costs. The benefits were to be shared with workers in the form of higher wages, more steady employment, and improved working conditions.

As in profit sharing, employers, stockholders, and employees have benefited from improved quality, lowered costs, and improved effectiveness of managers. Supervisors are able to devote more time to planning, organization, and coordinating and motivating workers and less time to directing and controlling workers. A study of ten firms that had installed the plan found that they had increased their efficiency by an average of 23 percent.

As a rule, few companies are interested in union-management cooperation to the degree required by the Scanlon Plan. These plans usually have been initiated and promoted by the union in the plant. In general, they have been adopted by companies in serious financial trouble where both management and employees have much to gain through cooperation.

Other Incentive Plans. Companies utilize many different types of plans and programs to stimulate employee interest in the company, and to increase productivity, reduce waste, and lower costs. It is common practice to conduct periodic and special sales contests, to make awards for regular and punctual attendance, and to reward outstanding safety records. Many companies encourage employees to purchase their common stock in the hope that it will stimulate employee interest and a feeling of partnership. Many companies encourage employee participation in reducing costs by rewarding them for their suggestions. Formal suggestion plans enable employees to receive cash payments for suggestions adopted by the company. The amount of the payment is related to the amount of savings that result from the suggestion.

Fringe Benefits

Wage and salary supplements have become an important part of employee compensation. Surveys by the U.S. Chamber of Commerce and the U.S. Bureau of Labor Statistics indicate that benefits amount to 25 to 40 percent of payroll. These surveys also indicate that benefits vary by industry, geographic region, organization size, union status of employees, and the composition of the firm's labor force by age, sex, and educational level.

The following list of wage and salary supplements includes some of the more common membership rewards in organizations:

1. Nonproduction awards and bonuses:
   a. Suggestion awards
   b. Profit sharing
   c. Christmas bonuses
   d. Safety awards
2. Payments for time not worked:
   a. Holidays with pay
   b. Jury duty time
   c. Rest periods
   d. Sick leave
   e. Vacations
   f. Voting time
3. Extra payments for time worked:
   a. Overtime premiums
   b. Shift premiums
4. Payments for or contributions toward employee security:
   a. Accident and disability insurance
   b. Hospitalization insurance
   c. U.S. government—Old Age and Survivors Insurance
   d. Employee stock purchase plans
   e. Pensions
   f. Workmen's compensation
5. Across-the-board wage and salary adjustments:
   a. General wage and salary increases
   b. Longevity or seniority rewards
   c. Cost-of-living adjustments
6. Employee services:
   a. Cafeteria
   b. Athletic teams and recreational programs
   c. Educational scholarships and loans
   d. Free meals
   e. Parking facilities

The number and variety of various wage supplements seem almost endless. Organizations find it extremely difficult to determine which of this large selection are preferred by employees. A benefit that may be important to one employee may be unimportant to another. For example, older employees tend to place a high value upon retirement benefits, while younger employees tend to prefer larger pay checks and fringe benefits that can be enjoyed immediately, such as vacations.

Since these fringe benefits represent a sizable cost to the organization and since the benefit preferences are different for each employee, some companies have adopted the "cafeteria" approach to benefits. Under this method, a company first determines the percentage of each employee's total pay that will be given in the form of benefits. It then calculates the cost for each available benefit. Finally, each employee selects a "package" of benefits, with a value equal to the amount permitted for the purpose. This approach enables the company to provide maximum employee satisfaction for money spent.

HOW THE SUPERVISOR MANAGES COMPENSATION

While most compensation policies seem to be made at high managerial levels or through negotiation with a union, supervisors are very important in administering wages and salaries. It is the supervisor who is in daily contact with the workers. By listening to what their subordinates are saying about pay, supervisors can become the first to know of dissatisfaction arising out of alleged inequities. For example, during times when wage rates are rising rapidly, it is easy for a company's wage rates to fall behind those of other companies. When this occurs, employees usually grumble and complain. An alert supervisor who senses a potential morale problem and reports it to higher management will enable the company to take corrective action.

In a similar manner, supervisors can identify pay inequities that develop between different jobs. These inequities arise when one job increases in value relative to other jobs because there is either an increase in demand for that job or a decrease in the supply of persons qualified to do the work. For example, if there are fewer persons interested in becoming secretaries, the price of that job will tend to rise relative to the price of other clerical positions. An alert supervisor will sense dissatisfaction among the secretaries arising out of pay rates that are too low. This supervisor will also be aware of the reasons why secretaries may be quitting to work elsewhere.

It is also the supervisor who can best tell when an incentive system is not functioning properly or when employees feel that the fringe benefits are not meeting employee needs.

SUMMARY

Wage and salary payments usually make up a large part of an organization's total costs. The supervisor is very important in controlling these costs and in making certain that the organization receives maximum return for each dollar expended.

The objectives of a compensation program are (1) to attract and retain qualified employees, (2) to maintain a wage and salary structure that employees will perceive as being fair, (3) to establish a wage and salary structure that will reflect the relative worth of one job as compared with another in the firm, (4) to compensate individuals according to their performance, and (5) to use a combination of cash wage payments and noncash fringe benefits that will provide maximum motivation.

DISCUSSION QUESTIONS

1. What is meant by the term *compensation*? Are psychic rewards, such as recognition for a job well done, a part of compensation? If not, how do they fit into a firm's reward system?

2. What role does a supervisor play in administering a compensation system? What role does a personnel department play? Who is finally responsible for making sure that employees are compensated equitably?

3. What are the objectives of a good compensation program?

4. What techniques are used to implement a compensation program?

5. What determines wage and salary levels in a firm?

6. What is the purpose of a wage or salary survey?

7. How does an organization set rates for jobs so that each is paid a fair rate when compared with the rate paid other jobs in the organization?

8. How does performance appraisal help a company determine how much to pay employees?

9. What three important requirements must be met if a company wishes to pay employees on the basis of performance?

10. When is it preferable to pay employees on the basis of output? On the basis of time worked?

11. What are the requirements of a good incentive plan?

12. When is a group incentive preferable to an individual incentive?

13. What is *profit sharing*? What is *productivity sharing*?

14. What is meant by the "cafeteria" approach to granting fringe benefits?

CASE 14-1.   The Underpaid Foreman

George Caldwell, maintenance supervisor of the Rohr Chemical Company, sat down at his desk and looked again at his paycheck. He had only a few minutes earlier distributed the weekly paychecks to his crew of fifteen carpenters. He was very angry to discover that eight of them had received checks larger than his own and that the checks of the other seven were only a few dollars less.

When he accepted this supervisory position a few years ago, he had been told that his earnings would average 15 to 20 percent more than those of his crew. However, it had not been working out that way for almost a full year since sales began to increase and the plant went on a six-day, and often a seven-day, workweek.

Craftsmen are paid time and a half for work in excess of eight hours in any one day or over forty in a week. In addition, they receive doubletime on a seventh consecutive day. On the other hand, Caldwell receives no extra pay for overtime. As a member of the management team, he is expected to work whenever the need arises. It is considered a part of the job.

Caldwell calculated that even when his crew worked a standard eight-hour day, he worked nine to nine and one-half hours. He had to be on the job at least a half hour before the start of his shift in order to check with the supervisor on the previous work shift, and he had to stay on at least a half hour at the end of the day to coordinate with the supervisor taking over the next work shift and to complete his reports. The inequity became even greater when his crew worked overtime. They had an option as to whether or not they wished to work, but he had to be there all the time!

He decided to speak to his superior about this.

QUESTIONS

1. Why is Caldwell displeased with his compensation?

2. Why doesn't he receive overtime pay?

3. Do you believe that he should be compensated in a manner similar to that of his crew? Why?

4. What benefits and privileges does Caldwell enjoy as a member of management that he would not enjoy as a member of the crew? Are they worth the price?

CASE 14-2. The Energetic Salesman

Keith Swanson is a sales representative with Lindstrom, Inc., a national manufacturer of office copiers. He joined the company two years ago after graduating from college. After attending a two-week sales training and orientation course at company headquarters, he was sent to a large city in the Southwest to work under the supervision of the local sales manager.

The sales manager provided Keith with a brief orientation to the local office and the city. He reviewed again with him the company's compensation policy. Salespersons are paid entirely on commission, although the company provides a drawing account of $1,000 to stabilize an employee's income. In effect, if he does not earn commissions of $1,000 in any given month, he will receive a loan of the difference between what he earned and $1,000. The company will deduct the amount of the loan from future earnings over $1,000 in any given month. Keith was willing to accept the risks associated with this compensation plan because he was also promised that there would be no ceiling on his earnings. The harder he worked and the more competent he became as a salesman, the more he could earn!

The sales manager estimated that Keith should be able to sell or lease about $120,000 in copiers a year in his territory, although the last salesperson had achieved sales of only $85,000 from it. While commissions range from 12 to 18 percent depending upon the items sold, the average commission is about 15 percent. Salespersons provide their own automobiles. Annual depreciation, repairs, gasoline and oil, taxes, and license costs total about $2,500.

Keith got off to a good start and after the first month his earnings were never less than $1,000. At the end of his first year, he had made $160,000 in sales and had earned $24,000 in commissions. He had not only worked long hours visiting clients but also spent many hours planning sales calls, using the telephone when personal calls were not feasible or necessary, writing proposals for new installations, and sending follow-up sales literature and personal correspondence to clients.

About four weeks after the close of the first year, the sales manager called Keith into his office to tell him that the company was reducing the size of his territory in order to enable him to concentrate on potential clients not yet contacted. Keith was very disappointed to lose some of his present clients, but was also very reluctant to turn over to another salesperson several excellent prospects whom he had been cultivating during the year and who would probably make substantial purchases within the next year.

Keith gave his full attention to his newly reduced territory during the second year. He discovered that by concentrating on higher-priced items and those providing larger commission rates, he could more than compensate for the reduction in the size of the territory. At the end of the second year, he had increased his total sales to $165,000 and had earned commissions of $27,000. Keith's joy was short lived, however. Four weeks later, the company announced that commission rates on all items had been reduced by 1 percent, but that some items had been reduced by as much as 3 percent. A quick calculation revealed that if he were to make the same sales in the current year, his commissions would total only $23,500.

QUESTIONS

1. What do you think of straight commission as a method for compensating salespersons? Any advantage or disadvantages for the company? For the employee?

2. Why did the company reduce the size of Keith Swanson's territory?

3. Why did the company reduce commissions?

4. If you were Keith, what would you do now?

5. How could Lindstrom, Inc., have avoided some of the problems it encountered in this case?

15

MANAGING CHANGE

LEARNING OBJECTIVES

This chapter discusses resistance to change and shows how that resistance can be overcome. After you have read this chapter, you will

1. Understand why people resist change
2. Be able to predict change resistance
3. Understand the three phases of a successful change
4. Know how to use ideas from other chapters to obtain desired change
5. Understand how participation, communication, and needs and anxieties of employees affect successful change

In organizations, change results in the alteration of what people think and do. Change is the shifting of values, attitudes, perceptions, or behaviors to new modes. Ultimately, it can require people to adopt a new self-identity —to become something different. Because supervisors spend considerable effort to get employees to act or think differently (i.e., increased motivation, improved morale, or higher production rates), the term supervision refers to the change process to a large degree.

Since change is one of the few factors that appear to be inevitable, understanding and overcoming resistance to change becomes a crucial skill for supervisors. The focus of this chapter is on determining why people resist change and developing effective change approaches or strategies to help overcome such resistance.

WHY PEOPLE RESIST CHANGE

As indicated in Table 15-1, change is resisted for many and varied reasons. In many cases a particular change is resisted because of a perceived fear and the resulting tendency to protect oneself. If an employee feels that a new time and motion study of his or her job will result in "tighter" standards, that employee may resist any attempt to restudy the job because of the fear of potential economic loss. In similar ways, individuals may fear the loss of power or influence through reorganization efforts. Interestingly, many changes are resisted because of distorted perceptions; merely the belief that a new organizational structure will be one in which employees lose control or influence will cause change resistance. Employees who *feel* threatened or

---

Table 15-1. Some Sources of Resistance to Change

1. Perceived fear of
   a. Increased standards
   b. Economic loss
   c. Loss of power or influence
2. Distorted perception of change impact
3. Expected benefits and costs of change approximately equal
4. Would require development of new organizational and interpersonal relationships
5. Sense of being manipulated or forced to accept change
6. Habit of doing things in a familiar way
7. Possible violation of group production norms

---

attacked may then resist any alterations in the organization's structure. The fact that a new structure will in no way diminish their influence does not reduce their resistance so long as they *perceive* a threat; the employees' perceptions become their reality.

For many employees, changes may be resisted because the reasons for such changes have not been made explicit. Stated simply, the employee may feel that "there's nothing in it for me." From the employee's view, a change that results in an increase in effort or time or the development of new informal relationships should result in substantial benefits to warrant such an expenditure of effort. Often, both the positive and the negative aspects of a change are about equal, and therefore most employees resist such changes because the potential benefits merely match the expected expenditure of time and effort. Thus it is important for employees to feel that there is something in it for them and that the benefits substantially outweigh the costs. For example, few employees will change jobs for only small differentials in pay because of the significant outflow of effort needed to develop new working relationships. Unless there is a substantial increase in pay or benefits, the costs exceed the value of making such a job change. On the other hand, employees will change jobs if present relationships with a supervisor or co-workers are poor and prospects of improved relationships in a new job are substantial.

Change resistance can also stem from the feeling of being manipulated or having another person's will imposed. In our culture, changes that are merely announced or imposed by upper-level managers are frequently resisted for no other reason than that the employee had little input into that decision. Much like a child saying "You can't make me do that," employees frequently resist changes because of the actions taken by their supervisors.

The preceding discussion has indicated several of the numerous reasons why people resist change. However, merely recognizing that change resistance takes many forms is of relatively limited value until the particular cause of resisting change is specified. A misdiagnosis of the cause of change resistance can result in inappropriate actions by a supervisor. For example, if a supervisor feels that a particular employee has a distorted perception about an impending change, an obvious strategy would be to clarify the misperception by communicating what the actual situation will be. However, if the employee's perception is not in error, then increased communication and feedback could, in fact, confirm the fear and need for self-protection. For reasons such as these, it is important to predict change resistance accurately.

PREDICTING RESISTANCE TO CHANGE

One useful method for getting at the basis of most resistance to change includes an analysis of how an impending change would affect (1) <u>what</u>

people do, (2) whom they would talk and associate with, and (3) the resulting feelings and emotional reaction they would have to new work and interpersonal patterns. By focusing on what people actually do, questions of changes in skill, effort, or responsibility come to the surface. Then, by looking at how the change will affect whomever the individual is in contact with, the interpersonal relationships become known. This step also includes recognizing alterations in the influence process. Finally, this analysis should help the supervisor predict any new attitudes, beliefs, or feelings of the employee.

If the change is one that results in more positive feelings or beliefs, little resistance may be expected. By contrast, if changes in what individuals do and whom they interact with have negative implications, the resulting feelings can be predictive of substantial change resistance.

Another way of predicting the change process is to consider change as a field of opposing forces—some forces are supporting change and others are resisting it. Figure 15-1 depicts a situation in which the length of each arrow represents its relative force in supporting change (*S* arrows) or resisting change (*R* arrows).

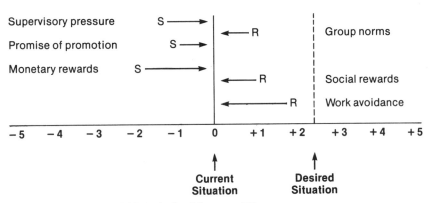

Figure 15-1   Force Field Analysis of Proposed Change

In Figure 15-1 the supporting forces (*S*) are exactly counterbalanced by the resisting forces (*R*). By increasing the supporting forces or decreasing the resisting forces, the situation can move toward the desired outcome. The recommended approach is to *decrease* the resisting (*R*) forces to avoid the "coiled-spring effect." This effect occurs when more supporting forces are added, which results in squeezing the resisting (*R*) forces back, as in a coiled spring. The resisting forces push back with even greater force as they are squeezed ever more tightly. By contrast, a reduction in *R* forces allows the change to take place with no increase in the supporting forces; moreover, less energy is needed to maintain the change than would be required with a tightly compressed spring.

For the purposes of this chapter, it should be assumed that an analysis of the situation has revealed the sources and amount of expected change resistance. In selecting a course of action to overcome resistance to change, it is helpful to understand the sequence of effective change steps.

CHANGE SEQUENCE

Several years ago Kurt Lewin, the well-known psychologist, described a process of change that focused on the critical stages through which a successful and significant change must proceed. The process he described has remained one of the more useful tools for understanding the change sequence. For Lewin, the change process occurred in three stages.

First, the person to be changed must be <u>unfrozen</u> by creating a motivation to change; this is much like saying that a person must be "prepared" for the change. There are several ways in which the unfreezing process can take place. One method of unfreezing an individual is to contradict what the individual believes. The purpose of such contradiction is to move the individual from a "solid state" to a "fluid state."

EXAMPLE

An employee may enter the job believing that the new supervisor is very easy-going but may later discover that the supervisor really is a very tough taskmaster who expects great amounts of effort from all employees. In this instance the earlier perception becomes contradicted.

Other approaches of unfreezing include increasing guilt and anxiety by communicating that the individual is inadequate or has failed to meet a reasonable obligation. In addition, unfreezing can occur through the reduction of threat or by removing blocks that have kept the individual from changing earlier. For example, an employee who is fearful of a change in the future may be reassured by the supervisor in order to reduce the employee's fear.

After the unfreezing process has been completed, the <u>change</u> process occurs. In this second stage, a new set of activities, responses, or behaviors occurs. These new activities or ideas can be adopted either because the individual desires the new change or because he or she is forced to comply. In both cases, meaningful change can occur only after the unfreezing process has been completed.

The third stage of the overall change process consists of <u>refreezing</u> the new behavior into a stable pattern. At the refreezing stage, the newly acquired beliefs or behaviors are rewarded in the various relationships that person holds. For example, a belief in Theory Y assumptions (see Chapter 3) can be refrozen in a supervisor who observes, through the comments and behavior of subordinates, that many of them are anxious to take responsibility and become involved in their work. The reconfirmation of these Theory Y assumptions may lead the supervisor to incorporate these assumptions into his or her own personality. For example, in a training program at International Harvester, supervisors from a very Theory X-oriented department were given Theory Y training. Tests of attitude indicated that the training had the effect of creating Theory Y beliefs. After returning to the job, however, a follow-up study showed that the attitudes reverted to stronger Theory X beliefs than had existed before the training.

Using the change sequence analysis, the training unfroze old ideas and changed the supervisors toward Theory Y. But before refreezing the new attitudes, the return to the old environment again unfroze the Theory Y concepts and refroze the original Theory X attitudes. Apparently, Theory Y ideas were contradicted and Theory X concepts were rewarded.

The change sequence of unfreeze-change-refreeze indicates that sustained change does not occur without preparation and follow-up. This implies that it will be difficult to change an individual without at the same time taking into account the environment or support systems (support or contradict) that affect that individual. Knowledge of the sequence of change is useful in determining the appropriate way to implement a desired change. The next section discusses various change strategies. The successful implementation of these strategies follows the change sequence just described.

CATALOG OF CHANGE APPROACHES

Throughout this book we have made various suggestions for obtaining desired behavior from subordinates. In a general way, an increase in motivation, an improved decision-making ability, or any variation in the work environment that causes employee behavior to differ from the original can be labeled as a change strategy. Other change strategies that have been discussed in various chapters are cataloged below.

Prescriptive, or Therapeutic, Approaches

Many writers on organizations have taken the position that they understand what the worker should be feeling or thinking. These authors believe that they know what "should be," and in many ways they prescribe how supervisors should behave. In this regard, McGregor with his Theory X and Theory Y concepts suggests that Theory Y is usually superior. Maslow describes a hierarchy of needs, which he states exists in everyone. Herzberg takes the position that all persons have motivator and hygiene needs; it is possible to motivate persons only by providing both motivators (achievement, recognition, enjoyable work, etc.) and hygiene factors (working conditions, pay, company policy, etc.). In its pure form, management by objectives implies that subordinates should participate in decision making and goal setting and that supervisors will permit such participation; this is based on the belief that a supervisor is willing to be influenced by the comments and ideas of subordinates.

In each of these cases, there is a belief as to what an individual or organization "should be." The intent or thrust of the change effort is to correct a problem or deficiency to fit the prescribed approach so that the individual or organization can operate more effectively.

Rational, or Logical, Approaches

Another category of change approaches, or strategies, consists of those associated with a rational analysis of each situation. These strategies include providing increased compensation for desired performance. In a similar fashion, providing a reward to an employee for successful completion of desired activities could be called a change strategy (see Chapter 4 on motivation).

By altering a person's or a group's goals, a change usually occurs in observable activities. Thus the goal-setting process can affect behavior; it is classified as a change strategy because of this (see Chapter 7 on goal setting). An added rational change strategy is to alter what people do on the job. Changes in behavior will result when new work assignments or tasks are given to subordinates.

Additional logical change strategies include the alteration of performance expectations or the roles of employees. Role changes can be accomplished by making alterations in the job description, in the work norms, and in the feedback given to individuals about their successful performance on the job. Thus, by redefining successful role performance, changes in behavior should result. An allied strategy for change includes altering what people understand through improved communication. By being more precise about what we mean, breakdowns in communication can be avoided, information can be transferred more accurately, and the needs of all parties may be more fully understood and adequately taken into account (see Chapters 5 and 6 on communications).

A change strategy affecting the behavior of supervisors can be found in the decision-tree presentation for effective selection of a leadership strategy (see Chapter 2 on leadership). This model matches an appropriate leadership style with the requirements for quality and group acceptance of decisions. Its utilization provides an effective framework for changing supervisory behaviors.

Changing the Situation and Training Approaches

A third category of change efforts includes altering significant aspects of the organization, with a resulting change in employee behavior. Using this approach, alterations in organizational structure can significantly alter responsibilities and behavior of individuals through centralization or decentralization (see Chapter 8 on organization).

The adoption of a new technology will also affect the behaviors of individuals in the organization. For example, differences in the product, the number and skill levels of employees, the span of control, and so forth, will be necessary if a company changes from custom or unit production to mass production. Thus changes in technology usually create significant changes in the operation of the organization.

Additional change strategies in this category include counseling, as well as the entire area of employee development (see Chapter 10 on development). Moreover, it can be argued that this book is in itself a change effort, since it focuses on increasing or changing the reader's understanding through the explanation and presentation of supervisory skill approaches. These new ideas and concepts can serve to change supervisory behavior so that it will be more effective.

Coercive Approaches

The final category of change strategies includes bargaining, or negotiation (see Chapter 17 on unions). Through the bargaining process, certain conflict situations can be resolved. The change strategy results in a change from a state of conflict to one of understanding or cooperation among parties who hold different positions.

The use of threats or force to obtain changes in behavior is also a change strategy. Among coercive strategies are threats of pay cuts, demotions, poor-performance reviews, reduction in overtime opportunities, and so forth. Although unacceptable as a change strategy in our society, physical coercion could also be included in this category.

The above catalog of change approaches, or strategies, has outlined various means for effecting the organizational or personal change discussed throughout this book. The following section describes the characteristics inherent in successful change efforts.

CHARACTERISTICS OF SUCCESSFUL CHANGE

Observations of significant and sustained change efforts have revealed some definite patterns that distinguish them from unsuccessful ones. In the preceding section, various concepts and techniques for thinking about and implementing change were cataloged. However, an attempt to change behaviors does not necessarily result in obtaining a successful change.

The characteristics of successful change include the following. First, the organization or individual to be changed must have a need to alter the usual behavior or way of operating. If this need does not persist initially, then an outside group or individual may help identify or even instill the need in the person or group to be changed. For example, an organization that has faced severe profit loss will usually experience a need to change, and thus it will be receptive to change efforts. Alternatively, outsiders, such as governmental or interest groups, could bring pressure on the organization to adopt new policies in consumer protection or in environmental areas; these pressures create a tension or need in the organization to resolve the demands. In both instances, the organization experiences a need for change; this is an important precondition for the change process. It leads to the "unfreezing" aspect of the change sequence discussed earlier.

Second, successful change efforts concentrate on specific goals. An individual or a group experiencing change needs an idea of the particular outcome desired; it is useful to be able to understand what the outcomes should be. This knowledge gives focus and purpose to the change effort. For example, a company experiencing revenue losses should be able to specify a particular goal, such as to cut employee absenteeism and turnover by 8 percent in six months. A more nebulous and general feeling that someone should "do something" without specifying what should be done is much less likely to result in change.

Third, successful change efforts are usually founded on an increased sense of self-confidence among the group or individual being changed. Heightened self-confidence is useful in helping the person or group feel that "we can do it." For example, in many change efforts the steps required to effect a large change are preceded by small requests that the group can quickly and easily accomplish. These early accomplishments or successes are necessary to help increase the individual's or the group's belief that the larger task can be accomplished. Moreover, earlier success in attacking a problem increases confidence in the initiator of the change and thus makes larger requests more acceptable.

Finally, successful and sustained change efforts integrate the new activity or belief into the personality and value system of the individual or group. This is similar to the "refreezing" component of the change sequence described earlier. Such integration is accomplished by making the new belief or behavior useful or functional to the needs of the person or group. For example, a new employee may adopt the norms of the group toward work output. "Carrying one's own weight" means that the employee can be accepted by the group; the development of new social ties can be reinforcing or rewarding so that the norm becomes an accepted value. In this way a previously low-performing employee may develop higher performance levels and integrate them into his or her own value system. Thus the work environment may reconfirm or "refreeze" this new higher output level.

How can the above characteristics be built into a successful change program? A supervisor can implement such a program by (1) fostering employee participation, (2) providing accurate communication, (3) understanding employee needs and perceptions, and (4) reducing employee anxieties.

Fostering Employee Participation

The involvement or participation of employees in the change process serves several purposes. It helps ensure that relevant information will be available which can increase the probability of developing a high-quality decision. Furthermore, by encouraging participation of subordinates, the acceptance of the change is increased. Participation tends to reduce change resistance.

EXAMPLE

The Harwood Manufacturing Company produced pajamas under an individual piece-rate system. Individual production records were posted each day, and pay was directly based upon the number of units completed each week. The plant was unprofitable. In part, this was the result of low productivity caused by inefficient methods and low work satisfaction.

The company undertook a major change in the plant. In one group the change was made in the customary way—the jobs were changed by management and a new piece rate was established. The members of this group were then informed of the change and authoritarian leadership was still used. Members were not informed beforehand of the change. They were not consulted in any way, and they did not participate in making any decisions concerning the change or piece rate.

The same change was introduced much differently in a second group. Meetings were held before any change was suggested or implemented. Employees were informed in great detail of the critical need to reduce costs. Each member participated directly in the design of the change, setting of the new piece rates, and implementation of the general plan.

In the first group, very little production improvement resulted. Members engaged in a deliberate restriction of output; there was no cooperation with the supervisor in implementing the change; much hostility and aggression against the supervisor and company were manifest; many grievances were filed against the new methods and piece rates; practically no increase in output occurred; and 17 percent of the group quit during the first forty days.

Results in the second group were dramatically different. Production returned to normal within a few days after the agreed-upon change was implemented; attitudes toward the supervisor and company were very good; no hostility or aggression was evident; forty days after the change, productivity had increased approximately 14 percent and no member of the group quit during that period.

Providing Accurate Communication

Full participation in the change process requires accurate and full communication. Full communication will permit the real nature and impact of the change to become known. Two-way communication will enable verification of statements and intentions. Thus, accurate communication will permit all parties to understand the proposed change, its likely consequences, the perceptions surrounding the change, and the information needed to accomplish it. (See Chapters 5 and 6 on effective communications).

Understanding Employee Needs and Perceptions

If the supervisor is to implement an effective change program, the needs and perceptions of employees must be determined. One of the better ways of gaining insight into employee needs and perceptions consists of having the supervisor put himself or herself in the place of the subordinate and ask the questions of how the change will affect job duties and personal contacts while at work. Such a focus will help increase the supervisor's understanding of employee views.

Reducing Employee Anxieties

With the knowledge of employee needs and perceptions plus participation and good communications, the supervisor is in a position to reduce employee anxieties. Several suggestions can be made concerning reduction of anxieties. First, a trial period can be implemented to assure employees that problems arising during the implementation of the change can be corrected or that the change itself can be dropped. Also, the supervisor may decide to reduce fears of failing or monetary loss by not collecting performance information during the initial change period. This will allow the persons affected by the change to learn the requirements of the new procedures and how to adapt to them. Moreover, by providing a regular mechanism or procedure for raising problems associated with the change, employees' anxieties can be reduced because they understand that attention will be given to their needs and problems. Follow-up programs provide a good mechanism for determining the impact of the change.

By being aware of the characteristics of successful change efforts and following the suggested steps for implementing change, a supervisor can increase the likelihood that a proposed change will be implemented successfully. Failure to include these concerns in the change effort will almost always result in only short-term compliance or active resistance.

SUMMARY

This chapter discussed various reasons why individuals and groups resist change, and it presented a method for predicting change resistance. This method asked how a proposed change would affect what individuals or groups do, with whom they interact, and what their beliefs about altering prior behavior patterns will be. Then a model of change sequences was described: unfreeze-change-refreeze.

A cataloging of various change strategies that have been considered in other sections of this book provided a number of approaches to bring about desired change. Finally, the characteristics of successful change efforts were discussed, and four steps for implementing change were presented. By comparing a proposed change effort with the suggested steps for effective implementation of change, the supervisor can predict the likely success of a new program or procedure.

DISCUSSION QUESTIONS

1. Why do people resist change? From personal examples, list five reasons why people resist change.

2. Why is it important to understand why people resist change? Do some people resist change more than others?

3. To predict whether change resistance will occur, what three aspects of the situation should a supervisor analyze?

4. In the unfreeze-change-refreeze model, describe the role of refreezing. Give examples. Can sustained change exist without refreezing?

5. Give an example of a therapeutic change of approach from this book. How does this approach compare with the logical change approaches?

6. What are *coercive change approaches*? Compare coercive approaches with training or situational change approaches. Give examples of each.

7. Most successful change approaches have certain characteristics. List the four characteristics of successful change presented in this chapter. Analyze a successful change with which you are familiar and pinpoint the four characteristics of successful change.

8. How does the concept of change describe the supervisory process?

CASE 15-1.   Royal Chocolate Candy Company

As a manufacturer of high-quality chocolate candies, the Royal Chocolate Candy Company had enjoyed a good reputation in its local market area. The candies produced were sold in company-owned stores, and the company was known for its attractive packaging and tasty products.

The production of the candy itself was predominantly automated, but the wrapping and packaging required that the individual pieces be wrapped by hand. Wrapping each piece of chocolate by hand was a very repetitious process. The company installed several short conveyor belts where groups of nine to ten employees stood on both sides of the belt and picked off of the moving belt those chocolate pieces that should go into a particular candy assortment. As the candy moved along, the employee would remove a piece of candy from the conveyor and place it in a small pleated paper cup. The wrapped piece of candy was then placed in its appropriate spot in the assortment box.

Since the work required relatively little thought, the employees seated at the assembly line chatted and joked with each other during a major part of the day. The foreman who observed this constant chattering felt that since so much time was available for socializing, the productivity of the employees must suffer. As a way of trying to reduce this constant socializing, the foreman had partitions installed between the work stations so that the employees were screened off from each other. This isolated the employees from one another and made it virtually impossible for them to converse while seated at their work stations.

At about the same time, a change in the assortment tray for the candy was made. Rather than merely indicating on the box that an approximate number of jellies, nougats, caramels, and so forth, were included in a package, the box contained a plastic tray with the indentions of the various candy shapes imprinted on it. The effect of this change was substantial. While the employees previously were able to arrange the candy according to their own preferences (e.g., in circles, rectangles, or just simply sections of nougats, caramels, and jellies), the new change required that a specific piece of candy be included in the particular compartment designated for it. This reduced the employees' flexibility in packing the box. The work was thus limited to merely matching a candy shape with the similar indentation in the tray.

QUESTIONS

1. Predict whether there will be resistance to the new changed working conditions.
2. What factors of importance have been changed?

3. If there is change resistance, how might it be overcome?
4. Do the changed working conditions suggest a change in the employees' skills or personal characteristics? Discuss.

CASE 15-2.   West Central Community College

Since the founding of West Central Community College eighteen years ago, Mrs. Martha Murray had served as the secretary for the Arts and Sciences Division of the college. She was fifty-three years old and was generally regarded by the other secretaries as part of the "old guard" who "knew everything there was to know" about the college. When asked, Mrs. Murray was not above telling what she knew, either.

Over the years, Mrs. Murray had developed a filing system which she alone understood. The dean permitted this system to be maintained because Mrs. Murray was both efficient and dependable. Her record of absenteeism was exceptional. It was rare that it took her over three or four minutes to locate any document he requested. It was not clear whether or not the system or her personal memory was responsible for the outstanding performance, but for whatever reason she performed her job admirably. When asked to share her knowledge of the system's workings with other secretaries, she always found excuses. She either claimed that she was too busy or said that it was unnecessary for others to learn her system, since she was able to fulfill any requests the dean might make.

At the start of the current academic year, a new assistant dean, Carolyn Rainey, was appointed to help the dean with the duties of registration, scheduling courses, and so forth. It was important that Ms. Rainey have access to the files, and Mrs. Murray complied with her requests with the same efficiency that was given to the dean. Ms. Rainey thought, however, that a new filing system based upon a decimal system of categories would improve the efficiency of the office. In addition, it would enable her to locate needed information without making requests of Mrs. Murray. She discussed the matter with the dean and received his approval for the new system. She then announced to Mrs. Murray that the new system would be implemented in two weeks' time. She not only provided Mrs. Murray with a manual that indicated the filing categories to be used in the future but told her that she should set up the filing system according to that method.

After one month the new system still was not installed. Mrs. Murray continually found problems with the new method, and she had not forwarded any forms to Ms. Rainey's desk showing that the location of the information was now where the manual said it should be.

QUESTIONS

1. Analyze the change strategy employed by Ms. Rainey. What might she have done to increase the probability that Mrs. Murray would co-operate?

2. Was the change necessary? Why did Ms. Rainey want to make such a change in the filing system?

3. Why was Mrs. Murray resisting the change? What gains or losses were at stake for her?

4. What should Ms. Rainey do now? What should Mrs. Murray do now?

16

THE SUPERVISOR AND PUBLIC POLICY

LEARNING OBJECTIVES

This chapter discusses the major laws with which the supervisor has constant contact. After you have read this chapter, you will

1. Know which provisions of the various laws on collective bargaining affect the supervisor's job
2. Know which provisions of the laws affect wages, hours of work, and employee benefits
3. Know which provisions of the laws affect occupational safety and health
4. Know which laws relate to equal employment opportunity

Americans have always placed a high value upon individual dignity and initiative. During the past century, there has been a tremendous change in the size, complexity, and interdependence of all types of organizations in our society. Employees have found it increasingly difficult to cope with the power and complexity of organizations—especially with their employers and with labor unions. At the same time, a higher standard of living and a higher level of education have raised expectations as to the quality of life to be enjoyed in our society. Numerous laws, administrative rulings by government agencies, and court decisions, which attempt to maintain a balance between the needs of these organizations and the needs of the individuals working in and with them, have flowed from federal, state, and local government bodies during the past fifty years. They encompass almost every aspect of both the internal and the external affairs of organizations.

The purpose of this chapter is to help middle- and lower-level supervisors understand those areas of government regulation that bear upon their performance of their personnel management responsibilities. Discussion is limited, with a few exceptions, to the major federal legislation.

The principal topics discussed are the law of collective bargaining; wages, hours of work, and employee benefits; occupational safety and health; and equal employment opportunity.

THE LAW OF COLLECTIVE BARGAINING

The enactment in 1935 of the National Labor Relations Act, commonly known as the Wagner Act, heralded a new era in collective bargaining for managers, workers, and unions. This act was the first major federal legislation giving workers the right to bargain collectively with their employers. It also established an administrative agency to oversee implementation of the many complex provisions of the law. The Wagner Act was amended by the Labor-Management Relations Act of 1947 and by the Labor-Management Reporting and Disclosure Act of 1959. These three laws contain the major collective-bargaining legislation in the United States and establish the legal framework of all subsequent federal and state legislation. Those portions of the collective-bargaining laws of concern to supervisors are described below.[1]

---

[1]For a partial text and brief analysis of the Labor Management Relations Act, see Sterling H. Schoen and Raymond L. Hilgert, *Cases in Collective Bargaining and Industrial Relations: A Decisional Approach* (Homewood, Ill.: Richard D. Irwin, 1978), pp. 3–57.

National Labor Relations Act

The National Labor Relations Act, also known as the Wagner Act, gave employees the right (1) to organize and join labor unions; (2) to bargain collectively through representatives of their own choosing; and (3) to engage in concerted activities, such as strikes and picketing, to achieve their collective-bargaining goals.

This act also prohibited certain activities by employers which might have the effect of thwarting workers in their attempt to bargain collectively. Specifically, it became an unfair labor practice for an employer to

1. Interfere with, restrain, or coerce employees in the exercise of their rights to unionize
2. Dominate or interfere with the formation or administration of any labor union or contribute financial or other support to it
3. Discriminate in regard to hire or tenure of employment or any term or condition of employment in any way that would encourage or discourage membership in any union
4. Discharge or discriminate against an employee because he or she has filed charges or given testimony under the act
5. Refuse to bargain collectively and in good faith with union representatives

Labor-Management Relations Act of 1947

The Labor-Management Relations Act, also known as the Taft-Hartley Act, was passed in 1947 as a major amendment to the Wagner Act. It contains four principal provisions of importance to supervisors. First, it endeavors to reduce union power and equalize bargaining strength between employers and unions. To accomplish this, the act makes it an unfair labor practice for a union to

1. Coerce or restrain employees by such activities as mass picketing, preventing nonunion or nonstriking employees from entering a plant or by violence
2. Cause an employer to discriminate against an employee for either wanting or not wanting to join a union
3. Refuse to bargain in good faith
4. Engage in strikes or boycotts designed to (a) require an employer or self-employed person to join a union or force an employer to bargain with one union when another is already serving as the certified representative, (b) attempt to force an employer to stop doing business with, or handling the product of, another employer (secondary boycott), (c) engage in jurisdictional strikes by forcing an employer to assign certain work to one union's employees rather than to another

5. Charge excessive or discriminatory initiation fees
6. Engage in "featherbedding" practices (requiring payment for services not rendered)

Second, it identifies the rights of employees as individuals apart from the rights of those employees as union members. To accomplish this, it explicitly provides that employees have the right to refrain from, as well as engage in, collective-bargaining activities. The Taft-Hartley Act levies restrictions upon the ability of unions to control union membership and to control whom employers hire. Specifically, it eliminates the closed shop. Under a closed shop, an employer agrees to hire only those persons who are union members at the time of employment. It also provides that the union and employer might negotiate a union shop. Under a union shop, an employee need not be a member of the union at the time of employment but must become one within some period of time after hire. The Taft-Hartley Act specifies that it not be sooner than thirty days after hire. This act contains the very controversial Section 14(b), which grants state legislatures the right to outlaw closed shops, union shops, and all union membership requirements in collective agreements. Nineteen states have enacted so-called right-to-work laws under this provision. These laws stipulate that no worker can be required to join a union in order to obtain or hold a job.

Third, it identifies and recognizes the rights of employers, a matter that had been overlooked in the earlier law. For example, although employers are still required to bargain with certified unions, they can now freely express their views concerning union organizations, as long as there is "no threat of reprisal or force or promise of benefit." Employers may also refuse to bargain with supervisors' unions, and they can also file labor practice charges against unions.

Fourth, it includes a provision to protect the rights of the public by enabling the president of the United States to delay a strike for up to eighty days in instances where a strike would create a national emergency.

Labor-Management Reporting and Disclosure Act of 1959

The Labor-Management Reporting and Disclosure Act, also known as the Landrum-Griffin Act, was enacted in 1959 to remedy certain deficiencies in the management of unions and to safeguard the individual rights of union members. It provides in its "bill of rights" that unions must conduct periodic elections; that all members be given an equal right to nominate candidates for union office; that they be allowed to participate in union meetings; that all votes be by secret ballot; and that they have the right to take legal action to enforce their rights. It restricts the size and manner of levying union dues, initiation fees, and assessments. It also restricts the union in the manner and procedures used to discipline members, and it protects against intimidation by union officers in the exercise of their rights under the law. Finally, it obligates the union to furnish each member with a copy of the collective-bargaining agreement.

The Landrum-Griffin Act also amended the Taft-Hartley Act by placing tighter restrictions on organizational picketing by unions and on the use of bribery of union officials and similar tactics by employers to thwart union members in their attempt to bargain collectively.

WAGES, HOURS OF WORK, AND EMPLOYEE BENEFITS

Federal regulation of wages, hours of work, child labor, and employee benefits is a comparatively recent development, although it is now an integral part of our entire economy. Prior to the Fair Labor Standards Act of 1938, such laws pertained only to government employment and a few specific industries; however, since 1938 this act has been amended seven times, and several other laws have been enacted to supplement it.

Fair Labor Standards Act of 1938

The Fair Labor Standards Act of 1938, also known as the Wage-Hour Law, provides that employers engaged in interstate commerce must pay time and a half to nonmanagement employees for all hours in excess of forty worked in a week. While this law was enacted principally as a means for "spreading the work," time and a half premium pay and the forty-hour week have become the accepted standards of our society.

The Wage-Hour Law also sets minimum wages in interstate commerce. The 1977 amendment increased the industrial rate to $2.65 on January 1, 1978, and stipulated increases to $2.90 in 1979, $3.10 in 1980, and $3.45 in 1981. Based upon past experience, the U.S. Congress will undoubtedly continue to increase the minimum rate in subsequent years.

If minors are employed, they must be over eighteen years old to work in hazardous occupations and above sixteen or fourteen in all others, depending upon the type of employment and by whom employed.

Another law, the Walsh-Healey Public Contracts Act, regulates wages, hours of work, and working conditions for those employed by government contractors. It requires them to pay the prevailing wage rates of the area; to pay time and a half for hours worked in excess of eight a day and forty a week; and to maintain safe and sanitary working conditions.

Social Security Act of 1935

In the 1920s a few companies pioneered formal retirement programs, which provided for a fixed retirement age, typically sixty-five, coupled with a guaranteed, but usually very small, pension. The Social Security Act created a federal program to provide a minimum retirement income for almost everyone. It was subsequently amended to include the payment of total disability benefits to eligible workers of any age and medical benefits at age sixty-five.

Since Social Security benefits provide only a base level of protection, many companies supplement them with a private pension plan. Most of these plans are financed entirely by contributions from employers. The Employee Retirement Income Security Act (ERISA) was passed in 1974 to remedy certain serious problems experienced by employees with their company's private retirement plan. In the past many workers lost their pensions either because they quit or were discharged before retirement or because their company went out of business. To correct this deficiency, ERISA requires that employers vest pensions. This means that employers must guarantee the payment of certain pension benefits, the amount depending upon length of employment.

The law also requires employers to set up a financially sound fund out of which retirement payments will be made. This funding of pension plans ensures the availability of money for paying benefits. Finally, ERISA makes private pension plans portable. Workers can transfer their vested pension rights earned with one employer to another employer.

State Unemployment Insurance Laws

Layoffs can have catastrophic effects upon both the standard of living and the self-esteem of workers. The Social Security Act attempted to alleviate some of the hardships of unemployment by helping the states set up unemployment insurance programs. These programs are largely financed by employers through a payroll tax. They provide benefits to unemployed workers based upon past earnings. The amount of the benefit typically is less than 50 percent of prior earnings. [2]

---

[2]Since benefits paid by these unemployment insurance plans usually are inadequate to meet basic living needs, many companies and unions have established Supplementary Unemployment Benefit (SUB) plans financed by a second payroll tax. These SUBs, when combined with the state unemployment insurance benefits, are designed to bring an employee's unemployment benefits very near to his or her take-home pay when employed.

OCCUPATIONAL SAFETY AND HEALTH

Widespread concern for worker safety and health dates back to about 1910 with the passage of workmen's compensation laws by many states. Although dramatic improvements have occurred since that time, industrial illness and injury remain a very serious problem. For example, every year about one out of every eight workers becomes ill or is injured; 2 million workers are disabled; fourteen thousand die in industrial accidents; and about 100,000 die from occupationally related illnesses. Occupational injuries and illnesses cost almost $10 billion each year, and almost 50 million man-days of work are lost. Renewed interest in safety and health in our society during the past two decades, accompanied by an increasing incidence of occupational disease, injury, and death, has resulted in our first comprehensive federal legislation setting minimum standards in industry.

State Workmen's Compensation Laws

State workmen's compensation laws make management directly responsible for accidents and illnesses arising out of and in the course of a worker's employment. They require that the employer compensate the worker for medical costs, loss of earnings, and permanent disability resulting from loss of limbs, hearing, eyesight, and so forth. Employers typically purchase insurance that provides the required benefits.

Occupational Safety and Health Act of 1972

The Occupational Safety and Health Act of 1972 (OSHA) places on employers a broad responsibility for providing workers with a safe and healthy work environment. It also requires that they abide by specific standards defining what is "safe" and "healthy" for each industry, occupation, and job. These standards include such elements of a job as noise, sanitary facilities, and physical safety. The standards are detailed and strict and in many instances are difficult and costly to implement.

Responsibility for Safety and Health

It is the responsibility of all managers to ensure that the workplace is safe and healthy. Top-management attitudes are very important, for they determine, in great measure, the attitudes of all other employees. The attitudes of employees at every level are determined by the attitudes of their immediate supervisor. The importance of management attitudes is well illustrated by E. I. Du Pont, which has always placed heavy emphasis upon safety. The accident rate of this company has consistently been much lower than the accident rate of the chemical industry. In 1974 Du Pont's accident rate was approximately one-twentieth that of the industry as a whole.

Developing and Maintaining Safe Work Practices

Supervisors can employ various techniques for developing and maintaining safe work practices:

1. Train new employees. Training means teaching employees the correct way to perform the job and at the same time motivating them to continue to follow the desired procedures once they have learned them. The probability that workers will follow safe work procedures is increased if they understand the reasons for them and the dangers inherent in following the undesired procedures. For example, machine operators are more likely to wear their safety goggles if they understand that a flying metal chip can blind them.

2. Safety comes first. Make it clear that while high productivity is important, speed must not be at the expense of safety.

3. Seek participation from workers. Consultation with workers not only produces good ideas about safety but also builds and maintains interest and enthusiasm.

4. Use constructive discipline. Reward safe practices. Behavior that workers perceive as being rewarding tends to be repeated. Point out departures from approved safe procedures, explain dangers inherent in them, and advise employees of company policy concerning safety. Take disciplinary measures if lesser measures fail.

5. Check for unsafe work conditions and for unsafe worker behaviors. Working conditions and technology change constantly in response to changing production demands. The supervisor should regularly monitor the effect of production processes on safety. Equally important, the workers' state of mind affects their behavior on the job. If an employee is emotionally upset because of something that occurred either on or off the job, the possibility of having an accident increases. The supervisor who is observant of employee behavior and sensitive to its consequences can counsel the employee or temporarily transfer that person to another job.

6. Set a good example. Members of management are influential in their work group. Subordinates observe what their supervisors say and do, and they imitate their behavior—both good and bad. Thus a supervisor who observes the company's no-smoking rule will find it easier to obtain the compliance of subordinates than will the supervisor who flaunts the rule.

EQUAL EMPLOYMENT OPPORTUNITY

Equal opportunity in organizations continues to be one of the most urgent problems facing management during this last quarter of the twentieth century. The numbers and the needs of minorities are as great as ever. Supervisors have been given both the legal and the social responsibility to recruit, hire, train, promote, discipline, compensate, and otherwise manage their subordinates without discrimination. National policy requires that they take affirmative action to eliminate discrimination in employment on the basis of race, color, religion, sex, and physical handicap, and discrimination against older people is prohibited. In addition, employment barriers based upon such factors as noncitizenship and homosexuality are being challenged.

Equal Employment Opportunity and the Law

Many categories of minorities are protected by federal, state, and local laws designed to provide equal employment opportunity. A brief review of the major federal legislation of importance to managers follows.

Equal Pay Act of 1963. This act requires that employers pay men and women the same wage within a plant for work on jobs that require equal skill, effort, and responsibility and that are performed under similar working conditions. Differentials in pay based on a seniority or merit system, a system that measures earnings by quantity or quality of production, or any other factor than sex are permitted.

While most organizations pay the same rate for jobs with the same title, some have maintained separate pay schedules for each sex. For example, universities have typically paid women faculty members at a lower rate than men, both by not promoting them as fast and by paying them less within each faculty rank. More commonly, discrimination against women occurs when different titles are used for substantially the same job. Thus a man might be identified as an "assistant to" a plant manager, while a woman performing comparable work would be given the title of "secretary" or "executive secretary." She might, in addition, receive a salary that was somewhat lower than that of her male counterpart.

On the other hand, jobs that appear to be identical may not actually be so. For example, a job that requires a substantial amount of continuous lifting may compensate women at a lower rate than men if the men perform the heavy physical work while the women perform the less demanding.

Civil Rights Act of 1964. This act makes it an unlawful employment practice to discriminate in the hire and conditions and privileges of employment on the basis of race, color, religion, sex, or national origin. The law is enforced by the Equal Employment Opportunity Commission (EEOC). As interpreted by regulatory agencies and courts, the law requires more than passive compliance. It imposes a duty upon organizations to act affirmatively to increase the number of minorities. The courts and regulatory commissions are increasingly examining the results that organizations are achieving in their employment activities. Thus, if a company in a community with a substantial Hispanic-American minority has only a token number of Hispanic-American employees, the courts may inquire into the company's recruitment, selection, training, and other personnel management practices. The courts may order the company to revise its practices so that the inequality will be reduced. Recent action by the EEOC and the courts goes beyond the elimination of discrimination in hiring for low-level jobs. The focus is shifting increasingly toward obtaining a proportional representation of minorities and women at all levels of the organization, including management.

The EEOC and the courts may order the organization to take immediate remedial action. This includes (1) the payment of back wages to compensate workers for income they lost because of discrimination and (2) the requirement that the company rectify past discrimination. For example, if women constitute only 15 percent of a given job category but it is concluded that they would have constituted 30 percent had there been no discrimination, the company may be required to take appropriate remedial action, such as hiring two women for every male until the inequality is remedied.

Age Discrimination in Employment Act of 1967. This act prohibits an employer from discriminating against persons who are from forty to sixty-five years old, because of their age. However, it was amended in 1978 to raise the age at which an employer can require workers to retire voluntarily from sixty-five to seventy. This law has had considerable impact upon employment practices. For example, several companies have been required to pay back wages and rehire employees whose employment had been terminated because of age.

Rehabilitation Act of 1973. This act requires organizations with government contracts or subcontracts in excess of $2,500 to take affirmative action to hire the handicapped. It also prohibits discrimination on the part of contractors against individuals as long as they are qualified to perform the work. Employers are expected to make a reasonable accommodation to the applicants' or employees' limitations. Thus, most buildings will be required to be equipped with such features as ramps and/or elevators, doors wide enough to accommodate a wheelchair, toilet facilities and fixtures suitable for the handicapped, and elevator buttons designated in braille. The number of physically and mentally handicapped is estimated at 11 million, and thus the law will have a considerable effect upon both the design of physical structures and the design of jobs.

Supervisors and Affirmative Action

Supervisors are expected to take positive measures to implement the equal employment opportunity objectives of their company and the legal requirements of the law. Affirmative action starts with recruitment and extends through the entire employment relationship.

Recruitment. In the past, recruiting has typically been directed toward whites. Many minority and disadvantaged persons never learned how to look for a job, and many were also convinced that the desirable jobs were not open to them. As a result, special recruiting measures must be taken to convince these persons that jobs actually are open to them. Employers utilize many techniques to reach minority applicants, including advertising in minority newspapers and over minority radio stations; cooperating with minority community leaders and organizations; setting up recruiting offices in minority neighborhoods; cooperating with minority career-oriented organizations such as the Urban League (blacks), Catalyst (women), and SER/Jobs for Progress (Hispanic-Americans); listing job openings with the public employment service; visiting high schools and colleges with sizable minority enrollments; and publicizing the company as an "equal opportunity employer."

The EEOC, the state and local agencies, and the courts have ruled that preemployment statements and advertisements that have the effect of deterring women and handicapped, minority, and older persons from applying for a job are unlawful. Thus a company is prohibited from including statements such as the following in advertisements: "Male Wanted," "Woman Wanted," "Age 25 to 35," "Age 40 to 50," "Retired Person Wanted," "Must be American Citizen."

Selection. The selection process is critical to equal employment opportunity. Traditionally, it has resulted in screening out many qualified women and minority persons. Unsympathetic and insensitive interviewers, complicated and long application procedures, the use of tests that did not measure what they claimed to measure, all discouraged these persons from pursuing jobs for which they were qualified or for which they might have become qualified through additional training.

The EEOC and the courts have ruled that many questions asked by interviewers and included in data sought on application forms are unlawful where the effect is to discourage persons from making an application or where the information is used to discriminate against various protected minority persons. Thus it is unlawful to ask questions concerning such matters as place of birth, age, physical handicaps, pregnancy or anticipated pregnancy, marital status, sex, race, type of military discharge, religious preference, or arrest and conviction record unless directly related to the function and requirements of the job. It is also unlawful to insist upon a preemployment photograph or birth certificate. The Supreme Court ruled, however, in 1976 that preemployment tests that have the effect of excluding blacks from jobs are not illegal so long as the discrimination is not intentional.

Job Description and Requirements. The qualifications specified for jobs tend to vary according to the relative supply of applicants and the demand for additional workers. When there are many applicants relative to the need for workers, organizations raise their standards; when there are few applicants relative to the demand, organizations tend to lower their standards. Companies frequently demand more education, more experience, and better communication skills than many jobs require. In some instances the qualifications demanded of applicants can be revised to meet the objective demands of the job. Thus a job may not require a college degree of the person who holds it; one year's experience, rather than two, may be adequate; required training time may be reduced from six months to one. In other instances a job can be redesigned so that a person with less education or experience may be able to perform it.

Training. Many minorities come to a job with little or no work experience. A supervisor may find that it is necessary to teach not only the necessary technical skills but also the habits of punctuality and perseverance. Individuals who have never experienced the demands of industrial discipline tend to find it difficult to come to work on time every day and to meet the rather rigid job and behavioral demands of the workplace.

Promotion. Affirmative action requires not only the hire but also the subsequent placement, transfer, and promotion of minority persons in order that they may have the opportunity to utilize their skills and abilities. The development of career ladders that indicate to all employees how they might advance within the organization is not only a strong incentive to excellent performance but also the means for helping employees develop themselves. Career ladders are especially effective if supplemented with training opportunities on the job, or through special courses offered either in the company or in the community.

Promotions are blocked sometimes not only by lack of training and by career ladders that relegate women and minority persons to dead-end jobs but also by collective-bargaining seniority rules. Seniority is the principle by which people are laid off as well as promoted. Women and minority persons have usually been the last to be hired. Thus they have also been the last to be promoted and the first to be laid off during cutbacks in production. The Supreme Court in 1977 ruled that seniority systems established before enactment of the Civil Rights Act of 1964 were not illegal even though their effect was discriminatory, provided that the seniority systems were not intentionally designed for discriminatory purposes.

Some Controversial Issues in Equal Employment Opportunity

Equal employment opportunity is in a very unsettled state. The "ground rules," as established by federal, state, and local legislation, the courts, and various government agencies, change frequently. Six major issues will continue to confront managers during the next decade.

Affirmative Action vs. Reverse Discrimination. To remedy inequities caused by many decades of discrimination, many organizations have made commitments to take positive measures to increase the number of minority and female employees. These commitments typically include intensive recruiting programs and accelerated training programs to qualify these persons for promotion. These companies have adopted policies and procedures designed to hire and upgrade minority persons who are not fully qualified to occupy a position at that time, but who through training can become qualified.

Affirmative action sometimes leads to charges of reverse discrimination, which is interpreted as hiring and promoting persons less qualified over others who are more qualified. In 1978 the U. S. Supreme Court in a landmark case (Regents of the University of California v. Bakke) ruled that the University of California could not use quotas in admitting minorities to its medical school, although it could use race as one of the factors in making admission decisions. Many equal opportunity advocates, as well as critics, disapprove of quotas. As a result of the Bakke case, race has become a legitimate factor to be considered in making employment decisions.

Minority Representation in a Work Force. A second issue centers on the question, What constitutes an appropriate representation of minority persons in an organization's work force? For example, should each minority be represented according to its proportion of the national labor force or according to its proportion of the labor force of the community in which the plant is located? Should each minority be represented in proportion to the number of applicants for jobs at the plant or according to their job category or skill level? Must each minority be represented at every job level (semi-skilled, skilled, lower management, middle management, etc.) and, if so, on what basis shall fair representation be calculated?

Social Responsibility vs. Efficiency. A third issue confronting managers focuses on the question, How does an organization balance its responsibility to help remedy the effects of past discrimination against the need for flexibility and efficiency? Special recruiting and training is costly. The high absence, accident, and quit rates of workers who have had no previous experience with the world of work is expensive and sometimes disruptive.

Seniority vs. Ability. The principle of seniority is important in determining the order of layoff during production cutbacks, rehire, and promotion in both union and nonunion work groups. It is especially important in unionized organizations, which usually state in a union-management agreement that layoffs, rehire, and promotion shall be according to length of service. Since minorities and women typically have been the last to be hired, they are also the first to lose their jobs during layoffs and the last to be hired or promoted.

Women. The traditional concepts of what constitutes "women's work" and "men's work" are breaking down. Women are seeking employment in occupations that have normally been reserved for men. They are becoming electricians, carpenters, automobile mechanics, doctors, lawyers, truck drivers, and—yes—even managers and supervisors. Men and women must be considered for employment and promotion on the basis of their ability to perform the work.

Older Workers. Although our culture is youth-oriented, the average age of our population is rising. Longer life expectancy, better health, and the reduced demand for physical effort on most jobs have produced a condition where more older workers both desire to work and have the ability to perform well. Organizational policies that require individuals to retire at any age, but especially before age seventy, have come under attack from those who believe that the ability to perform the work and not a person's age should determine who is hired, promoted, or laid off.

SUMMARY

Public policy has, during the past fifty years, been directed toward increasing regulation of both the external and the internal affairs of organizations. This chapter has focused on major laws controlling collective bargaining; wages, hours, and benefits; occupational safety and health; and equal employment opportunity.

DISCUSSION QUESTIONS

1. What rights were given workers when the Wagner Act became law?

2. What employer practices were prohibited as a result of the Wagner Act? Would it be an unfair labor practice for an employer (a) to refuse to hire an applicant who had a long history of union activity while working for previous employers? (b) to spy upon a union or its members? (c) to refuse to negotiate with a union whose members had voted to join the union?

3. How did the Labor Management Relations Act of 1947 change employer-union relations? What union practices were prohibited by the law?

4. What is a *union shop*? A *closed shop*?

5. Why was the Landrum-Griffin Act passed by the U.S. Congress?

6. What are the principal features of the Fair Labor Standards Act?

7. What are the principal features of the Social Security Act?

8. How can supervisors develop and maintain safe work practices?

9. What are the main laws governing equal employment opportunity? What are the principal features of each?

10. What role do supervisors play in implementing affirmative action in their organizations?

11. Discuss the controversial issues in equal employment opportunity.

CASE 16-1. Chase Chemical Company

Alice Blake is the office manager of the Chase Chemical Company where she supervises thirty-six clerks, stenographers, secretaries, teletype operators, and statistical tabulating machine operators, and one receptionist. Three clerks, one secretary, and one teletype operator are male. Seven members of the group are black, one is Hispanic-American, and another is Japanese. Alice has requested an appointment with Peter Hansen, the company's personnel manager, so that she and Pete can review her affirmative action program during the past six months. She especially wishes to discuss with him several troublesome cases about which she feels very insecure and hopes to obtain advice.

Her most recent problem concerns Charlene Lewis, who is the receptionist in the main lobby of the plant. Charlene was in Alice's office this morning seeking an increase in pay. She claimed that her salary of $550 per month was too low and that other employees performing substantially the same work were receiving higher salaries. She also stated that the company was keeping her on the job because it needed a black person in a highly visible position for public relations reasons.

Alice reviewed her personnel file, which indicated that Charlene had started one year ago at $500 per month and that she had received a $25 increase on her six-month appraisal review and another $25 as a result of an across-the-board cost-of-living salary adjustment. Alice informed Charlene that the salary range for the job was $500–$600 per month and that she was now at the midpoint of that range. Alice told her that her work was satisfactory, but not outstanding; she also pointed out that her absence and lateness record were marginal. She commended her on her excellent management of the reception desk. As to Charlene's comparing her salary with that of others performing similar duties, Alice pointed out that those who receive higher salaries are also able to type at a minimum rate of thirty-five words per minute, a skill that Charlene does not possess.

Charlene was not satisfied with this explanation and stated that she was worth more money. According to her, the company needed blacks and other minorities to meet its affirmative action commitments. She said that a company about two blocks away had offered her $575 per month for doing the same work.

Alice also wishes to speak to Pete about a recent application for employment from Ruth Jordan, a typist whose physical handicap requires that she use a wheelchair to move about. Her qualifications are excellent; however, the company would be required to purchase a special chair for her at a cost of about $300. It would also be necessary to move about six desks in order to widen an aisle to accommodate a wheelchair. In checking with the medical department, Alice learned that it would be necessary to widen the door to the washroom and remodel the facilities. She heard that a law passed in 1973 might require the company to hire Ms. Jordan.

Three weeks ago two secretaries, each with more than ten years' work experience, spoke with Alice about having been passed over for promotion to more responsible positions in the company only because they were females. Anne Hendricks told of having trained several young men only to have one of them become her supervisor when he learned the work. Ruby O'Leary spoke of having applied for a more important position on several occasions in the past. She said that in each instance she was told that women are not emotionally stable enough to work under the stress associated with managerial responsibility. Both Anne and Ruby indicated that they would probably file charges against the company if they did not hear from her soon.

Alice also plans to inquire about a dress code in the office. She is interested because one of the secretaries tripped on a low step while wearing high-platform shoes. She twisted her ankle and tore her dress. She has been off work for three days, and during a telephone conversation with Alice this morning asked how she should file a claim for reimbursement for the ruined dress. The step seemed clearly marked, and there is a railing to help persons to steady themselves. Alice also is concerned about how a handicapped person in a wheelchair could get past the step.

Finally, Alice wants help from Pete concerning the three black women who met with her two weeks ago and complained that they were missing out both socially and professionally in their jobs. They said that they noticed that she spent more time socializing on the job with the other employees, especially during morning and afternoon break periods and during lunch. They said that various company and departmental functions are discussed during these times, but that they miss out on many of these conversations. They also said that they do not seem to receive as many special assignments and projects as some other women do. They feel that these special projects not only are a welcome change from the usual office routine but also provide an opportunity to learn some of the skills that would qualify them for promotion and pay increases.

Alice believes that these problems are important and that she needs to discuss them fully with the personnel director.

QUESTIONS

1. Discuss the merits of the positions taken by each of Alice Blake's subordinates.

2. How would you recommend that the company respond to each individual?

17

THE SUPERVISOR AND THE LABOR UNION

LEARNING OBJECTIVES

This chapter discusses labor unions and collective bargaining in organizations. After you have read this chapter, you will

1. Understand why unions have become what they are today
2. Know why workers join unions
3. Know how supervisors feel about unions
4. Understand why the presence of a union affects the supervisor's job
5. Know what role the supervisor plays in negotiating and administering a labor contract

Unions have had a long and stormy history in the United States. Even before the Declaration of Independence, carpenters, printers, shoemakers, laborers, and other skilled workers formed separate associations to resist reduction in wages and provide members with financial assistance in the event of misfortune. The first authenticated strike was called in 1786 by the Philadelphia printers, who provided benefits for their striking members. These unions were very weak; they were confined to local areas; and they either disbanded once they had achieved their objective or collapsed if employers staged a counterattack during periods of economic depression.

In spite of strong opposition by employers and a generally unfavorable political and social climate in the United States, unions have slowly grown during the past two centuries, to the point where they possess considerable internal stability on the one hand and great influence in our society on the other. While many U.S. managers wish and hope that unions will disappear from the political, social, and economic scene, it is very apparent that they are a permanent institution. They possess considerable influence in local, state, and federal policy decisions. They also possess great economic power in negotiating with the management of individual firms.

Achieving good union-management relations is no easy task. It requires sensitivity, wisdom, and hard work on the part of all managers in an organization to demonstrate in their daily work relationships that the union is accepted as a responsible institution. In conducting their daily affairs, managers must look upon the union not only as an additional variable that they must consider in making decisions but also as an active force that participates with them in making these decisions.

UNIONS TODAY

It is difficult to obtain accurate statistics relating to union membership in the United States. It is generally agreed, however, that there are about 21 million persons in unions, including 19.5 million in national unions and 1.5 million in industrial local unions not affiliated with any national union.

These 21 million union members constitute about 22 percent of all persons in the civilian labor force. They represent about three out of every ten workers in nonagricultural establishments. They also represent about 35 percent of all employees in nonsupervisory and nonprofessional occupations in industrial employment.

Unions have dominant representation in those industries where technology is most advanced, where capital is used most abundantly, and where technological progress is most rapid. Thus, approximately 80 percent of all skilled, semiskilled, and unskilled blue-collar workers are unionized in such industries as steel, automobile, rubber, aerospace, agricultural implements, brewing, paper, government, printing, chemical, electrical, pharmaceutical, construction, and transportation.

The union movement is essentially a blue-collar movement; approximately one-half of the country's 30 million blue-collar workers (craftsmen and semiskilled and unskilled assemblers and operators) are now in unions.

While the union movement is predominantly a blue-collar one, this is no longer the case with the United States labor force itself. In 1956 the number of white-collar workers surpassed that of blue-collar workers for the first time in our nation's history—and the gap has been widening ever since. Such sectors as trade, services, finance, and government have continued to expand while the blue-collar sector, particularly manufacturing, mining, and transportation, has declined as a result of improved technologies and reduced consumer demand.

Unions have not been as successful in recruiting white-collar workers as in recruiting blue-collar workers for several reasons. First, white-collar workers tend to identify with management. They tend to work in close proximity with managers; they tend to share the values of managers; and they aspire to be managers. If they are not promoted into a managerial position, they are more likely than their blue-collar associates to ascribe this to the lack of ability on their part, or some other circumstance, rather than to inequity or arbitrariness on the part of their superiors. In addition, most white-collar workers, especially professional employees such as engineers, doctors, college professors, and nurses, believe that they can gain more by individual bargaining than by collective bargaining.

Second, white-collar workers think of themselves as having a higher status than blue-collar workers. Since the union movement is generally a blue-collar movement, they traditionally have rejected unions. They think of such union tactics as strikes, picketing, and boycotts, along with the use of violence and undemocratic internal management, as being inappropriate. Women, who now constitute almost 40 percent of the labor force, especially have found unions unacceptable.

Finally, the orientation of labor unions tends toward liberalism and economic egalitarianism, which runs counter to the social, political, and economic philosophy of many white-collar workers.

WHY WORKERS JOIN UNIONS

Human behavior is complex, and individuals join unions for many reasons. Our study of Maslow, McGregor, Herzberg, and others in Chapters 3 and 4 provides a useful framework for understanding worker interest in unions. Individuals endeavor to satisfy the needs and the wants that are important to them; dissatisfaction on their jobs with the extent and manner in which these needs and wants have been gratified has stimulated many of them to turn to unions.

Physiological Needs

Although satisfying our physiological needs comes first, this apparently is no longer a dominant reason for joining unions in this country. Few people who are working have great difficulty in satisfying at least their most basic survival needs in our relatively affluent society. People who are unemployed are the ones most frustrated in their attempts to satisfy their minimal physiological and biological needs. They, however, do not belong to unions; they are not even good candidates for membership.

This does not mean that workers have little interest in higher wages and other economic improvements. In fact, the desire for these benefits probably remains as strong as ever. The important point is that the desire for these benefits stems from the need to satisfy their higher-order needs. Money satisfies more than just the physiological needs. Our society is one in which each succeeding decade seems to bring higher levels of education, a broader perspective on national and world phenomena, and a higher standard of economic well-being. All of these lead individuals to believe that their personal world will become better with the passage of time. With these rising expectations on the part of individuals comes a feeling that their real income will increase, that their working conditions will improve, and that their sense of dignity and self-worth will be enhanced on the job. All of these things have been occurring in a national environment that has stressed both the right to enjoy individual freedom and the right to participate in making decisions about one's own affairs. Many workers have been motivated to satisfy their (1) safety, (2) social, (3) self-esteem, and (4) self-actualization needs through union membership.

Safety Needs

Satisfaction of safety needs constitutes the major reason for union membership. The union is an employer-controlling mechanism. Labor-management contracts are negotiated agreements. Most management decisions concerning wages, hours, and conditions of employment become a matter of negotiation. When an organization is unionized, management no longer makes these decisions unilaterally. Employees through their membership become a "partner" in establishing many personnel and other management policies and procedures concerning almost every aspect of their work relationship with their employers. Thus unions place considerable restriction on management decisions.

Unions, through participation in formulating management policies with respect to workers, and through the continuous challenge of management decisions and behavior, provide workers with considerable protection against management decisions that are perceived to be arbitrary and threatening to their job security and rights, status, dignity, or opportunity for growth and advancement.

Social Needs

Unions also help workers meet their social needs. Large organizations, and even many small ones, tend to be highly impersonal. The union, for these workers, offers a sense of identification and community. As members of an influential organization, they are able to develop a feeling of acceptance and belonging, and they can enjoy the society and respect of other individuals whose values, beliefs, and sentiments are similar to their own.

Some unions have done much to foster a feeling of fellowship among members. Union membership stimulates and provides opportunities for social interaction in organizations. Employees find this valuable in those instances where social interaction is difficult to achieve either because individuals are widely scattered geographically or because they are separated from one another in a plant by noise, the pace of work, or physical barriers.

Unions promote a wide variety of off-the-job activities designed to bring their members together and help them develop a feeling of social identity in a world that many find impersonal and cold. Unions are quite open about this objective. Some carry the word "Brotherhood" or "Lodge" in their titles, and almost all internal union communications are addressed to "Dear Brother" or "Dear Sister" and closed with "Fraternally yours."

The need to belong and be accepted by one's fellow workers is a very powerful need. Furthermore, individuals spend most of their waking hours in close contact with other individuals in their work group. A union can bring strong social pressure upon members to conform to its values and norms of behavior. The individual who remains aloof from the union is an outsider and tends to be excluded from the many informal social interactions between members both on and off the job. To the degree that employees are emotionally unable to identify with management or to the degree that management frustrates the attempt of employees to identify with it, they turn to unions for a feeling of belonging and acceptance.

Self-Esteem and Self-Actualization Needs

The union provides some employees with an opportunity for the realization of their self-esteem and self-actualization needs. A small, but important, number of individuals seek and attain positions of leadership within unions. These are people who have considerable need for achievement and power. They have been passed over for managerial positions in their organizations either because their supervisors are unable to recognize their abilities and interests or because their supervisors feel that their political, social, or economic philosophy would make them unacceptable for a managerial position.

Unions engage in a wide variety of activities that go beyond the strict collective-bargaining relationship. They provide various social, cultural, and educational activities for their members, and they are very active in politics at all levels of government. They encourage and provide support for members to become active in local politics and to serve not only on union committees but also on committees in the various branches of government. Thus unions provide an outlet for many individuals who have a strong need to exercise leadership and power.

Union membership is most effective in satisfying the safety and social needs of large numbers of workers. It also satisfies the self-esteem and self-actualization needs of a smaller, but very important, group of workers who have high aspirations for recognition, responsibility, achievement, and growth in their work careers and who have a strong need for power and influence.

MANAGEMENT ATTITUDES TOWARD LABOR UNIONS

Managers have typically been critical of the philosophy, objectives, and practices of unions.

Sharing of Power

We have seen that collective bargaining decreases the area of management discretion. Every limitation placed upon management action in the collective agreement and its day-to-day administration reduces the managers' ability to act unilaterally. Managers often complain that unions insist upon sharing in the decision-making process, yet it is they who are held ultimately responsible for the success or failure of the enterprise.

Most managers resist having to share power with others, whether it be a union, a government agency, or a subordinate. They view their role as that of making decisions without challenge from subordinates or their representatives. They perceive the union as a threat both to their position and to their personal identity. These feelings become acutely strong when managers experience situations in which the union leadership bypasses them and negotiates with others higher in the organization. For example, first-line supervisors feel a loss of status when union officers bypass them to negotiate grievances with higher-level executives.

Different Social, Economic, and Political Philosophy

Managers disagree with the social, economic, and political philosophy of most unions. They value individual initiative and performance; they favor merit and ability over length of service in making decisions concerning promotion, transfer, and layoff; they believe firmly in the free-enterprise system with minimum government regulation. They oppose the income redistribution measures favored by most union leaders; they resist the strong emphasis placed upon security; they believe in individual as opposed to group decision making; they tend to be authoritarian as opposed to egalitarian in their approach to management; and they oppose the concept that everyone should be treated alike and should be compensated in the same amount without regard to the performance of the individual and the needs of the organization.

Reduced Efficiency and Flexibility

Managers genuinely feel that unions represent a serious threat to the welfare not only of their organization but also of the entire society. They see unions as reducing efficiency and flexibility by restricting output, decreasing work loads, promulgating make-work rules, emphasizing seniority to the detriment of ability, and interfering with the normal functioning of the free-market system in setting a price for labor services.

Creation of Conflict

It is quite evident that while the interests of employees and managers are in many ways identical, in other ways they are in conflict. Almost everyone can agree on the need for maintaining a high level of productivity in an organization. Almost everyone can also agree on the need for providing employees with the type of work environment in which they can pursue their major goals, satisfy their major needs, and experience a high level of general satisfaction. However, the implementation of high productivity on the one hand, and satisfaction of employee needs on the other, can place managers and workers in severe conflict on specific issues. The presence of a union in an organization sharpens the focus of that conflict. It tends to equalize the bargaining position of the parties, and it provides a mechanism for continual challenge of the organization's personnel management policies, procedures, and practices.

Outsiders

Managers have typically viewed unions as "outsiders" holding no status within the organization. They have viewed the union as merely another power structure having its own goals and objectives which are not only in opposition to those of employees and managers but also independent of them.

The presence of a union introduces an additional variable into the employer-employee relationship. The union is an organization with goals and objectives that may be quite different from those of the company, and it frequently embarks upon courses of action that managers view as contrary to the interests of the company. Managers often look upon a union not only as an outsider but also as a "trouble maker," which creates animosity within an otherwise harmonious organization. They also feel that the union usurps employee loyalty, which rightfully, and otherwise, would go to the organization.

Managers acknowledge that they have a responsibility for meeting the reasonable expectations of their subordinates. They point out, however, that these employees constitute but one of several competing interests to which they must be responsive if the enterprise is to succeed. Managers must be attuned to the demands made upon them by customers, stockholders, suppliers, competitors, and government agencies, as well as subordinates. They feel that they must be free in responding to these many and often competing demands.

Management Response to Unions

While managers typically dislike unions, their response to them varies widely depending not only upon their personal philosophy but also upon the union's own basic policies for dealing with management. Open conflict on the one hand, and full acceptance of the union as an active partner on the other, constitute the extreme positions taken by managers. Most managers follow what has been termed the policy and practice of accommodation.

This position is best expressed by the statement, "If this is what our workers want, I guess we shall have to go along with it."

The union is accepted as an institution to which managers must adapt. Harmony is sought whenever possible. The company presses firmly to maintain its sphere of interest and influence and at the same time tries to limit that of the union. It is ever alert to prevent the union from usurping its "right to manage" and to keep collective bargaining limited to wages, hours, and conditions of employment. The company avoids open confrontation whenever possible but does not avoid it when matters of "principle" are at stake. The day-to-day relationships between the company and the union are friendly and conciliatory, with the company and the union making mutual concessions in the interest of harmony, so long as precedent and principle are not at stake.

THE MANAGER AND COLLECTIVE BARGAINING

When Employees Form a Union

Union-organizing campaigns are hotly contested by employers. The issues surrounding the decision to join or not join the union occupy the full attention of almost everyone. These discussions occur not only at the workplace but also on the parking lot and in the cafeteria and locker rooms. Sometimes the parties carry the battle outside the company to the local news media. Emotions run high, and the barrage of words may be accompanied by strikes, lockouts, work slowdown, and sometimes even violence.

If the workers vote to join a union, managers at all levels typically feel that they have lost more than an election! They feel that they have been let down, even deserted, by those whom they had considered to be their loyal employees. They are generally in no mood to sit down with the representatives of their employees to negotiate a collective-bargaining agreement.

Negotiating the first collective agreement is a frustrating experience for most managers. The hostilities generated during the organizing campaign have not yet been dissipated; the egos of the company representatives have been deflated, while those of the "victorious" employees and their union representatives have been enhanced. Although these managers may be accustomed to negotiation in other areas of their business, negotiating personnel policies concerning wages, hours, and conditions of employment is new to them. Union negotiators, on the other hand, are skilled bargainers —it is part of their business; they can be tough; they know "all the tricks of the trade." Finally, union representatives make many demands that raise costs, restrict the managers' freedom of action, and revise many long-standing policies and practices.

The Role of the First-Line Supervisor

Supervisors play a major role in determining both the outcome of a union-organizing campaign and the quality of the union-management relationship during and after the initial negotiations. All managers, but especially supervisors, must be aware that our labor laws restrict what they are permitted to do and say during this critical period. For example, managers may not engage in any of the five unfair labor practices previously listed. These include such activities as attending union meetings or questioning employees either publicly or privately about union activities in the company; refusing to hire applicants because of previous union activity; intimidating employees by removing certain privileges, cutting out overtime, transferring employees to a less desirable shift or job, or demoting or discharging them; making any statement that might be interpreted as a threat or promise of benefit; questioning workers about their feelings toward or opinions of the union.[1]

Supervisors are especially confused as to how they should behave both during an election campaign and following the advent of a union. It is important that all supervisors attempt to understand why their subordinates decided to join a union—namely, why their subordinates feel rather strongly that one or more of their major needs is not being met satisfactorily on the job. Supervisors often attribute their subordinates' action to seduction or strong-arm tactics employed by the union leaders during the campaign, or to the gullibility or perversity of their subordinates. Instead of blaming others for employee interest in unions, they would be wise to examine their leadership behavior and the policies and practices of their company for an explanation of their subordinates' behavior. It is important that they not allow strong negative feelings, which typically surround a union-organizing campaign, and the subsequent negotiations to interfere with building good work relationships with those around them. It is particularly important that they meet the new union representatives ''half way.'' Building a satisfactory union-management relationship is a challenging undertaking, which commences with understanding and respecting the new union leadership in the plant.

Working with the Union

All managers, but again, especially first-line supervisors, find that the arrival of a union greatly complicates their lives. They must now spend

---

[1]On the other hand, managers are not prevented from expressing their point of view. For example, they may express their opinions toward unions; justify, explain, and extol company policies, practices, and wage rates; answer union questions, arguments, or charges; advise employees as to their rights under the law; discuss the history and current policies and practices of unions in general and of this union in particular; express a desire that employees would vote against the union, etc.

many hours each week negotiating decisions that they had formerly made unilaterally in a matter of minutes. They feel that their status has suffered, too. It is not uncommon for union representatives to bypass lower levels of management in order to work directly with top managers. This especially occurs when higher-level managers refuse to give lower-level managers either the information or the responsibility necessary for making decisions. The arrival of a union usually causes top management to centralize decision making in the area of personnel management in order to reduce the probability of error and increase the probability of consistency in making decisions.

First-line supervisors particularly feel the brunt of the new situation, for it is they who make most of the decisions affecting the unionized employees and it is they who must first respond to employee grievances and negotiate with union representatives. It is also they who are the point of contact between their unionized subordinates on the one hand and members of higher management on the other. Their unique position in the organization makes them important in determining the quality of the union-management relations in their company. First, because of their direct and frequent contact with unionized employers and their representatives, they possess a great amount of information needed by higher-level managers in negotiating the collective agreement. Second, supervisors administer the terms of the agreement. How well they do this will, in large measure, determine the quality of life in the work group for supervisors and their subordinates alike.

THE SUPERVISOR'S ROLE IN CONTRACT NEGOTIATIONS

The collective-bargaining agreement negotiated between management and union representatives and approved by union members constitutes a basic document containing many of the company's personnel management principles, policies, procedures, and practices. The agreement represents a series of compromises that have been agreed to, though often unwillingly, by management. It is nevertheless a statement that is binding upon union management and employees alike. Although no two contracts are exactly the same, the typical agreement provides for statements of personnel policy and procedure on the following topics:

Purpose of the agreement
Management rights
Union recognition
Union security, including checkoff of union dues
Hours of work and overtime
Wages
Vacations and holidays

Seniority
Promotion, transfer, layoff, and rehire
Leave of absence
Grievance procedure and arbitration
Strikes and lockouts
Working conditions
Safety and health insurance and medical benefits
Contracting other work
Termination of the contract and contract renewal

Supervisors work and live with the contract every day. They obtain a vast amount of experience in applying it. It is important that those higher up in the company who periodically renegotiate the contract receive the benefit of the supervisor's knowledge and experience. It is customary for the labor relations negotiators to meet with supervisors and review the contract with them clause by clause as part of the preparation for negotiations. A few companies even include the supervisors in the bargaining sessions as observers in order to both educate them and obtain ideas from them.

ADMINISTERING THE AGREEMENT

Collective-bargaining agreements are negotiated under conditions of considerable tension and pressure. They are often signed at the "eleventh hour" immediately preceding a strike deadline. Words have different meanings to different people; and when viewed in the bright light of day, words often mean something different from what they did earlier during the heat of a last-minute rush to beat a contract-termination deadline. Thus it sometimes becomes difficult to interpret the meaning of a contract clause.

In other instances the supervisor finds it difficult to apply the standards laid out in the agreement. For example, most contracts include a statement to the effect that management will maintain reasonable standards with respect to safety, health, and working conditions. Many agreements stipulate that the company must provide adequate heat, light, and ventilation; that it will control noise, dust, dirt, and toxic fumes; that it will provide safety equipment such as goggles and special clothing; that it will provide adequate safety guards on machines; and that it will maintain a professionally staffed first-aid station. While the clause may be quite specific in enumerating the measures the company must take to maintain employee health and safety, it does not specify precisely what it is that constitutes a reasonable standard of ventilation in the plant or office, who shall be issued safety shoes at company expense, or whether a particular machine is adequately protected with safety guards. The question of whether or not the company is meeting the intended standards of the parties is a question that a supervisor will ordinarily be unable to answer.

In all such cases the supervisor should consult with his or her superior. This is important for several reasons: (1) the supervisor did not attend the negotiations, does not know the full background of the clause, and is unaware of the intent of the parties to the negotiations; (2) the issue may involve other people in other departments, and it is necessary to consider the full impact of any discussion upon the entire organization; (3) decisions establish precedent, and it is important that an undesirable precedent is not established; and (4) clarification of the intent of the clause may have to be negotiated at high levels between the parties.

The Shop Steward

The supervisor's principal contact with the union occurs with the shop steward, also sometimes called the committeeman or committeewoman. The steward is typically elected to that position. This is a difficult position because the steward owes loyalty to employees as union members, to the union leadership, and to management. The steward serves the needs of employees by representing their interests to management, usually through the grievance procedure. The steward also represents union members when they have questions or problems with their union or its leaders.

The steward, while holding that position in the union, customarily remains a full-time employee of the company and is expected to perform as such. Furthermore, while remaining a subordinate of the supervisor in the work relationship, the steward becomes that supervisor's equal in the presentation and processing of grievances. This relationship is further complicated by the fact that the supervisor and the steward may wish to work together on an informal friendly basis to keep both their jobs running smoothly.

The steward occupies the lowest position in the union-management hierarchy. In many ways the steward's position in the union is comparable to that of the first-line supervisor in the company. Both are often referred to as the "person in the middle" in their respective organizations. Stewards owe loyalty to the union officers, who view them as their principal communication link with union members. Stewards perform many functions in addition to processing grievances. They solicit members, collect dues, promote union social functions, and promote the union's political activities both within the union and within the community.

It is important for the supervisor to understand that the shop steward is very sensitive to the treatment he or she receives from management. Supervisors find that "going half way," or even further, usually pays big dividends in building an open and trusting work relationship with stewards. The steward can be a source of help in carrying out leadership responsibilities, or the steward can be a source of great frustration. Whether the department runs smoothly or roughly depends in great measure upon the cooperation received from the shop steward.

MANAGEMENT AND UNIONS: A FINAL LOOK

Managers frequently look upon the union as a negative force in their endeavor to achieve high productivity for the organization, job satisfaction for employees, and feelings of achievement and self-worth for themselves. This view of unions may be incomplete and inaccurate. Supervisors should not forget that, while the existence of a union may make their jobs more complex, in many ways it also makes their jobs easier. When a union is present, the company must examine its own personnel management objectives, policies, procedures, and practices, and it must communicate them to employees. The union, especially through the steward, can serve as an additional means for keeping in touch with employee attitudes and the state of employee morale. Unions also provide supervisors with an additional channel through which to communicate management policies and practices to workers. This is especially helpful in large organizations.

While unions are usually associated with restriction of output, delay of decisions, and so forth, they can be a valuable aid in increasing productivity and implementing change. Union leaders and union members are employees, too. Their loyalty to the organization is not necessarily diminished or diverted by the presence of a union. Management, in carrying out its leadership responsibilities, for the most part determines the type of role a union plays in the company.

SUMMARY

Although labor unions constitute only about 22 percent of the total civilian labor force, membership is concentrated among blue-collar workers in strategic industries. Unions exercise considerable influence in making government policy decisions. They also have great economic power in negotiating with the management of individual firms.

Workers join unions to satisfy their major needs. Unions are most effective in enabling them to satisfy their safety and social needs. They help satisfy the self-esteem and self-actualization needs of a smaller, but very influential, number of employees.

Managers typically are critical of the philosophy, objectives, demands, and tactics of unions. They are reluctant to share power with union leaders and members. They feel that unions are "outsiders" and that unions therefore have no place in their organizations. They believe that unions reduce efficiency and flexibility and create unnecessary conflict. Their most common approach to unions is that of accommodation.

The federal government undertook regulation of the collective-bargaining process in 1935 with the passage of the National Labor Relations Act, which established the right of employees to organize and bargain collectively through representatives of their own choosing. This act was amended twice, with the passage of the Labor-Management Relations Act of 1947 and the Labor-Management Reporting and Disclosure Act of 1959.

The adjustment to working with a labor union is difficult for most managers. Negotiating the first contract is a trying experience for them. Learning to accept the principle of negotiation in making decisions about people is also difficult for most managers. The behavior of first-line supervisors both before and after the arrival of a union is a critical factor in determining the quality of union-management relations in a company.

The collective agreement establishes the basic relationship between management, union leaders, and employees. It establishes policies, procedures, and practices for almost every aspect of the management of employees in the bargaining unit. The first-line supervisors are also influential in the day-to-day administration of the contract. Their principal contact with the union is through the steward. It is important that managers, especially first-line supervisors, establish a good work relationship with the union steward.

DISCUSSION QUESTIONS

1. Among what workers and in what industries are unions the strongest? Why have unions experienced considerable difficulty in organizing white-collar workers?

2. Why do workers join unions?

3. How do managers typically feel about unions? Do you agree with them? Why, or why not?

4. Why are first-line supervisors important in achieving good union-management relations? Why is the position of first-line supervisors difficult in unionized plants?

5. What personnel management policies and procedures might be affected by union-management negotiations and the resulting collective agreement?

6. What are some of the problems associated with administering an agreement after negotiations have been completed and the agreement has been signed by both parties?

7. What is a *shop steward*? What are the functions of a steward? Why is the steward important in determining the quality of union-management relationships?

CASE 17-1.   A Union at Blair?

Ronald Boles, a member of the staff of the Bureau of Labor Relations of Midwestern State University, has undertaken a study of a union-organizing campaign currently under way at the Blair Lamp and Fixture Company. His research is part of the bureau's study of the quality of employee relations in the state. He is conducting a series of interviews with representatives of both the employees who have organized the campaign and the members of management.

The Blair Lamp and Fixture Company normally employs about two hundred persons in manufacturing, maintenance, and warehousing. About fifty of these employees are women. Most of these workers are semiskilled or unskilled, except for seven maintenance craftspersons and eight production technicians. Production is subject to rather wide seasonal, as well as cyclical, fluctuations. At the time of the organizing campaign, forty persons are on layoff.

The following conversations have been drawn from notes made during interviews.

Henry Temple (union president and production assembler):   The plant is long overdue for unionization. We've been pushed around by supervisors, the sales manager, and even Bob Blair [President of the company] ever since the company landed that big contract with the United Furniture Company five years ago.

Boles: What do you mean by "pushed around"?

Temple: All we ever hear is "production, production, production." Last year they even hired a young kid out of college to speed up production. He runs around all day with a stopwatch and one of those new calculators timing how long it takes us to make every motion we make. He even tells us how to do our work. That's pretty hard to take if you've been around here for twenty years like some of us.

George Swanson (union vice-president and shipping clerk):   On top of that, we have some of our people with many years of service on layoff while five friends of the plant superintendent with only about two years' service are still on the job. Those long-service people have earned the right to work, and we're not going to stand for it.

Has anyone told you about the three women who got promoted about six months ago? They had only been here about a year or two but were promoted over some people who had been here for many years.

Boles: Were these women better qualified?

Swanson: Hell, no. They know how to swing the hips, that's all. There are at least eight other women and five men who can do the job as well, or better, and who have longer service.

Boles: Does pay have anything to do with your current organizing campaign?

Kenneth Frye (maintenance electrician in charge of organizing the maintenance crew): It's all those pay problems that will win the election for us next week.[1] This is the lowest-paying company in town. Management is continually saying to us that competition is tough. They keep talking about foreign competition. When they don't talk about that, they talk about having to move south to reduce labor costs. Hell, we're only about twenty-five cents over the minimum wage. That makes us about 20 percent lower than other companies. We need another seventy-five cents just to catch up.

Even worse, some of the pay rates around here are really crazy. I know that there are some people in the plant who are getting more money than the rest of us. It's not what you know, but who you know that counts around here.

Boles: Anything else?

Temple: Ron, let me tell you about supervision. You would think that these foremen had no idea what it's like to be a laborer. They yell and bark orders like top sergeants. There's one out there in the plant who starts every order with, "While you're leaning on that machine, why don't you ———?" Now you know that that's no way to talk to a person. We're entitled to a little respect out here, and by God we're going to get it.

Mr. Blair tells us that the company can't afford to pay us decent wages, but you ought to see how he and the rest of management live it up—chauffeured Cadillac, condominium in Florida, the whole works. Would you believe that top management goes to a resort in Canada every summer for one week on a so-called planning trip? However, we don't really care how they spend their money, just so we get ours, too.

Frye: We need a union, but I hope that we can keep it independent. I've been a member of one of the big international craft unions, but I don't like their bosses, the politics, and everything else that goes with a big union. But we'll go that route if management forces us to. There are a couple of outside unions that would love to move in.

We need a union steward who can stand up to management. We have nobody to listen to our complaints—and we have a lot of them. Incidentally, working conditions are not good here, either. This is the dirtiest shop I've ever worked in. Nobody listens to us around here, except maybe that new personnel man, but I don't think he can do anything. The president decides everything.

---

[1]The National Labor Relations Board will conduct an election which will give these employees an opportunity to vote on whether or not they wish to be represented by a union.

[Boles has also met separately and individually with several members of management to discuss the employees' organizing campaign.]

Boles: Mr. Blair, why do you think your employees are attempting to organize a union?

Robert Blair (president): It's mostly outside agitators. They are always hanging around trying to stir up our people. If you were to go into the bar down the street right now, you would find one or two organizers haranguing our employees about what a lousy place this is to work. There is probably one out at the plant gate now, too. They never leave us alone.

Boles: In other words, you believe that it is strictly a matter of outside agitation.

Blair: Well, I know that there are a few union sympathizers in the plant, too. But they are the people who don't want to work but who want to make big money. I just don't understand their problem. We do our best by them. Competition is keen, however. We need high production and we need to keep our costs down.

Boles: Do you think that it is only a matter of money?

Blair: Well, from time to time I hear rumors about foremen who supposedly have told some loafer to "shape up or ship out." But we treat our people well. We give them a two-week vacation every year; we give them free hospitalization insurance; we even give them time off to attend a funeral. I just don't understand what all the complaints are about.

Charles Sharp (production manager): I'd say that Bob was a little generous in his comments to you about our foremen. I came here a year ago from another company. I can only say that we have some pretty rough characters out there. I've been getting together with them once a week for an hour to try to get them to change. A couple of the old-timers out there are living in the Dark Ages. Maybe you can tell me what I should do with my foremen.

Henry Taylor (personnel manager): Chuck is right about our foremen. I came at the same time he did, but Bob still doesn't seem to trust me. I think that deep down he knows we should be changing—that's why he hired us, but he doesn't really know how to do it. We need to improve the leadership skills of all our operating managers. I'm afraid that the union might win the election next week.

QUESTIONS

1. Why are the production, maintenance, and warehouse workers interested in a union? What unsatisfied needs are they expressing in this organizing campaign?

2. Comment on the opinions expressed by management personnel.

3. If the opinions and feelings of the employees interviewed by Ron Boles are typical, what would you predict about the results of the forthcoming representation election?

18

EFFECTIVE GRIEVANCE PROCEDURES

LEARNING OBJECTIVES

This chapter discusses effective grievance procedures in both nonunion and unionized work groups. After you have read this chapter, you will

1. Know the characteristics of an effective grievance procedure
2. Know how a grievance procedure in a unionized work group functions
3. Know how a grievance procedure in a nonunion group functions
4. Know how to prevent grievances
5. Know how to resolve disputes
6. Know why keeping records concerning grievances is important

Grievances seem to be an inevitable consequence of organizational life. However, the disruptive consequences that follow attempts by supervisors to ignore or suppress them are not inevitable. Sensitive and experienced supervisors do not feel threatened by them; instead they seek out grievances and attempt to resolve them before they get out of hand. This can be a very time-consuming and frustrating responsibility, especially for first-line supervisors, who are usually the first in management to hear and adjudicate grievances; it is also toward them that many of the grievances seem to be directed. As difficult as this responsibility may be to carry out, it is important that it be managed with great skill and patience.

A distinction is often drawn between a complaint and a grievance. A complaint refers to any feeling of dissatisfaction, injury, or injustice concerning any aspect of the work relationship. Most complaints are taken care of informally by superiors in the normal course of working with their subordinates. In the language of employee relations, a grievance is a complaint that has been formally submitted in writing to a supervisor, or sometimes to a union steward if the company is unionized. The distinction between a complaint and a grievance is a fine one. A complaint becomes a grievance when an employee feels that an unresolved problem is so serious that he or she seeks to have it settled under the formal procedures established for that purpose. Again, if the company is unionized, either the employee or the union may file a grievance under the terms of the collective agreement. Some grievances develop from a strong feeling of having been ignored, overridden, or dismissed without due consideration by a member of management; others arise out of differing interpretations of a personnel policy or procedure; and still others result from differing interpretations of the terms of a collective agreement or from the alleged violation of an employment standard.

Grievances usually start as minor irritations. If supervisors enjoy an open and friendly relationship with their subordinates, the dissatisfied employee will usually discuss his or her dissatisfaction with them. Most of these small problems are readily resolved. Sometimes the problems do not end there, however. On occasion, supervisors are unable to satisfy the expectations of a complaining employee either because the supervisor lacks the authority to make a decision or because the supervisor believes that the employee's request is unreasonable or contrary to established company policy. Under such circumstances, dissatisfactions sometimes develop into formal grievances.

CHARACTERISTICS OF AN EFFECTIVE
GRIEVANCE PROCEDURE

If a grievance procedure in either a union or a nonunion situation is to be effective, it must possess certain characteristics. First, it must be simple. It must be easily understood by both employees and supervisors so that the mechanics of the process will not interfere with its implementation.

Second, it should give prompt action in every case. An employee who voices a complaint or files a grievance feels aggrieved. If the procedure is dragged out over a long period of time, the employee is likely to become frustrated and dissatisfied. The original problem may be a minor one, but if an answer is not forthcoming, the importance of the matter becomes exaggerated in the employee's mind. Unreasonable delay itself becomes the source of a grievance.

Third, the plan should be definite. Employees should know that the initiation of a grievance will result in certain actions on the part of management. If the procedure is definite, there is less chance that a grievance will be sidetracked somewhere in the organization before a satisfactory answer is found. If responsibility is clearly fixed at all levels of supervision, management representatives know the extent of their authority as well as their limitations. When supervisors know that their decisions are accepted as an important part of the total process, they are more likely to come up with constructive solutions.

Fourth, the entire procedure should be reduced to writing. Many grievance procedures in nonunion work groups are not included in the policy handbook for employees. Employees are supposed to know that they can bring their "problems" to their supervisors at any time! A written statement makes the procedure more definite and less subject to misinterpretation.

Fifth, employees must be assured that filing a grievance will not bring retaliation by their supervisors. One of the most prevalent fears among nonunion work groups is that if they register a grievance, they will be discriminated against by their supervisors. This fear must be overcome if the grievance procedure is to be effective. It can only be overcome through the experiences of employees who have had grievances settled through the process and have not suffered retaliation at the hands of their bosses.

Sixth, a staff specialist from the personnel department should be available to assist managers at all levels in their attempts to adjudicate the grievance. In nonunion work groups, the personnel department is often called upon to assist employees also by informing them of their rights to file a grievance and lending them technical assistance in preparing and filing the grievance.

292

The Personnel Department. Most companies require that their supervisors seek assistance in processing grievances from labor relations specialists in the personnel department. This is important for several reasons:

1. Many grievances involve not only the individual employee and the supervisor but also the entire work group or even the entire organization.

2. The supervisor's decision must be consistent with company policies, terms of the collective agreement, and prior management decisions.

3. Decisions become precedents for future decisions, and both employees and supervisors look to prior decisions in guiding their behavior.

4. Labor relations specialists can provide valuable assistance to operating managers in negotiating with employee representatives.

GRIEVANCE PROCEDURES IN UNIONIZED WORK GROUPS

Grievance procedures in unionized work groups differ substantially from those in nonunion work groups. First, the grievance procedure in unionized groups is part of a contractual agreement between the parties. Second, the union serves as an advocate in processing and negotiating employees' grievances. Third, the union can bring considerable power to bear in arriving at a settlement of a grievance. Fourth, most collective agreements provide for the arbitration of those disputes that the union and management are unable to resolve by themselves.

Grievances and the Union Steward

Union officers and stewards are elected to their positions. Unions are political institutions, and officers hold their positions only so long as they satisfy the expectations of union members and are reelected. These leaders often feel a need to prove (often shortly before a union election) that they are vigorously representing their constituents' interests. Furthermore, shortly before the negotiation of a new union contract, union leaders may feel a strong need both to build cohesion within the membership and to indicate union solidarity to company negotiators. The union may, in both of these situations, make a concerted drive among employees to learn of their dissatisfactions and to present them aggressively to management. While the number of grievances received by a supervisor is often used as a gauge of that supervisor's leadership qualities, in times such as these the number and type of grievances filed might be a better representation of the internal state of union affairs than of the quality of the supervisor's relationship with his or her subordinates. And under these circumstances, the union steward may be more interested in prolonging the unrest created by considerable numbers of unresolved grievances than in negotiating a settlement.

A major determinant as to whether or not a minor problem will result in a formal grievance is the type of relationship that the supervisor enjoys with the union steward. On occasion this relationship is an uncomfortable one because the steward is unable to handle the power inherent in that position. On the whole, however, stewards are reasonable people who attempt to strike a reasonable balance between their loyalty to the company and their loyalty to the union. A supervisor who treats the steward with respect usually discovers that his or her relationship with the union and the ability to resolve grievances at the first step of the grievance procedure will be enhanced considerably.

The Grievance Procedure

A grievance procedure is written into almost every collective agreement to provide a set of rules under which disputes can be settled in an orderly manner without an open conflict. The grievance procedure usually involves four steps:

1. The employee talks with his or her immediate supervisor. (Many contracts stipulate that the employee may bring a complaint to either the supervisor *or* the union steward.) If the employee goes to the supervisor, the supervisor may discuss the problem without the steward being present, however. (The supervisor should request that the steward be present if the problem involves the union or any part of the contract.) If the employee takes his or her complaint to the steward, the steward may present it to the supervisor either orally or more formally as a written grievance, with or without the employee being present. (The supervisor should request that the employee be present for a discussion of the problem; but the supervisor cannot insist that the employee be present, even though this is always preferable.) If the parties cannot resolve the problem, it is reduced to writing and becomes a formal grievance, which may then be appealed.

2. If the grievance is appealed, it moves to the second step where the chief steward, or business agent, of the union enters the proceedings along with the superintendent or other designated middle management of the company. They attempt to negotiate a satisfactory solution to the problem.

3. If the company and the union representatives cannot agree in the second step, the grievance moves to the third step. This is the last opportunity for settling the problem within the decision-making structures of both the company and the union. The union executive committee or grievance committee negotiates with the appropriate top-level company representatives, including the plant manager, vice-president for production, or vice-president for personnel.

Almost all grievances are resolved through negotiation between management and union representatives. A few, however, remain unresolved. About

97 percent of all collective agreements provide that unresolved cases may be submitted to arbitration.

4. Arbitration is typically the final step in the grievance procedure. The union and management, during contract negotiations, agree that disputes that cannot be settled to their mutual satisfaction during the first three steps of the grievance procedure may be submitted to an impartial outsider who will hear their testimony and render a decision that will be final and binding upon both parties.

The typical grievance procedure in a unionized company is illustrated in Figure 18–1.

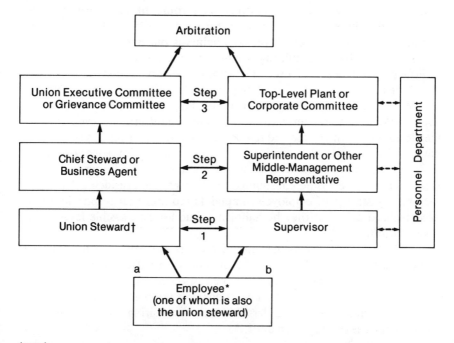

*a or b.
†Subordinate of the supervisor,
  except in capacity of union steward.

Figure 18-1   Typical Grievance Procedure in a Unionized Company

GRIEVANCE PROCEDURES IN NONUNION WORK GROUPS

Over three-fourths of the labor force are members of nonunion work groups. Whether the type of work involved be office, shop, or sales, these employees need an effective means for communicating their dissatisfactions to their supervisors. However, managers of such groups often believe that everyone belongs to "one big happy family" and that either their subordinates do not have any complaints or that those subordinates who do have complaints are troublemakers.

Open-Door Policy. Some managers attempt to handle employee complaints by announcing that their "door is always open" to anyone who wishes to talk with them. This method of adjusting complaints has several weaknesses and usually breaks down in practice.

First, few employees possess the courage required to confront middle and top managers in their offices (even if they are able to get past these managers' secretaries). Members of middle and top management usually underestimate the social gulf separating them from rank-and-file employees.

Second, these executives are frequently inaccessible at the time a problem arises. Listening to employee complaints is but one of their many responsibilities. The complaint that seems urgent to an employee often seems of little consequence to an executive who, at the very moment an employee is seeking an appointment, is feeling pressured by a major planning, policy, or strategy problem involving productivity and profits. Top-level executives live, think, and act at an entirely different organizational level. It is an inefficient use of their time and talent for them to perform tasks that can be handled by lower-level executives. For example, the investigation of the facts in a human relation problem is often a laborious and time-consuming task—generally too time consuming for a busy vice-president. The satisfactory adjustment of employee complaints requires that responsibility be decentralized and that they be handled at the lowest possible level in the organization.

Third, when top management encourages employees to bypass their immediate supervisor, the status of that supervisor suffers. He or she finds it increasingly difficult to command the respect of subordinates. Furthermore, supervisors ordinarily look with disfavor upon anyone who bypasses them. Subordinates usually understand this; and fearing reprisal, they hesitate to make use of the "open door."

MS. JONES HAD A GRIEVANCE

Let us examine Ms. Jones's grievance, which occurred in a nonunion work group having a formal grievance procedure. Her grievance is especially interesting because she eventually appealed her case to the president of the company.

Ms. Jones worked as a statistical clerk in the home office of a large insurance company. She was an excellent worker and had been with the company for about three years. Her supervisor spoke with her recently about spending too much time during working hours in conversation with employees of another department and also about eating lunch with the employees of the other department. He told her that visiting friends in other departments to talk about personal matters on company time was contrary to company rules. He also said that she should not eat lunch with employees of the other department, since the supervisor of the other department objected to the practice.

Ms. Jones stated that she had a number of friends in the other department and that she liked to eat her lunch with them. Since there was no rule about where employees were to have lunch, she had assumed that she was free to eat with people of her own choice. She stated further that she had spent working time on the other floor because she was captain of one of the women's bowling teams, and she had to collect money each week for the team. She pointed out that this practice had been accepted for many years, and that other women also collected money during working hours.

After hearing her side of the story, the supervisor made the following decisions: (1) that Ms. Jones should make arrangements to eat her lunch in her own department rather than with her friends in the other department, and (2) that she should discontinue visiting the other department during working hours.

At the end of this interview Ms. Jones stated that she was not satisfied with the decisions, and she requested that she be permitted to discuss the matter with the division manager. The supervisor said he would arrange an appointment as soon as possible, which he did.

When the situation had been explained to the division manager, he called the personnel manager, explained the problem, and asked him to sit in on the interview with the employee. The division manager then stated that he agreed with the supervisor and that Ms. Jones should comply with the instructions she had previously received. Ms. Jones was not satisfied with the decision because it seemed to be unfair and arbitrary to her. She indicated that she wished to appeal the matter to the president.

The matter was taken to the president by the division manager, the department manager, and the personnel manager. During this discussion both sides of the case were again explained in detail. The president pointed out that there was no policy governing the collection of money for the women's bowling team or for any other employee activity. He directed the personnel manager to make an immediate recommendation on this matter so that all employees would be treated alike. He also pointed out that employees had never been required to eat lunch in their own departments, and that the young lady could continue to have lunch with her friends.

The department manager conveyed the president's decision to Ms. Jones. The personnel manager was present at this interview in an advisory capacity. Ms. Jones was satisfied with the final disposition of her grievance.

The president asked the personnel manager to develop a policy relative to the collection of money for employee activities in the future.

PREVENTING GRIEVANCES

Some disputes are unavoidable. Organizations bring together individuals with different personalities, interests, and goals; and these individuals are expected to reconcile their differences with each other and with the organization in order that the organization may achieve its goals. Tensions and frustrations are inevitable. Managers and supervisors can forestall some of the complaints and grievances that might be expected to develop and can minimize the impact of many others that occur. Techniques for preventing complaints and grievances include the following:

1. Selection and placement. Employees should be assigned to jobs for which they are suited, and which will therefore be less frustrating to them. Sometimes a job can be simplified, enriched, or otherwise changed to match the abilities, interests, and skills of the employee. Individuals should not be promoted to jobs for which they are not qualified and in which they are not interested. For example, the best mechanic may not make the best supervisor.

2. Coaching and training. Supervisors should be sensitive to the training needs of their subordinates. Many frustrations occur because workers are unable to perform the work satisfactorily. They sometimes perform unsatisfactorily because they do not understand the organization's and the supervisor's expectations of them in terms of both job performance and personal behavior.

3. Communication. Supervisors can prevent many grievances by listening to what their subordinates are *really* feeling and saying. It is important that they communicate policies and rules; it is equally important that they learn how their subordinates perceive their work, their supervision, and the company. Some companies utilize formal attitude surveys to determine how employees feel about their jobs. Employees are asked to fill out questionnaires anonymously. These questionnaires enable management to keep in touch with worker sentiments and to bypass communication blocks within the organization. Such attitude surveys are no substitute for open two-way person-to-person discussions between subordinate and supervisor, however.

4. A clinical approach to grievances. Grievances may be approached either legalistically or clinically. The clinical approach means that supervisors will try to understand why the employee or employees are expressing the dissatisfaction. Does the cause lie with the individual or individuals, within the policies and practices of the organization, or within the behavior of the immediate supervisor or other members of management? This approach also stimulates the supervisor to ask how the situation might be resolved to treat everyone equitably and to prevent its recurrence. The clinical approach is concerned with solving problems rather than with fighting battles.

RESOLVING GRIEVANCES

To help ensure that complaints and grievances will be settled to the satisfaction of all concerned, the supervisor should observe the following problem-solving procedure:

1. Get the facts.

   a. Talk with the individuals concerned. Observe the rules for face-to-face communication (see Chapter 11). A supervisor's anger and hostility are frequently aroused by either the content of the employee's complaint or the manner in which it is expressed. It is important that supervisors remain cool, friendly, and problem-oriented. They should not allow their anger or other negative feelings to impair their ability to listen to those who are expressing their own negative feelings.

   b. Review applicable company policies, procedures, practices, and customs. They set the framework within which any decision must be made.

   c. In unionized situations, check the collective agreement and decisions on any other similar grievances previously settled within the company.

   d. Check the records and work history of the individuals, where appropriate.

   e. Consult with the immediate supervisor and the labor relations specialist in the personnel department to determine the plant-wide implications of the complaint and to obtain help in handling the problem.

2. Define the problem. Complaints and grievances often are not what they at first appear to be. For example, an employee's complaint about wages might reflect the fact that the company's rates are too low or that one or more jobs are not properly classified. On the other hand, the complaint could also be an expression of frustration over some personal problem, such as inability to pay off a large amount of personal debt. Or the complaint might be that individual's way of expressing unhappiness with the work situation, such as lack of recognition for excellent performance, failure to receive an anticipated promotion, or boredom with a routine and unchallenging job. The supervisor must assemble the facts, evaluate the feelings and opinions expressed by the dissatisfied individual, weigh all the evidence, and finally make a judgment as to the cause and nature of the employee's dissatisfaction.

3. Seek alternate solutions. Most problems have several possible answers or solutions. Some solutions are better than others, and sometimes there is even "one best solution." In seeking a solution to a grievance, the supervisor should first explore as many alternatives as possible. It is at this point that discussing the grievance with other supervisors and with the labor relations specialist can be especially productive. Having identified several possible solutions, the supervisor should analyze the feasibility of implementing each. The following factors should be considered:

    a. Company policies and procedures

    b. Federal, state, and local laws

    c. Collective agreement

    d. History of collective bargaining and the policies and practices of the labor union

    e. Past practice

    f. Costs

    g. Effect on the morale and expectations of both management and non-management personnel

    h. Future plans

    i. Personalities of individuals involved

    j. Community relations

    k. The general social, political, and economic "climate"

    l. Short-run and long-run considerations

4. Make a decision. After analyzing the alternative courses of action, the supervisor must select the one that will be most satisfactory under all the circumstances. The decision should be fair to everyone concerned and consistent with both past decisions and anticipated future decisions.

While not acting hastily, the decision should be made and communicated promptly. If the supervisor or company is in error, it should be admitted graciously. If the employee's grievance is unfounded or if the company does not agree with the employee's point of view, it should be explained considerately.

5. Follow through. Having made the decision, the supervisor should take prompt action to remedy the causes of the complaint or grievance. In some instances the supervisor must inform his or her supervisor that the employee or union is appealing the grievance.

A NOTE ON KEEPING RECORDS

When dealing with grievance procedures, supervisors should keep full and accurate records of their personnel management activities and decisions. Federal, state, and local laws with respect to hire, promotion, transfer, training, discipline, safety, health, and retirement of employees require the maintenance of accurate records. The collective agreement establishes policies, procedures, and standards which the company agrees to follow and maintain. Supervisors are often required to explain or defend to government agencies, union stewards, arbitrators—and also their bosses—actions taken and decisions made with respect to subordinates. For example, supervisors may be required to prove that they did not discriminate with respect to hire, promotion, or pay on the basis of sex, race, or age; that they did not violate the safety and health standards required under the Occupational Safety and Health Act or the collective agreement; that they did not violate the standards of the Wage and Hour Law, the National Labor Relations Act, or a host of other laws.

Supervisors also require good employee records in order to counsel subordinates and make a variety of administrative decisions concerning such matters as compensation, promotion, and training.

Finally, it is important that supervisors keep records of understandings, agreements, and decisions made with respect to both informal complaints and formal grievances. They should keep records of interviews, including the topic discussed and the agreements entered into. Decisions and agreements become precedents. Sometimes grievances are appealed and are even submitted to arbitration. It is difficult to explain or defend an action without adequate records. While the personnel department maintains a file on each employee, only the employee's superior has all the information necessary for taking action and making decisions.

SUMMARY

Grievances seem to be an inevitable consequence of people working together in an organization. Most grievances start as minor irritations that are successfully resolved by the supervisor and the subordinate. When the supervisor is unable to satisfy the expectations of a subordinate, a formal grievance may result. The quality of the relationship between a supervisor and the union officers, especially the union steward, affects the number and type of grievances with which a supervisor must contend. Sometimes, however, the number and type filed by employees and the union are determined by power struggles and other internal union problems over which the supervisor has no control.

While grievance procedures are desirable for all work groups, they are most prevalent where employees are unionized. Most collective agreements provide for the arbitration of grievances that cannot be settled through collective bargaining.

A grievance procedure should (1) be simple, easy to understand, and easy to administer; (2) provide for prompt action; (3) be definite and clearly define the responsibilities of all parties; (4) provide for reducing the grievance to writing if it is not settled at the lowest step; (5) assure employees that there will be no retaliation for having filed a grievance; and (6) provide for expert assistance from the personnel department.

A good problem-solving procedure to observe in adjusting grievances is as follows: (1) get the facts; (2) define the problem; (3) seek alternative solutions; (4) make a decision; and (5) follow through on the decision to remedy the cause of the problem.

Ideally, complaints are resolved before they become formal grievances; and grievances, once filed, are adjudicated to the satisfaction of all parties at the first step of the grievance procedure. Adjusting grievances is one of the major responsibilities of every manager. However, because of their position in their organizations, first-line supervisors devote more of their time to this activity than do their superiors.

DISCUSSION QUESTIONS

1. What is a *complaint*? What is a *grievance*? At what point does a complaint become a grievance? Given an example of each.

2. What are the characteristics of an effective grievance procedure? Why is each important?

3. What role does the personnel department play in the grievance procedure? How can this department help the manager with a grievance to process?

4. What role does a union steward play in the grievance procedure? How can the steward make the handling of a grievance either easier or more difficult than normal?

5. What steps are involved in a grievance procedure? Can you describe how a grievance is processed up through the various steps? What is *arbitration*? Why is arbitration a major step in a grievance procedure?

6. Why is a grievance procedure important in a nonunion work group? How does a grievance procedure in a nonunion work group differ from that in a unionized work group?

7. What is an "open-door policy"? What are the difficulties in using it effectively?

8. How can an organization minimize grievances?

9. What are the steps to follow in a problem-resolving procedure for resolving grievances?

10. Why is it important that a supervisor maintain good records on the performance and behavior of his or her subordinates?

CASE 18-1.   Who Vacations on the Fourth of July?

On January 4, 1976, Todd Archer was recalled to his regular job as a detail scheduling clerk in Section A of the production planning department at the Fairless Works of the United States Steel Corporation. In a reduction in force in 1975, he had been transferred to Section B of that department as an assistant scheduling clerk. While in Section B, he was assigned the four weeks that he had requested for vacation during 1976: weeks beginning July 4, September 5, November 21, and December 19.

At the time that Archer was transferred back to Section A in his regular job, the Section A vacation schedule had already been established. Two other employees, one of whom was junior to Archer in duration of employment, had also selected the week beginning July 4. Archer's supervisor refused his request to keep his July 4 vacation and told him that he would have to select another week. The other three weeks remained unchanged. The plant superintendent and the plant manager supported the supervisor's position. Archer filed a grievance requesting that he be granted the week of July 4 as vacation.

Archer and the union argued that recalled employees had always obtained their vacation choices in the past on the basis of seniority. Since he had longer service than the other employees, he claimed that he was entitled to the week he chose. The union cited Section 12(B) of the collective agreement, which includes three principles to be observed in establishing or changing an employee's vacation schedule:

1. Vacations will be granted at times most desired by the employees so far as practicable;

2. Longer service employees will be given preference in choice of vacation periods; and

3. The final right to allot vacation periods (and to change such allotments) is reserved exclusively to the Company in order to assure orderly operation of the plants.

The supervisor and his superiors argued that it would be impractical to let Archer "bump" the junior man out of his vacation because it would create a "domino" effect resulting in a serious threat to orderly operations. The collective agreement requires only that senior employees be given preference "so far as practicable." They contended that the company must limit to two the number of detail scheduling clerks who may be on vacation during any week from Section A; therefore, it was not possible to accommodate Archer's request for vacation the week of July 4.

QUESTIONS

1. How important is seniority in Archer's vacation problem?

2. What is meant by "so far as practicable" in the collective agreement?

3. The company reserves the final right to allocate vacations, under the collective agreement, "in order to assure orderly operation of the plants." How would you apply that phrase to this case?

4. If you had been Archer's supervisor, what would you have done?

5. If you were an impartial arbitrator, how would you decide this case?

CASE 18-2. The Automated Fare Boxes

Prior to the spring of 1976, the bus company in the city of Racine, Wisconsin, was privately owned and operated. The company used several mini-buses to carry passengers. In the spring of 1976, the city of Racine purchased the bus company and started operating it as a public carrier. It hired Taylor Enterprises, Inc., to manage the bus system. Shortly thereafter, several large coaches were purchased, and passenger fares doubled from fifty thousand fares a month to one hundred thousand per month.

To accommodate this increased ridership, the company purchased new automatic fare boxes, which are much more complex than the manual boxes that had previously been used. The difference in the degree of sophistication between the fare boxes is partly reflected by the fact that while the old boxes cost about $40, the new automatic models cost $1,400.

Since the introduction of the automatic fare boxes, the company has required all of its drivers to fill out a "run report" at the end of each scheduled run. The report is filled out by the driver while the bus is stationary prior to the start of a new run. The driver records the time of day, the amount of money deposited in the box, and the number of tokens accumulated. This information is obtained by looking at the meters on the fare box and then recording the required information on the "run report."

THE DRIVERS' COMPLAINT

The bus drivers claim that their jobs have been changed as a result of being required to fill out "run reports," and their union—the Teamsters, Chauffeurs & Helpers, Local 43—filed a grievance in their behalf. The drivers claim that the information collected for the "run report" constitutes a survey, and that they therefore are entitled to an additional twenty-five cents per hour when they conduct surveys for the company, as provided in a memorandum of understanding dated November 28, 1975, which stated that "when surveys are required, the driver shall receive an additional twenty-five cents per hour."

THE COMPANY'S REPLY

The company disagrees with the drivers. It contends that the drivers are not conducting a survey and that, instead, they are merely recording the information that is collected on the fare boxes. The drivers are not required to question any passengers; they are not even required to talk to passengers in reading the meters on the fare boxes and recording the data on the "run report."

The company points out that most other transit systems require their drivers to record such information as part of their normal job duties. These drivers receive no extra compensation for completing such reports.

Finally, the company argues that the contract stipulates that the company has the right to "introduce new or improved methods," to "change existing methods and to determine the methods, means, and personnel by which such transit operations are to be conducted." The company has the right to require drivers to fill out the "run reports" as a part of their normal job duties without extra compensation.

QUESTIONS

1. Has the company changed the job of bus driver?

2. In comparing the old job with the new one, does it warrant an increased rate of pay? If so, how much?

3. What is the significance of the statement that other transit systems require bus drivers to complete "run reports" as a normal part of their job duties?

4. How would you decide this case? Explain your reasoning.

VI

The Supervisor's Personal
and Career Development

19

TIME: THE NONRENEWABLE RESOURCE

LEARNING OBJECTIVES

This chapter discusses the effective use of personal time. After you have read this chapter, you will

1. Be able to assess the way you spend your time
2. Know how to use a specific method for setting priorities and scheduling work
3. Know how to conduct time-efficient group meetings
4. Know how to reduce interruptions in your workday
5. Know how to read more efficiently
6. Know how to troubleshoot your time problems by using the chart provided

Time is one of our most valuable nonrenewable resources. It cannot be stored; it cannot be amassed. Time allowed to pass without serving any purpose is a resource lost forever. To manage time does not necessarily mean to use it to work for profit. Time devoted to rest, relaxation, recreation, hobbies, and other noncareer pursuits can be as rewarding as the pursuit of the career itself. In fact, for most persons, a balanced commitment to both career and noncareer pursuits is necessary for a rich and satisfying life.

The authors hope that you will become conscious of the value of your time and that you will manage its use with the same care that you manage your monetary, material, and human resources. The personal payoff for managing time effectively is increased productivity, improved performance, better use of abilities and talents, and the opportunity to engage in new and rewarding career and noncareer pursuits.

Although most of us would agree that the effective use of time is important, good time management is critical for the effective supervisor. Without the ability to manage his or her own time, the supervisor will encounter substantial problems in finding time to supervise others. Moreover, poor management of time on the job will handicap the supervisor in managing the time available for family life and noncareer pursuits.

MANAGEMENT OF TIME: UTILIZING THE RESOURCE

Table 19-1 lists eight essentials for effective time management. The failure to do the things outlined in the table results in an ineffective use of time. Note that of all the causes of time inefficiencies, only a few result from sources that the supervisor *cannot* control. Stated positively, the supervisor

---

Table 19-1. Essentials for Effective Management of Time

1. Know how your time is spent
2. Set priorities
3. Schedule your time realistically
4. Delegate effectively
5. Lead meetings effectively
6. Control interruptions
7. Manage your reading load
8. Improve communications skills

---

controls the bulk of causes for difficulties associated with time usage (i.e., setting priorities, scheduling, delegating responsibilities, conducting meetings, improving reading and communications skills, and so forth). The following sections will help you become more aware of how much time you have, how you use it, and how you can make decisions regarding its effective use.

How You Spend Your Time

"What do I spend my time doing?" Most supervisors cannot answer that question accurately. They have only a vague or faulty knowledge of the allocation of their time resource. But one thing they are certain of is that they do not have enough time; they feel that they are overworked. Significantly, almost all believe that, once they know how they spend their time, they will be able to get more done in less time and with less effort. In other words, almost *everyone* can improve his or her effectiveness by analyzing time allocations and making appropriate changes.

In assessing the way you spend your time, examine the supervisor time audit form in Figure 19-1. This form will help you audit your time during a typical week. Usually, the supervisor time audit will reveal some rather valuable information about your job. Specifically, it enables you to determine how you spend your time resource; ultimately, it helps specify the demands placed upon you. Knowledge of this is essential for effective supervisory performance.

At thirty-minute intervals throughout the day, the form in Figure 19-1 asks you to specify the activity you are performing (ask yourself, What am I

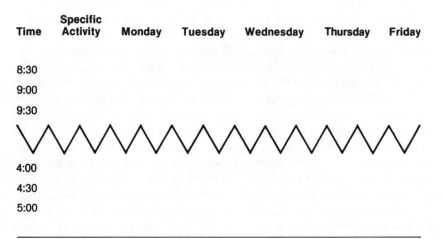

Figure 19-1 Supervisory Time Audit

doing?). After you have written down what you are doing, take this information and analyze it to gain even more insight about yourself and your job. Ask yourself the following questions:

1. Does the way I spend my time reflect my personal and job priorities?
2. Whom do I direct my activities toward?
3. How much time do paperwork and group meetings take?
4. Could I delegate more?
5. What activities do I seem to repeat?
6. What *must* I do well?
7. Do I lose time because I procrastinate?
8. Are there any blank spaces between tasks that could be utilized?
9. Am I performing each task efficiently?

The answers to these questions will not only focus on how you spend your time but also point out what supervisory skills are necessary to perform the job well. Thus the supervisory time audit will help you identify necessary job skills, whether these be technical, decisional, interpersonal, or informational.

The following recommendations will help you increase your efficiency. These recommendations emphasize those areas that the supervisory time audit disclosed as having special significance for you.

Set Priorities and Schedule Work

A supervisor should begin work each day, week, and month with a set of goals and priorities clearly in mind. For example, by planning the week's output on Monday, and then following each day with an assessment of what has been completed to date, the supervisor can begin to organize his or her efforts in such a way that the highest-priority items are accomplished. Try this system: label those absolutely essential items as "three-star" priorities (e.g., meet sales goal for the month); label the second category of items as "two-star" priorities (e.g., update old reports); and label the last category of items as "one-star" priorities (e.g., wash car). Then spend all your time and energy working on "three-star" items. Whatever time is left can be devoted to "two-star" items. Forget the "one-star" items until *all* the two- and three-star items have been completed. Before you complete one job, however, start to think about the next one you will be tackling. In this way you can reduce the time customarily lost in moving from one job to another.

It is important to establish schedules and deadlines that provide for the accomplishment of the essential work. This means that some of the less critical items will be crowded out and simply go undone (as was suggested above). When you stop to think about it, there are usually several things on your schedule each day that will have little consequence if they are *never* completed. A further advantage of this system is that it strikes a major blow at the problem of procrastination. By setting clear goals and establishing schedules and deadlines, major decisions must be made immediately rather than delayed perpetually. Furthermore, if you have the resolve to face up to difficult problems and do not hold yourself to perfectionism as a performance standard, you will have overcome the major causes of procrastination.

There are other good reasons for establishing priorities and determining a specific work schedule. A list of priorities enables supervisors to say no to the requests made of them by subordinates and others. As a result, they avoid taking on many of the obligations and tasks that were initially assigned to subordinates or others. Finally, a schedule and list of priorities help the supervisor avoid the difficulties involved in operating in a climate of crises. "Management by crises" is a direct result of being overworked by an inability to say no. In general, an ability to keep priorities firmly in mind can help a supervisor avoid new obligations that consume much time, but contribute little.

Delegate

We are all familiar with the saying "Let George do it," but most supervisors fail to understand just how vital it is to take that advice to heart. A supervisor must realize that the delegating of responsibilities is important for personal effectiveness and for the development of subordinates. By delegating responsibilities the supervisor is free to spend more time on planning. Delegation also increases the motivation of subordinates by actually making their task more interesting and challenging. Also, supervisors should not talk themselves into believing that merely by working hard they can be more effective. Many a supervisor shoulders the work best done by subordinates and then forces himself or herself to take home the work more properly expected of the subordinates. This is one cause of eight hours of work expanding to fill twelve hours.

The supervisor can become a more effective delegator by using the following suggestions:

1. Express confidence in the general abilities of subordinates.
2. Permit subordinates to make small mistakes but require them to learn (develop) from these mistakes.
3. Avoid a tendency toward perfectionism and the time-consuming overcontrol it brings.
4. Don't be afraid that subordinates will view delegated tasks as "yours" and thus resent your delegating them.

5. Delegate authority commensurate with responsibility.
6. Establish a follow-up procedure to monitor results.

The supervisor who uses these suggestions will not only overcome many problems (real or imaginary) associated with delegation but will be able to delegate more effectively and thereby take the single most important action to make the best use of the available time.

For example, a manager can delegate time-consuming, but essential, tasks to his or her secretary. The secretary can take responsibility for making all sorts of reservations, appointments, phone calls, and so forth, and in encouraging the manager to use a dictating machine rather than write letters out in longhand. Also, a secretary can free a manager from proofreading letters after they have been completed and typed. Fortunately, increasing the responsibilities of the secretary may have positive motivational benefits as well.

Exercise Leadership in Group Tasks and Meetings

Having a schedule for oneself is important, but having a schedule *and* a plan for a group meeting may be even more important, since more persons are involved. Effective use of group meetings requires that a supervisor, acting as a group leader, have an agenda clearly in mind prior to the meeting. Moreover, meetings should be scheduled prior to natural breaks, such as a meal or quitting time, to reduce the tendency to "fill the time available" or to drag on endlessly. Research has shown that effective group leadership results when a person realizes that the role of leader is quite different from that of group member. Specifically, the group leader should help state the problem, summarize the contributions group members have made toward the solution of that problem, and make certain that all group members have an opportunity to speak and inquire as to whether the group has reached a conclusion. Note that these inputs do not require a leader to take a position; instead, the leader is there to help the group reach a conclusion.[1] Finally, since it has been found that groups usually come up with more accurate problem solutions, a good supervisor realizes that it is appropriate to use groups for major decisions in which high-quality solutions are necessary. Where speed is essential, where group commitment is not needed, or where the decision is not crucial, it is not appropriate (from an efficient use of time standpoint) to utilize the group meeting (see Chapter 12, "Supervisory Decision Making").

---

[1] Readers may recognize this as being consistent with the type E leadership style described in Chapter 2.

When conducting a group meeting, there are several rules that summarize many important group leadership concepts:

A. Preparation for meeting

    1. Limit the number of participants to those persons who are needed to reach a decision on the topic confronting the group.

    2. Schedule the meeting properly: (a) allocate time according to the relative importance of each topic, (b) schedule meetings before natural quitting time, such as lunch.

    3. Determine the specific purpose of the meeting in your own mind.

    4. Develop and distribute the agenda in advance.

B. Leading the meeting

    5. Start the meeting on time. Do not wait for latecomers.

    6. Start with the most important item on the agenda. Then stick to the agenda; permit only emergency interruptions.

    7. Be sensitive to hidden agendas and the social-emotional needs of members.

    8. Summarize group progress and restate conclusions to ensure agreement.

    9. Make specific assignments for the next meeting.

    10. End the meeting on time to allow participants to plan their own time effectively.

C. Follow-up meeting

    11. Distribute the minutes or a summary of the proceedings. It is especially important to communicate group decisions to the group members.

By observing these rules, a supervisor will be able to lead meetings effectively.

Interruption Control

The telephone is an essential tool of modern industrial life. But while it is available as a tool to serve us, it governs our lives as well. Most supervisors cannot resist answering phone calls as they arrive. As a result, these people become the slaves of the telephone "master." Not only does the telephone interrupt us, but the time spent conversing with the caller is frequently filled with interesting but irrelevant pleasantries. Thus "phone power" is something a supervisor must understand if he or she is to make efficient use of time.

An added source of interruptions comes from employees. One major cause of employee interruptions is the failure to delegate responsibilities; as a result, employees are required to "touch base" prior to making any decisions on their own. In a different way, a desire to involve everyone in the decision requires frequent consultations with subordinates. Thus, one type of time inefficiency (e.g., lack of delegation) can lead to an additional time inefficiency (i.e., employee interruptions).

An additional source of employee interruptions stems from the commitment to an "open-door policy." While a supervisor's open door conveys a receptivity to passersby, it is used by a fellow supervisor or a subordinate who has nothing to do at the moment and wishes to spend several minutes discussing such nonwork matters as the latest football scores or a newly discovered restaurant. In this way, one person's lack of pressing business has resulted in preventing a second person from completing his or her task. This discussion is not meant to condemn the open-door policy under all circumstances, but supervisors should be aware of the time cost involved in such a policy.

How does a supervisor control these interruptions? The following suggestions should prove helpful. In general, a supervisor should be available for conferences with subordinates during specified hours. One possibility would be to hold the hours from 10:00 A.M. to 3:00 P.M. available for subordinates to inquire about matters that concern them. By reserving the early hours and the last two hours of the day, the supervisor is able to devote an appropriate amount of time to planning and organizing his or her own work.

A secretary's contribution in controlling the manager's interruptions cannot be overestimated. A competent secretary may screen (some authorities say "*should* screen") incoming telephone calls so that the manager is not burdened with low priority interruptions. The secretary can tell such callers that the manager is temporarily unavailable. The manager can return the call at his or her convenience rather than being interrupted continuously by callers. The secretary can provide the same function regarding subordinates and other visitors. In this way the manager retains greater control of his or her time.

Manage Reading and Develop Communication Skills

An obvious solution to the problem of having too much to read is simply not to read so much. Stated plainly, supervisors should be more selective in what they read—they should set reading priorities. To be more selective in your reading, look at a book's table of contents to get a general idea of the topics covered. Then, scan through the book to obtain a better idea of the general subject matter and the author's perspective and style. Finally, read only those sections or chapters that are of interest to you. To reduce the reading load, supervisors should practice the skills of speedreading. The more fundamental speedreading rules include the following:

1. Do not mouth or move your lips while reading.
2. Do not reread words or sections of the text.
3. Read entire phrases rather than individual words—this reduces the number of times your eye focuses on each line of print.
4. Skip the first or second word of each line—use your peripheral vision to comprehend these words.

An additional technique the supervisor may find useful is to read carefully only the introduction or first few pages and the conclusions of a report, article, chapter, or book; then the center section of the publication should be skimmed. For most persons, this will provide a very substantial idea of the content of that publication. By using these and similar techniques, a supervisor can expect to increase his or her reading speed from 300 to 500 percent.[2]

Regarding verbal communication, one of the most effective ways to reduce communications breakdown is to utilize feedback. In applying this technique, a manager should not simply ask subordinates *if* they understood what was said, rather ask them *what* they understood was said. Similarly, it is appropriate for the supervisor to summarize a subordinate's comments to make clear in the supervisor's own mind exactly what the subordinate has conveyed. (Communications problems and their remedies were explored in Chapters 5 and 6.)

TROUBLESHOOTING FOR EFFECTIVE TIME USE

To enable the supervisor to cope with time difficulties, Table 19-2 summarizes the various problems involved in time management, and it serves as a troubleshooting guide in focusing on the major causes and solutions. Table 19-3 provides a worksheet for organizing efforts to increase time effectiveness; it also helps determine action steps to resolve time usage problems.

SUMMARY

Everyone has *exactly* the same amount of time at his or her disposal each day, and yet some supervisors accomplish more than others. This difference in effectiveness can be explained largely by *how* this time is used. It is essential that supervisors realize that time is a resource to be managed and used wisely.

---

[2]These and other effective reading techniques are provided by such firms as Evelyn Woods Reading Dynamics. Also, a book from your local library on this topic will give a detailed explanation of these procedures.

Table 19-2. Troubleshooting Chart for Effective Use of Time

Problem	Possible Causes	Suggested Solutions
Lack of planning	Failure to see the benefit of planning	Recognize that planning takes time but saves time in the long run
	Orientation toward action	Emphasize results, not activity
Lack of priorities	Lack of goals and objectives	List goals and objectives. Discuss priorities with employees
Overcommitment	Too broad interests	Learn to say no
	Misplaced priorities	Put first things first
	Failure to set priorities	Develop a personal philosophy of time. Relate priorities to a schedule of events (three-star items before two-star items)
Management by crisis	Lack of planning	Use the same solutions as for "lack of planning" problem
	Unrealistic time estimates	Allow more time. Allow for interruptions
Haste	Impatience with routine	Take time to do it right. Don't waste time doing it over
	Dealing with the so-called urgent	Learn the difference between the so-called urgent and the really urgent
	Trying to do too much in too little time	Attempt less. Designate more
Paperwork and reading	Information overload	Read selectively. Learn to speed-read
	Failure to screen	Delegate reading to subordinates
Routine and unimportant detail	Lack of priorities	Set goals and stick with them. Delegate non-essential tasks
	Oversupervision of subordinates	Delegate; then give subordinates responsibility. Expect results, not particular methods
	Inability to delegate; feeling of greater security dealing with trivial routine	Recognize that without delegation it is impossible to get anything done through others
Visitors	Enjoyment of socializing	Do it somewhere else. Meet visitors outside your office. Go out to lunch if necessary. Hold on-the-spot conferences

Problem	Possible Causes	Suggested Solutions
	Inability to say no	Screen visitors. Say no. Be unavailable
Telephone	Lack of self-discipline	Screen and group calls. Don't talk long
	Desire to be informed and involved	Stay uninvolved with all but essentials
Meetings	Fear of responsibility for decisions	Make decisions without meeting
	Indecision	Make decisions even if some facts are missing
	Overcommunication	Don't plan or attend unnecessary meetings
	Poor leadership	Stick to the subject. Set group goals
Indecision	Insistence on getting all the facts	Accept some risks. Decide without all the facts
	Fear of the consequences of a mistake	Delegate the right to be wrong. Use mistakes as a learning process
Lack of delegation	Fear of subordinates inadequacy	Train them well. Allow mistakes. Replace if necessary
	Fear of subordinates' competence	Delegate fully. Give credit
	Work overload on subordinates	Balance the workload. Create new positions. Set priorities in proper order

Adapted from: R. Alec Mackenzie, *Managing Time at the Top* (New York: AMACOM), 1970.

Table 19-3. Time Troubleshooting Chart

My Time Usage Problems	Causes	Proposed Solutions	Action Taken	Results

By analyzing the supervisory time audit, the supervisor can determine how time is spent on the job. This information can be used to improve a supervisor's time efficiencies by implementing the various suggestions regarding setting priorities and scheduling, delegating, conducting meetings, controlling interruptions, and improving communications and dealing with the reading load.

The effective use of time is something a supervisor can easily improve. The results of these efforts are immediate, observable, and significant. Thus the efforts devoted to managing one's time are among the most satisfying of undertakings.

DISCUSSION QUESTIONS

1. Time has been called the great equalizer. Comment on this statement.
2. What is the value of a supervisory time audit?
3. Describe the method of setting priorities indicated in the chapter.
4. Describe appropriate and effective ways to increase the supervisor's delegation of responsibilities.
5. Describe leadership in group meetings from the standpoint of effective use of group time. What should a leader do prior to the meeting? How should the meeting be conducted? Does the leader have any responsibility after the meeting?
6. Describe three ways that interruptions in a workday can be controlled. What interruptions do you face in a typical day? How can they be reduced?
7. How can your reading efforts be made more effective? Do you read too much? Explain. Which materials should you *not* read?
8. Using the troubleshooting chart for effective time use (Table 19–2), select that area of your own behavior that is the greatest potential time waster. What steps can you take to improve this potential problem? Using the table, what are your greatest strengths for time management?
9. Ask yourself the question, What is the best use of my time right now?

CASE 19-1.   Branson High School

Branson High School is located in a rural consolidated school district in which the majority of the school's seven hundred students are bused. The principal, Edward Kraus, found himself extremely busy from his routine contacts with the students, thirty-one faculty members, four janitors, the school board, and parents. Mr. Kraus prided himself on being available to students, faculty, or parents who wished to speak with him personally about matters that concerned them. His open-door policy was real in that he would take whatever time was needed to listen to anyone who came in to talk to him. He was extremely empathetic with the members of his staff. He was generally well regarded as someone who encouraged a participative or democratic atmosphere.

Each day began with Mr. Kraus's arrival at school at approximately 7:30 A.M. Classes began at 8:00 A.M. Between 7:30 A.M. and 8:00 A.M. many teachers would appear to discuss questions they had regarding their schedules, facilities, problem students, and so forth. Mr. Kraus kept a schedule of his activities for the day, and his secretary scheduled additional meetings if he was unavailable and unable to be contacted by an interested person. They coordinated their schedules whenever it was convenient. As a typical day proceeded, Mr. Kraus was often late to appointments because his schedule was so full.

Because of the needs of the faculty and students, Mr. Kraus frequently found himself responding predominantly to crises that had arisen within the school. He rarely had time to engage in long-range planning or to initiate new programs or to evaluate current programs unless directed or required to do so by a faculty member or a directive from the central offices.

Although most persons felt that Mr. Kraus was conscientious, open, and hard working, they also had the impression that decisions were delayed and that his willingness to listen resulted in other people's priorities being substituted for his priorities. A teacher of American history commented that during a free period any faculty member could walk into Mr. Kraus's office without an appointment. In fact, even if other faculty members were discussing something with Mr. Kraus, they could often be interrupted by someone else at the door with a problem.

QUESTIONS

1. What could be the causes of having to react to so many crises?

2. What time management suggestions could you give to Mr. Kraus for implementation? What contributions could his secretary make?

3. What recommendations would you make for someone trying to strike a balance between being "responsive to the public" and being an effective administrator?

CASE 19–2. A Personal Time Management Plan

This chapter contains a series of time usage suggestions as well as a log for determining your current use of time. To develop a personal time management plan, follow these five steps: First, fill out the time log in

Figure 19-1. Second, review the chapter. Pay particular attention to the troubleshooting chart to identify various sources of time waste. Third, as a result of this review and your time log, identify which aspects of time management you now do well. Fourth, make a personal analysis of your time management weaknesses. Identify five specific steps you can take to increase your time usage as a result of this analysis. Fifth, make a list of items you wish to accomplish today and set priorities by using the 1 star, 2 star, 3 star method presented in the chapter.

20

PERSONAL GOALS AND CAREER DEVELOPMENT

LEARNING OBJECTIVES

This chapter discusses individual goals and the development of your career. After you have read this chapter, you will

1. Know which of the various life periods affect career development
2. Know what an organization expects of the employee
3. Know which competencies are needed for successful career development
4. Understand how to develop your own life goals
5. Know how certain career tips can assist your career

The topic of career development is important to persons who are about to enter the job market as well as to those who have been working for some time. As used in this chapter, the word <u>careers</u> will refer to the series of <u>work experiences</u> that a person has throughout his or her life. Effective career development requires that you have an intimate understanding of yourself and of your organization's needs so that desired career outcomes may be obtained.

In this chapter we will describe the various life stages that individuals pass through, discuss what organizations expect of individuals, analyze the career competencies a person must have in order to obtain desired career outcomes, and give a series of "tips" that can serve to aid a new employee.

LIFE PERIODS

Several writers have developed configurations of a person's life periods. The various life stages, as they relate to careers, are summarized in Table 20–1.

Table 20–1. Significant Life-Work Periods

Life Period	Approximate Age
I. Childhood and preparation for work	0–20
II. Early work years and becoming established	20–30
III. Stable work period: maintenance and self-experience	30–50
IV. Late career years: preparation for retirement	50–65*
V. Retirement	65+

*Although the legal aspects of forced retirement have changed, it is generally believed that retirement for most persons will remain close to sixty-five years of age.

It should be noted that the age designations in the table are only approximate and that a particular individual may enter these phases at a different age. The important point here is that these stages reflect the different needs and orientations of an employee. Because of this, the match between the personal and the organizational requirements will shift as an individual enters a new life period and alters certain concerns.

In Period I, childhood and preparation for work, the individual develops by identifying with key figures in the family, engaging in fantasies, developing interests, and testing his or her capacity. This parallels general schooling and self-examination through role playing; and in later years it includes a rejection of the necessary dependencies of early childhood. Near the end of this period, the individual begins making tentative career choices by taking new work, or seeking advice, or enrolling in formal course work.

In the early years of Period II, new fields are tried out as potential life work. Effort is focused on becoming established in a new field, and a beginning job is tried. At this time, skill development and new job responsibilities are sought; additionally, a supportive environment is desired because it enables individual autonomy to be maintained. Throughout this period the individual tests his or her ability to compete with others. An awareness of competitive abilities helps establish a person's aspiration level.

In Period III, a stable work period emerges where the individual focuses on maintaining a stable and long-term relationship with the organization. At this point in one's career, physical limitations become more evident, along with the realization that there will not be time to accomplish all the goals that seemed desirable in earlier years. This leads to a rethinking and self-examination regarding values, work, and personal relationships. Generally, the result is the development of a broader view of work and emphasis on developing others—usually younger employees. At this stage the individual usually desires recognition by the organization for his or her contributions.

In Period IV, preparation for retirement, the individual tends to be motivated by a secure position that offers an environment in which guidance, wisdom, and consultation are sought. During this phase, the individual tends to become more detached from the organization as preparations for retirement are made. Because of impending retirement, important motivators tend to be job security and recognition of continuing organizational contributions, as well as pension and health benefits. It is during this phase that a person must accept the reality that one only has a single life cycle.

With retirement in Period V, the overall pace of work and life is reduced. Occupational work and duties cease and the person participates in activities on a selective basis or only as an observer. Reduced activity comes as mental and physical capacities decline.

With each new period, the needs of an individual change. The result is that the match between individual and organizational needs shifts. In the early years when a person is in a trial period, a high degree of responsibility, challenge, and demand for creativity can be quite motivating. This is followed by a stable and longer-term relationship with an organization where long-term personal development and advancement become major concerns. Finally, a secure position and steady employment predominate as a person prepares for retirement. Thus it is important to recognize that an employee's behavior will be affected by the current life stage. For example, one might expect an older employee to have a less enthusiastic response to the addition of new responsibilities than would a younger employee. By contrast, a young employee may be less likely to accept a position that offers stable employment rather than one that provides an interesting and exciting immediate job assignment.

CAREER SUCCESS

"Career success leads to more career involvement and more favorable attitudes toward work and companies; these outcomes presumably lead the person to work harder and thus, to perform better in the future. Thus, success breeds success."[1] This statement by an expert on career development is intriguing. It suggests that, as one becomes more successful in a career, further opportunites and successes emerge which then breed more success. You may wonder how you can become part of this pattern. The answer lies in understanding personal and organizational needs and matching the two over a period of years.

In the preceding section we described various life periods. It is important to recognize the period of your career that you are now in, so that a reasonable match can be made between your needs and organizational requirements. But what does an organization require?

In general, organizational expectations can be reduced to six categories:

1. Confidence: The organization expects the individual to be able to identify problems and have the self-assurance to follow a problem through to its solution.

2. Loyalty and commitment: The organization expects the individual to place the organization's goals and values ahead of the individual's own selfish motives and, where necessary, to sacrifice some of his or her personal life.

3. Generate and obtain acceptance of ideas: The organization expects the individual to have a range of such characteristics as the ability to translate technical solutions into practical terms, the ability to diagnose and overcome resistance to change, the ability to use interpersonal skills, and the ability to influence others.

4. Personal integrity and strength: The organization expects the individual to be able to adhere to a personal point of view without appearing to be a deviate or rebel. This requires compromise when appropriate.

5. Acceptance of organizational realities: The organization expects the individual to understand the values and other nontechnical factors that constitute organizational life, such as the need for survival, recognition of group loyalties, informal power arrangements, and office politics.

---

[1] Douglas T. Hall, *Careers In Organizations* (Pacific Palisades, Calif.: Goodyear, 1976), p. 142.

6. <u>Capacity to grow</u>: The organization expects the individual to learn from expereience. Although mistakes are anticipated, repeated mistakes of a similar nature are not tolerated. Moreover, the individual must demonstrate an ability to mature and take on increasing responsibilities in the handling of interpersonal relationships.[2]

This list of organizational expectations reflects a range of requirements for a successful career. Note that technical competence, although important, is only part of one of the expectations. The need for communication (both written and oral) and for the maintenance of interrelationships should not be underestimated. A crucial part of a career is the ability to sell ideas and to write and voice persuasive messages.

Using the above information, you should have a reasonable idea of organizational expectations. How can you go about developing the basic competencies necessary for successful career development? The next section addresses this question.

DEVELOPING CAREER COMPETENCIES

Certain career competencies can affect a person's career. Crites has identified five areas that contribute to a person's career: self-appraisal, occupational information, goal selection, planning, and problem solving.[3] These abilities are fundamental for career development; happily, they are all skills that can be acquired.

Self-Appraisal

To develop an appropriate match between personal and organizational requirements, it is essential to have an idea of one's own makeup. How do you get to know yourself? One of the most effective ways of gaining information about yourself is from personal experience and through the use of guidance and counseling personnel. A student may utilize the college or university placement service, while employees may be able to take advantage of counseling services provided by their employer. In addition, there are certain exercises or group assignments that your instructor may provide for you.

---

[2]Adapted with permission from Edgar H. Schein, "How to Break in the College Graduate," *Harvard Business Review,* Vol. 42, (November–December 1964) p. 70, Copyright ©1964 by the President and Fellows of Harvard College; all rights reserved.

---

[3]John O. Crites, *Theory and Research Handbook, Career Maturity Handbook*, (Monterey, Calif.: McGraw-Hill, 1973).

An added source of personal understanding can come from feedback from your associates, your family, and your supervisors. You are more likely to get helpful feedback if you ask for it. You should ask for specific instances of your strengths or weaknesses rather than a general "OK" or "not OK" evaluation.

In using the feedback method, get feedback from several individuals and compare their responses. Try not to be defensive about this, since you have asked for their comments. Instead, repeat back to them what they have said to verify an evaluation (as we discussed in the chapter on interviewing).

Occupational Information

After you increase your self-knowledge, it is important to know something about the job market and specific job opportunities. Unfortunately, the sources of this information are not widely available for all occupations. One source, the *Dictionary of Occupational Titles*, can be found in most libraries. It describes the job requirements associated with most major occupations. In addition, the *Occupational Outlook Handbook*, compiled by the Department of Labor, can be useful in helping to project employment needs in the future. This kind of information can help you determine whether a particular occupation will experience growth and opportunites in future years.

Goal Selection

After learning about yourself and about job opportunities, it is important to set career goals so that you can move toward effectively matching yourself with a rewarding job. Goal setting gives you purpose and direction, and it allows you to select among the many alternatives available. Moreover, after a goal has been designated, it is possible to develop a strategy to attain the goal.

Certain difficulties can interfere with the developing of effective personal goals: (1) individuals may have doubts about their own abilities; (2) a person may be afraid to set out in one direction because this entails a choice between two attractive alternatives, forcing something to be given up; (3) some persons do not set goals because they do not know enough about their own abilities; and (4) some persons fail to set goals because they do not want to fail—if they never set a goal, they will never have to try to reach it. To overcome these interferences, it is important to learn about yourself (described above) and to recognize that goals can be changed. Today's selection of a goal can be changed tomorrow if new information or preferences emerge. Therefore, goal setting is merely a way of concentrating a person's energies on accomplishing those things preferred by that person. It is a way of gaining control of one's life.

To develop personal goals, try this exercise: Picture yourself five to ten years from now and write down on a sheet of paper the things that you would like to be doing or the position you would like to have at that time. List them rapidly and do not worry about phrasing them "properly." A form similar to that in Figure 20-1 can be used. Consider the amount of money, the amount of status, the kinds of relationships you would like to have, the accomplishments you would like to have achieved, and so forth. Following the completion of this list, go back and designate the most important items to you, and let these serve as your long-range goals. Then take a second sheet of paper and indicate the activities that will lead you during

---

For each of the following categories, indicate what you would like to have achieved five to ten years from now.

A. Career Responsibility: _____

B. Status: _____

_____

C. Financial Security:_____

_____

D. Personal Relationships: _____

_____

E. Individual Development and Education: _____

_____

F. Religion and Spiritual Development: _____

_____

G. Other (specify) _____: _____

_____

Figure 20-1   Personal Goal-Setting Worksheet

the next six months toward the longer-range goals you have already identified. This procedure, or one similar to it, can help you focus on the goals important to you. Also, it can indicate the shorter-term milestones involved.

Planning

After goals have been selected, planning can begin to identify the strategies designed to obtain the stated goals. At this stage it may become apparent that you will not be able to attain the goals that were identified earlier. If this proves to be the case, then you must go back to the goal-setting phase and set more-realistic goals. (For further discussion of the goal setting and planning process, see Chapter 7.)

Problem Solving

The planning process will indicate those obstacles that must be overcome and the means by which goals can be attained. Much of the information that was generated by the goal-setting and self-awareness activities can be used to help solve any problems that become apparent at this stage. (Chapter 12, "Supervisory Decision Making," includes additional suggestions for problem solving and overcoming obstacles.)

These five basic career competencies encompass fairly general requirements for effective career development. The following section gives specific career recommendations, or tips.

CAREER TIPS

As a prospective employee, you should choose an organization carefully. To do this, it is important to ask questions that will help reveal the nature of the job and the distinguishing characteristics of the organization. This means that you should not necessarily accept the first job that is offered. Prior to the interview, you should learn about the local reputation of the organization, its growth rate, and the nature of its product. During the interview, such issues as specific job assignments, responsibilities, available training programs, travel requirements, fringe benefits, and salary level should be discussed. This information can be useful in helping to reduce the possibility of making a serious error in selecting an organization. By gathering this kind of information, you can avoid later surprises on the job. Although some changing of organizations and jobs throughout one's career can be broadening, job changes that occur more frequently than every two years can be detrimental to an employment record.

Second, you should strive to obtain a challenging first job. The first job can be challenging due to both the nature of the tasks and the kind supervision you receive. As a result, it is important not only to gather information about the specific job and its responsibilities but also to learn as much as possible about your immediate supervisor. Some of the clues that will help you separate the more challenging jobs from those that are less challenging include asking: How soon do individuals normally get promoted from this particular job? What kinds of positions do the capable jobholders get promoted into? The answers to these questions will give you an indication as to whether this job will be likely to lead to added opportunities. In addition to inquiring about the content of the job, an interview with your prospective superior can be useful. Look for a supervisor who will "stretch" your capabilities and help you learn. Then, after taking the job, learn whatever you can from this person. Your supervisor serves as a model of work behavior, so listen and learn. If your supervisor is capable, he or she can help you learn how to be a capable employee. Unfortunately, if your supervisor is incompetent, the reverse is true.

Third, an obvious and effective way to increase career opportunities is to become known as an outstanding performer. To do this, work hard to prepare yourself in whatever job responsibilities you are given. Frequently seek feedback about your performance from your supervisor. The feedback you seek should be specific and directed toward improvement in any areas that need improvement. In this process you can utilize your supervisor's experience; at the same time you will tend to generate a positive view of your enthusiasm and conscientiousness. Recognize that the first six months on the job are crucial because it is during this time that many organizational perceptions about your ability and long-term capabilities will be made. It is *very* difficult to overcome poor performance reviews. This is very similar to what happens when a student begins the first semester or two with several D's or F's and thereafter must earn A's and B's just to maintain an "average" overall performance.

Fourth, you can foster "managerial mobility" by paying attention to the following items regarding your supervisor. (a) Try to become an important subordinate to a mobile superior. In your interview with a prospective boss, try to determine whether or not this person is mobile. As a rule of thumb, a mobile superior is a person who has had a promotion within the last three years. By becoming someone that your superior can rely on, your career can be tied to his or hers. Conversely, make an effort not to become an indispensable subordinate to an immobile superior. An immobile supervisor can serve to block your career efforts. (b) Take advantage of any opportunity for increased exposure or visibility in the organization. Get your name known, not only by performing well but also by being unafraid to take credit for your achievements. One method of accomplishing this is to seek and accept special assignments. In a similar way, you should be prepared to put your own name forward and volunteer for new responsibilities and positions. Do not turn prospective promotions or responsibilities down. In your relations with your supervisor, seek his or her support as a sponsor who will help you obtain the opportunity to show your abilities through challenging work assignments and promotional opportunities.

Managerial mobility can also be fostered by maintaining a wide set of options. A person develops a broader set of opportunities by having work experiences (including line experience) and by taking care not to become overspecialized. However, if it becomes apparent that a move to a new organization must be made, try to make that decision and announce your departure without being asked to leave. In this way you can leave with good relationships intact; it has become your decision to move on rather than another person's decision that you must go. Moreover, you should expect to have several careers in your working life. Therefore you do not have to feel dejected if a particular opportunity fails to emerge. Rather, you can follow up an alternative option and explore a whole new set of career choices. You should recognize that most persons change the direction of their careers on the average of three times throughout their working lives.

Fifth, you should seek help in career management. Utilize various sources that are available to you (i.e., those provided by various universities or alumni and alumnae, and even families, friends, and colleagues). If your spouse also has a career, the planning for your career opportunities must

Table 20-2.   Summary of Methods to Improve Self-Management of Careers

I. Develop basic career competencies
 a. Self-appraisal
 b. Obtaining occupational information
 c. Goal selection
 d. Planning
 e. Problem solving
II. Choose an organization carefully
III. Get a challenging initial job
IV. Be an outstanding performer
V. Develop managerial mobility
 1. Don't be blocked by an immobile superior
 2. Become a crucial subordinate to a mobile supervisor
 3. Always favor increased exposure and visibility
 4. Be prepared to practice self-nomination
 5. Leave an organization at your own convenience
 6. Plan for a multi-career
VI. Get help in career management
VII. Continually reassess your career

Adapted from Douglas T. Hall, *Careers In Organizations* (Pacific Palisades, Calif. Goodyear, 1976), p. 189.

take the needs of the other person into account. In these cases, mutual career planning becomes essential.

Sixth, it is fundamental to all career development that a person continually reassess current progress. It is reasonable to ask yourself how close you are to reaching the long-term goals you set for your career. Periodic analysis of your progress may require that certain changes be made. By recognizing that career development is a continuing process, you will be able to make the appropriate correction either in your behavior or in your goals. By focusing on your current life stage, you may be able to identify more easily the needs you require. This can help you take advantage of different opportunities as they arise throughout your working career.

SUMMARY

This chapter has focused on many aspects of career development. It described five life periods that can help individuals recognize various phases that affect their working life, discussed various organizational expectations, and presented five career competencies a person should develop. These competencies—self-appraisal, occupational information, goal selection, planning, and problem solving—provide the basis for making effective career decisions. The chapter concluded with a series of "tips" to aid the reader in obtaining desired career outcomes.

DISCUSSION QUESTIONS

1. What are the significant life-work periods indicated in this chapter? Which period are you in now? What period will you move into next?

2. Describe the implications of your next life-and-work period. Is it important to prepare for this new period? Why?

3. What are the general expectations an organization has of its employees?

4. How important is technical competence to successful career development? What other factors, if any, affect the career success of a worker?

5. Describe the career competencies indicated in the chapter. Are any of these competencies more important to you than others? Why?

6. Fill out the personal goal-setting worksheet included in the chapter. Was the process difficult or easy for you? Do you have short-term goals to move you toward accomplishing the goals you indicated in Figure 20–1?

7. How should you go about selecting an organization as part of your career development?

8. How can you increase your "managerial mobility"? What role does your supervisor play in this?

9. Should your first job be a challenging one? Why or why not? What steps can you take to ensure that you get the kind of job that you need for career development?

10. Where are you in your career now? Where do you want to be? What are you going to do about it?

CASE 20-1.   The Case of Larry McCarthy

For the past seven weeks Larry McCarthy has worked for the Miner Construction Company as a carpenter's helper. This position is the third construction job Larry has had during the past year. Prior to working in the construction field, Larry worked in an automobile assembly factory. He got that job after finishing high school with no clear idea of what kind of work he wanted or what he would like to accomplish. After several months as a worker in the paint department, he grew tired of the work and decided he would leave after paying for a new car he had purchased.

His second job was quite different from physical factory work. In his new job for the U.S. Postal Service, he had a clerical responsibility and for a few months seemed to progress well. After eight months on the job he received a minor promotion, but shortly thereafter he became restless and left the Postal Service to enter construction work. Each of the job changes was explained by Larry as part of his search to "find himself" because once he found work that he liked he expressed confidence that he would "really go somewhere." As part of this search, he attended night school while working for the Postal Service and took one course in music appreciation and one in political science.

Currently, Larry is aware that he is floundering in his search for a career but feels that he has not actually failed in any single job. His wife recently gave him a book that described methods of success on the job. She has encouraged him to return to his office work and apply the major ideas discussed in the book to his own career. The suggestions summarized in the book include wearing stylish clothes, spending time off the job with superiors, and becoming well known by important people in the organization. This last suggestion was one that struck a chord in Larry, since he was fond of saying that "it isn't what you know but who you know that leads to success."

QUESTIONS

1. What would you recommend that Larry do to "find himself"?

2. How would you rate the advice listed in the career development book given to Larry? Was anything left out?

3. If Larry continues on his current course, what would you predict his long-term career prospects would be?

CASE 20–2.   Your Personal Career Plan

This chapter began with a general presentation of career stages and then offered several career development suggestions. Review the chapter and your own personal situation and answer the following questions:

1. What career stage are you in now? What is the next career stage for you?

2. What preparations should you make for the next career stage? What changes in your life will these preparations require?

3. List the career development steps that you have mastered.

4. Which career development suggestions or tips could you improve?

5. List at least two activities you can do that will aid you in reaching your career goals.

VII
Some Parting Thoughts

21

PUTTING IT TOGETHER

LEARNING OBJECTIVES

This chapter discusses some of the trends that are occurring in our society and shows how they will affect the supervisor's job. The chapter concludes with a self-study, which will enable supervisors to assess their performance. After you have read this chapter, you will

1. Know about the opportunities that exist for supervisory talent, and the types of skills and abilities that supervisors should possess
2. Understand why workers are changing
3. Understand why the nature of work is changing
4. Understand why organizations are changing
5. Know more about your competence as a supervisor or your potential for becoming a supervisor

It is always risky to predict what will happen in the future. While we know that the future will be different from the present, it is very likely that it will be somewhat different from what we expect. In spite of the limitations of prediction, there are certain trends in organizations and in our society that will probably continue. It is these trends that we wish to address.

OPPORTUNITIES FOR MANAGERIAL CAREERS

The supply of managerial talent has been inadequate in both good times and bad times during the past four decades. Opportunities continue to be excellent for those who have the will to manage and the skills necessary for doing so. The first managerial position held by almost everyone is that of "first-line supervisor." Most individuals start at the bottom of the managerial ladder and work their way up.

Behaviors and skills learned in these positions provide the background necessary to rise up through the managerial hierarchy. These behaviors and skills include leading subordinates, making decisions, planning the work of the unit, organizing human and other resources, staffing the unit, and controlling the performance of people and other resources. In addition, managers must possess the added skills necessary to cope with work that involves (1) a fast pace and heavy pressure; (2) work patterns characterized by brevity, variety, and fragmentation; (3) emphasis upon action and the here and now; (4) heavy reliance upon verbal media; (5) maintenance of a communications network; and (6) a complex blend of rights and duties that must be continuously managed if they are not to "manage the manager." Moreover, managers must work with their peers and satisfy the expectations of their superiors. Finally, organizations are social systems in which interpersonal competence, politics, and even luck influence how high an individual will rise within the managerial ranks.

Individuals who hope to embark upon a successful managerial career should consider the conclusions of a leading business educator, consultant, and manager, who said that successful managers possess three important personal characteristics.[1] First, they have a strong need to manage. They have a strong desire to influence the performance of others and derive strong satisfaction from doing so. Second, they have a strong need for power.

---

[1] J. Sterling Livingston, "Myth of the Well-Educated Manager," *Harvard Business Review*, 49 (January–February 1971), 79–89.

They seek the authority and ability to command which comes with their managerial position. They also strive to gain the knowledge and expertise that provide the basis for power. Third, they possess a capacity for empathy, which is the capacity to understand and cope with the stressful interpersonal relationships that occur when people work together under pressure in an organization. They are aware of the feelings of other people and consider them in carrying out their responsibilities. This statement summarizes many of the characteristics needed to function effectively and take advantage of the available managerial opportunities.

WORKERS ARE CHANGING

In several ways workers are different from what they were two decades ago, and they will probably continue to change in the future. First, as a group, they are better educated. More people are graduating from high school and college than ever before. Even more dramatic is the great upsurge in the number of adults who are continuing their education on a part-time basis while remaining employed full time. Partly as a result of this training, workers have developed complex and major skills to meet the demands of increasing technology. These factors have enabled workers to develop broader personal and work interests.

Second, the work force has become more diverse. Higher levels of education have broadened the interests of people and have produced workers with many different tastes and life-styles. Increasingly, the work force consists of minorities and women who are qualifying for and accepting employment in positions formerly reserved for white males, and men are entering careers formerly considered to be primarily "women's work." Women are becoming carpenters, coal miners, and airline pilots, while men are becoming nurses, secretaries, and kindergarten teachers!

Third, workers are placing greater emphasis on equity and rights in their relationships with those who hold power. Workers have raised expectations about how they will be treated by their government and by their supervisors. Managers are being required to give increasing attention to civil rights issues, which include not only rights based upon race, religion, and color but also rights based upon age, handicap, alien status, and homosexuality. Even left-handedness may become a civil rights issue!

THE CHANGING NATURE OF WORK

The gradual reduction in the length of the workweek has been one of the major changes in industry during the past several decades. Although the length of the average workweek has not changed during the past few years, there has been considerable pressure to reduce it below the standard of forty hours. Some of this pressure is coming from those who believe that improved technology makes such a reduction mandatory in order to maintain full employment. However, those who believe that workers should have more leisure time have been equally vocal. Their argument rests primarily upon a belief that the importance of work has been overemphasized in our society.

As an indication of pressures for changes in the nature of work, organizations have been experimenting with ways in which they might adjust to the personal needs of individual workers. Thus they are experimenting with four-day, ten-hour-per-day, workweeks; flexible work hours; and shorter workweeks. It is anticipated that these efforts will continue.

As individuals acquire more education and skills, their employment opportunities broaden. They become more flexible in their ability to move from job to job, from organization to organization, and even from one career to another. Thus we expect that career paths and mobility patterns will continue to expand and be more flexible.

The distinction between white-collar and blue-collar work is becoming blurred. Changing technology has reduced the need for unskilled workers and for some semiskilled workers, and it has increased the need for skilled workers and technical and professional employees. These forces, plus the rising educational level of the work force and increasing emphasis on participation, have operated to reduce some of the distinction between managerial and nonmanagerial work—for example, by placing nonmanagerial workers on a monthly salary rather than on an hourly rate, eliminating the requirement that they punch a time clock, and granting paid time off to engage in community activities. The changing nature of work has been paralleled by new concerns and goals in organizations.

THE CHANGING NATURE OF ORGANIZATIONS

Organizations are increasingly being called upon to justify their existence on the basis of performance. Business has traditionally used the "bottom line," or earnings, as the ultimate measure of performance. Currently, not-for-profit organizations, including government agencies and social welfare organizations, are also placing increasing emphasis on performance. Managers at every level are being required to set goals, analyze activities, and compare actual results with initial plans for the benefit of stockholders, voters, or sponsors. New management information systems collect and analyze data more efficiently and rapidly than ever before. Managers who understand and use the new technology will continue to be in great demand, especially if they also are willing and able to transmit this information to their subordinates.

Organizations are becoming more individualized and differentiated. This is, in part, a response to the more individualized needs and expectations of employees. However, it is also stimulated by the greater openness of our society, which seems more supportive of experimental organizational forms. For example, company personnel policies and practices have become more individualized in order to meet individual employee needs.

Organizations are striving to create the type of work climate in which individuals can do their best. Redesigning jobs to provide personal challenge is one step in this direction. Another is the "cafeteria" approach to employee benefits. By allowing employees to select their individual "package" of benefits, employees not only participate in determining their own destiny but also derive personal enjoyment or benefit from money spent by the organization.

In summary, these changes—individual, work, and organizational—provide workers with an increased range of choices as to type of work, geographical location, career choice, and organization. These trends permit individuals to choose those careers and organizations that will enable them to work in the social climate and under the style of leadership that they find most satisfactory.

A SELF-STUDY

The title of this book, *Supervision: The Management of Organizational Resources,* suggests that the way in which supervisors work and the specific things they choose to do have a profound impact on their organizations. The more supervisors understand their job and themselves, the more sensitive they will be to the needs of their organizations and the more efficient they will be in doing their work.

The following nineteen groups of questions are presented to stimulate lower- and middle-level managers to analyze their own work, and to aid in the self-study process:

1. What kind of leader am I? How do my subordinates react to my managerial style? How well do I understand their work? Am I sufficiently sensitive to their reactions to what I do and say? Do I use an appropriate balance between encouragement and pressure? Do I stimulate their initiative? Do I promote their creativity?

2. What kind of relationship do I maintain with my peers and my superiors? Are my methods for establishing and maintaining a satisfactory relationship appropriate and constructive? Is there anyone with whom I should establish a better relationship? Do I devote too much or too little time to maintaining these relationships?

3. Where do I get my information? How do I get my information? Can I make greater use of my contacts with subordinates, peers, and superiors to get needed information? Can other people, such as staff specialists, obtain some of this information for me? In what areas is my knowledge strongest? In what areas is it weakest? How can I improve my knowledge?

4. What information do I share with my subordinates? How important is it that they receive my information? Do I keep too much information to myself? Do I hoard information because I believe it is too time consuming or inconvenient to share it? Or am I reluctant to share the power that information provides? How do I get more information to others so that they can make more and better decisions?

5. Do I permit subordinates to solve problems and make decisions on matters in which they have interest and competency? Do I develop my subordinates so that they are able to solve problems and make decisions? Am I competent to assess the worth of proposals made by my subordinates? Do I have problems in coordinating the activities in my unit because subordinates now make too many decisions independently?

6. Have I established with my superior the necessary goals and objectives for my unit? Are they stated in terms of the results I expect to achieve within the next six months or year? Have they been reduced to writing? Have I expressly shared these objectives with my subordinates?

7. Have I selected the right people to do the work in my unit? If not, what are their deficiencies and how can I reduce the impact of these deficiencies on the work that needs to be done?

8. Am I developing my subordinates in a way that will result in maximum productivity? Have I itemized their strengths and their weaknesses? Am I working with them to help them overcome their deficiencies and to maximize their strengths? Have I helped them establish both work and personal goals?

9. Am I motivating my subordinates to give their maximum effort to the organization? Does their work provide them with the opportunity to satisfy their personal goals? Am I appropriately rewarding the type of behavior in which I wish to see them engage? Does the design of the work provide them with the opportunity to experience feelings of achievement for esteem and self-actualization? Am I making appropriate use of money as a motivator?

10. Do I make decisions appropriately? Do I tend to act before I obtain enough information? Or do I wait so long for "all" information that opportunities pass me by?

11. Do I communicate appropriately? Do I know how to make the most of written communication? Do I rely excessively on face-to-face communication, thus placing some of my subordinates at an informational disadvantage? Do I seek feedback? Do I adjust my behavior appropriately based upon the feedback I receive? Am I a good interviewer?

12. Do my subordinates consider me approachable? Do I listen with empathy? Do I take appropriate action on their complaints? Am I willing to permit them to take their complaints to a higher authority if it is not within the scope of my

authority to take action? Am I willing to permit them to take their complaints to higher authority even though I may disagree with their position?

13. If my subordinates belong to a union, am I able to work with the union stewards and union officers?

14. Do I understand the various laws that apply to me as a supervisor?

15. Have I achieved a satisfactory balance between the stability necessary for accomplishing work and the innovation that makes it possible to accomplish work more effectively? Am I supportive of creativity on the part of my subordinates? Do I encourage change? Do I protect the reasonable interests of my subordinates when change occurs?

16. Do I make good use of my time? Do I plan ahead? Do I delegate properly? Do I give each activity, function, or type of problem an appropriate amount of time? Do I neglect any activity, function, or problem? Can someone else, such as a secretary, take responsibility for certain activities?

17. Do I overwork? Can my unit carry on when I am absent for an hour, a day, a week, a month? Am I too superficial in what I do? Am I too meticulous in what I do? Do I reserve an adequate amount of time for planning? Do I reserve time for being creative? Do key problems receive the attention they deserve?

18. Do I strike an appropriate balance between work and leisure? Between work and my family responsibilities? Between work and community activities?

19. Have I given adequate attention to the type of life I wish to lead? Have I considered my career goals? Have I thought about my next job in this organization or some other organization? Where do I hope to be five years from now? Ten years from now? How do I go about preparing myself for my next job and my ultimate career objectives?

This list of questions is long. The chapters of this book are designed to provide direction, if not answers, to them. The number and complexity of the answers indicate that managerial work is important to the organization, to the supervisor and to the employees.

INDEX